Preaching with Purpose and Power

Preaching with Purpose and Power

Selected E.Y. Mullins Lectures on Preaching

compiled and edited

by
Don M. Aycock

Mercer University Press
Macon, Ga. 31207

All books published by Mercer University Press are produced
on acid-free paper which exceeds the minimum standards set by the
National Historical Publications and Records Commission.

Library of Congress Cataloging in Publication Data

Preaching with purpose and power.

    Includes index.
    1. Preaching—Addresses, essays, lectures.
I. Aycock, Don M.
BV4211.2.P74   251   81-22388
ISBN 0-86554-027-6   AACR2

Contents

Acknowledgments

Many people helped to make possible this collection of selected E. Y. Mullins Lectures on Preaching. For graciously granting, or helping to secure the granting, of permissions to publish these selected lectures, I especially wish to thank the following: (Luccock lectures) Professor Robert Luccock of Boston University School of Theology; (Farmer lectures) Professor H. H. Farmer and Gladys S. Farmer of Hove, Sussex, England; (Mackay lectures) Professor John A. Mackay of Hightstown, New Jersey, and The Reverend Stanton Wilson of Princeton, New Jersey; (Adams lectures) the late Reverend Professor Theodore F. Adams of Richmond, Virginia; (Davis lectures) Henry Grady Davis, Jr. of Maywood, Illinois; (Miller lectures) William Miller, and Alan Seaburg of Cambridge, Massachusetts; (Phillips lectures) Ruth T. Phillips of Markdale, Ontario; and (for materials belonging to the seminary) Professor Roy L. Honeycutt, provost of Southern Baptist Theological Seminary, Louisville, Kentucky. In addition, I wish to thank Dr. Ronald Deering who helped secure several manuscripts; and the members of West Side—Portland Baptist Church (Louisville) who allowed me the freedom of both time and spirit in order that I might compile this collection of Mullins Lectures.

Don M. Aycock
West Side—Portland Baptist Church
Louisville
1981

Introduction

When the history of twentieth century American preaching is written, special attention should be given to the E. Y. Mullins Lectures on Preaching. Based at Southern Baptist Seminary in Louisville, Kentucky, these lectures have been presented by some of the finest preachers and teachers in America and England.

This lecture series was made possible by a grant to Southern Baptist Theological Seminary in 1935.[1] Mrs. Isla May Mullins added the sum of three thousand dollars to the ten thousand dollars previously given by her husband, and a former president of Southern Seminary, E. Y. Mullins. Dr. Mullins, himself a noted preacher, had an abiding interest in the quality of preaching. His grant to the seminary was for the expressed purpose of establishing a lectureship on "Preaching" at Southern Seminary for the benefit of future preachers.

Dr. George A. Buttrick was invited to inaugurate the lectures in 1937, but he was unable to accept the invitation.[2] So the first lectures were actually given in the 1941-1942 academic year by William Lyon Phelps, professor emeritus of Yale University. The lectures have

---

[1]Leo T. Crismon, "Mullins Lectures," *Encyclopedia of Southern Baptists*, vol. 2 (Nashville: Broadman Press, 1956), p. 930. See also the will of Mrs. Isla May Mullins (dated 1935) in the Boyce Library of the Southern Baptist Theological Seminary (Louisville).

[2]Joint Faculty Minutes, Southern Baptist Theological Seminary, 9 September 1937 and 5 December 1939.

continued annually, with five exceptions. No lectures were given in the academic years 1943-1944, 1949-1950, 1950-1951, 1958-1959, and 1964-1965.

Eight complete lecture series are available in unpublished manuscript form.[3] All or portions of eighteen series are available on reel-to reel tape.[4] Portions of five of the series have been published in the *Review and Expositor*.[5] Five series have been published in book form.[6] Some persons invited to give the Mullins Lectures were given the option of presenting lectures or sermons. Six series therefore were not lectures at all, but were sermons.[7] Six of the series of lectures and

---

[3]These include the lecture series of George A. Buttrick (1943), John A. Mackay (1948), Theodore F. Adams (1956), Paul Scherer (1957), Henry Grady Davis (1962), Samuel H. Miller (1963), Harold Cooke Phillips (1964), and William Muehl (1975).

[4]These include the lectures since 1960, with the exception of D. E. King's 1973 sermon-series.

[5]These include all or portions of the following series of lectures or sermons: George A. Buttrick (1943), in *R&E* 40:2 (1943): 151-66, and *R&E* 40:3 (1943): 279-95; Halford E. Luccock (1945), in *R&E* 42:3 (1945): 255-65, and *R&E* 42:4 (1945): 383-92; H. H. Farmer (1946), in *R&E* 43:3 (1946): 243-60, *R&E* 43:4 (1946): 403-18, and *R&E* 44:1 (1947): 34-49; John A. Mackay (1948), in *R&E* 46:1 (1949): 3-12; and Paul Scherer (1957), in *R&E* 54:3 (1957): 355-56, and *R&E* 54:4 (1957): 560-73.

[6]These include the 1952 lectures of T. W. Manson on the theme "Some Aspects of the Public Ministry of Our Lord." Manson first presented these lectures in 1939 at Yale University Divinity School (the Shaffer Lectures), then in a revised and expanded form, in 1951, at the University of Cambridge. Manson's lectures were published as *The Servant-Messiah: A Study of the Public Ministry of Jesus* (Cambridge: Cambridge University Press, 1953; reprinted by Baker Book House of Grand Rapids in 1977). The 1954 lectures of David A. MacLennan became his *Pastoral Preaching* (Philadelphia: The Westminister Press, 1955). Robert J. McCracken's 1955 lectures formed the substance of his *The Making of the Sermon* (New York: Harper and Brothers, 1956). Paul Scherer's 1957 lectures were published as chapters 1-4 of *The Word God Sent* (New York: Harper and Row, 1965). Scherer first presented these lectures at Union Theological Seminary (New York), and then at several other institutions, including the Mullins Lectures at Southern. The 1961 lectures of Horton Davies appeared as chapter 10 of *Worship and Theology in England: From Newman to Martineau, 1850-1900, Worship and Theology in England,* vol. 4 (Princeton: Princeton University Press, 1962). Joseph Sittler's 1966 lectures were published as his *The Anguish of Preaching* (Philadelphia: Fortress Press, 1967).

[7]These include the series of sermons by Charles L. Graham (1947), Elam Davis (1967), J. P. Allen (1968), Jack Finegan (1969), Edmund Steimle (1972), and D. E. King (1973).

sermons are not available at all.[8] Thus, all or portions of twenty-seven sets of lectures and sermons are available. A complete listing of all the lecturers, with their themes, and a note on their availability is given below.[9]

The E. Y. Mullins Lectures On Preaching

1. *1941-1942.* William Lyon Phelps, professor emeritus, Yale University. Theme: "The Experience of Christian Religion in Literature." (Not available.)

2. *1942-1943.* George A. Buttrick, pastor of the Madison Avenue Presbyterian Church, New York City. Lectures: "What Is The Gospel?"; "Power and the Man."; "The Craftsmanship of Preaching (A)"; "The Craftsmanship of the Preacher (B)"; "Preaching in This Present Age." (The first two lectures are in *Review and Expositor*; lectures three and four are mimeographed.)

   1943-1944. No lectures.

3. *1944-1945.* Halford E. Luccock, professor at Yale Divinity School. Lectures: "What Literature Can Do for the Preacher"; "A Hunger For Affirmations"; "The Still Sad Music of Humanity"; "The Greatest Literature of All—The Bible"; "Literature and the Sermon." (Lectures one and two are in *Review and Expositor*; three and four are not available.)

4. *1945-1946.* H. H. Farmer, professor of philosophy at Cambridge University. Theme: "The Source and Setting of the Sermon." Lectures: "Preaching and Worship"; "The Preacher and Persons"; "The Preacher and Culture"; "The Preacher and Books"; "The Bible and Preaching." (Lectures

---

[8]The unavailable series include the lecture- or sermon-series of William Lyon Phelps (1942), Charles L. Graham (1947), Elmer G. Homrighausen (1949), Harold Cooke Phillips (1953), Clarence E. Cranford (1958), and D. E. King (1973).

[9]This list is from my book, *The E.Y. Mullins Lectures on Preaching with Reference to the Aristotelian Triad* (Washington, D. C.: University Press of America, 1980), pp. 3-9, and is used by permission of the publisher.

one, two, and three are in *Review and Expositor;* four and five are not available.)

5. *1946-1947.* Charles L. Graham, pastor of the Crescent Hill Baptist Church, Louisville, Kentucky. Sermons: "Despising the Shame"; "God's Interpreters"; "Good Man"; "Belshazzar's Feast." (Not available.)

6. *1947-1948.* John A. Mackay, president of Princeton Theological Seminary. Theme: "Our World and God's Gospel." Lectures: "The Life of Man in the Light of God"; "God's Unveiled Secret"; "The Cosmic Christ"; "The Gospel of God for the Nations"; "Christian Action on the Frontiers of Strife." (Mimeographed.)

7. *1948-1949.* Elmer G. Homrighausen, professor of Christian education at Princeton Theological Seminary. Theme: "The Primary Task of the Church." Lectures: "Why Engage in Evangelism?"; "What Is Evangelism?"; "How Evangelize Today?" (Not available.)

   1949-1950. No lectures.

   1950-1951. No lectures.

8. *1951-1952.* T. W. Manson, professor at the University of Manchester, England. Theme: "Some Aspects of the Public Ministry of Jesus." (Book: *The Servant-Messiah.*)

9. *1952-1953.* Harold Cooke Phillips, pastor of the First Baptist Church of Cleveland, Ohio. Lectures: "The Preacher and the Gospel"; "The Gospel in Hosea"; "The Preacher and the Church"; "The Preacher and His Age." (Not available.)

10. *1953-1954.* David A. MacLennan, professor at Yale Divinity School. Theme: "Pastoral Preaching." Lectures: "Perspectives"; "Objectives"; "Resources"; "Methods"; "The Pastor Preaching." (Book: *Pastoral Preaching.*)

11. *1954-1955.* Robert J. McCracken, minister of the Riverside Church, New York City. Theme: "The Making of the Sermon." Lectures: "The Long-range Preparation of the Sermon"; "The Varied Character of the Sermon"; "Preaching as an Art"; "The Construction of the Sermon." (Book: *The Making of The Sermon.*)

12. *1955-1956.* Theodore F. Adams, pastor of the First Baptist Church, Richmond, Virginia. Theme: "A Preacher Looks at His Preaching." Lectures: "The Preacher Looks at Himself and His People"; "The Faith of a Preacher"; "Planning, Preparing, and Preaching"; "Preaching With Purpose and Power." (Mimeographed.)

13. *1956-1957.* Paul Scherer, professor of homilectics at Union Theological Seminary, New York City. Theme: "The Word in Search of Words." Lectures: "A Great Gulf Fixed"; "The Nature of Revelation"; "The Credibility and Relevance of the Gospel"; "Preaching as a Radical Transaction." (Mimeographed; and chapters 1-4 of the book, *The Word God Sent.*)

14. *1957-1958.* Clarance W. Cranford, pastor of the Calvary Baptist Church, Washington, D. C. Theme: "The Minister and His Task." Lectures: "The Pulpit Ministry"; "The Minister and His Bible"; "Don't Forgets for the Minister"; "The Minister and His World." (Not available.)

15. *1959-1960.* G. Earl Guinn, president of Louisiana College. Lectures: "Reformation Preaching"; "That the Ministry Might Not Be Ashamed." (The first lecture is not available; the second is mimeographed.)

16. *1960-1961.* Horton Davies, professor of religion at Princeton University. Theme: "The Power of the Victorian Pulpit." (Chapter 10 of *Worship and Theology in England,* vol. 4.)

17. *1961-1962.* H. Grady Davis, professor of homilectics at Chicago Lutheran Seminary. Theme: "Reappraisals of Preaching." Lectures: "The Personal Word"; "The Contemporary Word"; "The Individual and Community"; "The Moment of Recognition." (Mimeographed.)

18. *1962-1963.* Samuel H. Miller, dean of Havard Divinity School. Theme: "The Minister's Workmanship." Lectures: "The Word of God—and Words"; "The Vision of Reality—and Art"; "The Care of Souls—and Faith"; "The Insight of Saints—and Morals." (Mimeographed.)

19. *1963-1964.* Harold Cooke Phillips, pastor emeritus of the

First Baptist Church of Cleveland, Ohio. Lectures: "The Eternal Word"; "The Relevant Word"; "The Word of God"; "Communicating the Word of God." (Mimeographed.)

1964-1965. No lectures.

20. *1965-1966.* Joseph Sittler, professor of theology, Lutheran School of Theology of Chicago. Lectures: "The Role of the Seminary in the Formation of the Preacher"; "The Problems of New Testament Interpretation and the Task of the Preacher"; "The Anguish of Christology"; "Faith and Form." (Book: *The Anguish of Preaching.*)

21. *1966-1967.* Elam Davis, pastor of the Fourth Avenue Presbyterian Church, Chicago. Sermons: "The God Who Creates From Nothing"; "On Treating People as Persons"; "The Church and the Social Dilemma"; "God and Life." (Tape recording.)

22. *1967-1968.* J. P. Allen, pastor of the Broadway Baptist Church, Ft. Worth, Texas. Sermons: "What Kind of Gospel?"; "The Next to the Last Straw"; "Life's Indefinable Categories"; "Open Other Channels." (Tape recording.)

23. *1968-1969.* Jack Finegan, professor of New Testament and Archaeology, Pacific School of Religion. Sermons: "God, Jesus, and Life"; "With Whom There is No Variableness"; "Measuring Jerusalem." (Tape recording.)

24. *1969-1970.* Donald Macleod, professor of homiletics, Princeton Theological Seminary. Lectures: "Crisis in Preaching"; "The Identity of the Preacher"; "The Preacher at Worship"; "What Are You Doing in Church?" (Tape recording.)

25. *1970-1971.* Kelley Miller Smith, pastor of the Capitol Hill First Baptist Church, Nashville, Tennessee. Theme: "Preaching and Social Crises." Lectures: "What Social Crises?"; "Through a Glass Blackly"; "The Relevance of Structure." (Tape recording.)

26. *1971-1972.* Edmund Steimle, professor of homiletics at Union Theological Seminary, New York. Sermons:

"Lover's Quarrel"; "Children and Angels"; "The Waiting Game." (Tape recording.)

27. *1972-1973*. D. E. King, pastor of the Monumental Baptist Church, Chicago, Illinois. Sermon: "Creative Preaching." (Not available.)

28. *1973-1974*. John R. Claypool, pastor of the Broadway Baptist Church, Ft. Worth, Texas. Theme: "The Preaching Event." Lectures: "Preaching and the Preacher"; "The Authority of the Preacher"; "Listening and Preaching"; "From Preaching to Liturgies." (Tape recording.)

29. *1974-1975*. William Muehl, professor of homiletics at Yale Divinity School. Lectures: " A Sense of Loss"; "The Height of Creativity"; "The Depth of Judgement"; "The Breadth of Compassion." (Mimeographed and tape recording.)

30. *1975-1976*. Roger Fredrikson, pastor, First Baptist Church, Wichita, Kansas. Theme: "Renewal in the Church." Lectures: "Renewal"; "Following Him: What Will He Make Of Us?"; "Look Who's Coming To The Party." (Tape recording.)

31. *1976-1977*. James I. McCord, president, Princeton Theological Seminary. Theme: "Theological Education and the Preacher." Lectures: "The Anthropological Question"; "The Christological Answer"; "Liberation Theology." (Tape Recordings.)

32. *1977-1978*. Clyde Fant, pastor, First Baptist Church, Richardson, Texas. Theme: "The Authentic Voice In Preaching." (Tape Recording.)

33. *1978-1979*. Gardner C. Taylor, pastor, Concord Baptist Church of Christ, Brooklyn, New York. Lectures: "The Preacher and The Preacher's Themes"; "A Model For Preaching"; "The Soul of the Preacher"; "Can These Bones Live Again?" (Tape recordings.)

34. *1979-1980*. Ernest T. Campbell, former senior minister, Riverside Church, New York City. Lectures: "What Does It Take To Preach?"; "The Prophetic Dimension of the Pulpit"; "Why Sermons Misfire (Part 1)"; "Why Sermons Misfire (Part 2)." (Tape recordings.)

Halford E. Luccock

Halford Luccock was professor of homiletics at Yale Divinity School when he delivered the Mullins Lectures in 1945. A popular preacher and lecturer, Luccock was also well-known through his writings. Two of his most popular books are *In The Minister's Workshop* and *Communicating the Gospel*; the latter includes his Lyman Beecher Lectures at Yale in 1953. The lectures presented here (by permission) were first published in the *Review and Expositor*.

What Literature Can Do for a Preacher

Our focus here on the general theme of literature and the preacher is not literary criticism in itself, in which field I would be the least of all the saints, but literature as an ally of the spirit, an implement for maintaining and restoring the dignity of the human soul, and the reinforcing of the values inherent in the Christian revelation. The limited purpose, then, is literature as a factor and aid in the fruitful proclamation of the gospel.

The church is in a battle in which it needs the aid of every ally with which it can join. We would consider literature then in Emerson's words, "An ally to those who would live by the spirit." J. D. Adams, in his recent volume, *The Shape of Books to Come*, has put this need succinctly: "Ours is a generation surfeited with facts and starved for vision." Often it seems as though the chief, and indeed, the only, vision of many today is that of the flood of gadgets due to arrive in the magical world science will bring after the war. Every bus in the State of Connecticut has for months been carrying this advertisement: Have miracles at your finger tips tomorrow. It sounds like a degenerate form of the Westminster Confession in which the chief end of man is in his finger tips. We have our anatomy all wrong. The miracles our world supremely needs are those of the head and of the heart. And that is where real literature, as well as religion, comes in.

Let us consider two preliminary observations as briefly as possible.

The first concerns the preacher's use of literature. It is an emphatically negative observation. The preacher's use of literature is not to be confused with preaching about books or preaching bookish sermons. Preaching which deals primarily or very largely with books easily becomes an expedition across the Sahara Desert, the most arid journey on which a congregation can be dragged. It very often degenerates into a form of exhibitionism in which there will rush from the preacher's lips with the dependability of an Old Faithful Geyser, reference to So and So's brilliant analysis of the renaissance, or his scintillating shots at somebody else's criticism of Spengler's Cycles of Doom, and similar glimpses of things as shining and far away as Arcturus. Such preaching often becomes a sort of cannibalistic display of literary scalps the preacher has taken. We may all join fervently in the litany, "From such vanity, Good Lord, deliver us."

Often one wonders what some preachers would preach if nothing had been published the preceding week. Emerson once wrote in a letter, "It is an exhilarating thing to come across a genuine, Saxon stump of a man, a wild virtuous man, who knows books but keeps them in the right place in his mind, which is lower than reason." He adds, "Books are apt to turn the mind out of doors. You find men everywhere talking from their memories instead of from their understanding."

The greatest value of the study of literature, by which we mean here, creative literature, poetry, drama, and fiction, is what it does for the preacher *himself*, rather than primarily what it may do for his sermon. A preacher might well, for his own warning, paraphrase the lament of Cardinal Woolsey, as he reached the end of his skyrocket career: "Had I but served my mind with half the zeal I served my sermon barrel, I would not have been left intellectually naked in my old age."

The great danger is that of making a merely instrumental use of literature. We are all familiar with the danger in connection with religion itself. Much so-called psychological preaching makes a merely instrumental use of God. He becomes merely a means of accomplishing some other end. For instance, we are told if we can't sleep, try religion. If you are having digestive trouble, try the peace of God which passeth understanding. Thus, God becomes a sort of glorified aspirin tablet. The greatest experience of life is reduced to the level of a corner drug store.

So we may have a viciously instrumental use of literature, as though it were something that is useful in providing little bricks for sermonic houses, rather than its primary service, which is the enlargement of the preacher as a person. For the mind must be plowed like a field, and not filled like a bottle. Literature is a plow to make the field of the mind fertile, to turn it over to the life-giving sun and rain of human experience.

The failure in this first use of literature has been very arrestingly put by John Oman. He says, "My heart sighs when I see only homiletical literature, and little improving books on a minister's shelves. It does not beat very high when I see nothing save religious books of any kind, and it beats with a still slower pulse when I find on talking with the owner that he is mainly interested with ideas theological and affairs ecclesiastical, and that in the whole kindly race of men with vital thoughts that move so warmly in their hearts, their varied avocations, and the joys and sorrows they experience, he takes only a parson's interest."

Literature can keep alive the sense of wonder, of amazement, of sympathy, of fear, and deep disturbance. It is not stuff to put into sermons, but to help create the mind and the spirit, and the heart out of which sermons will naturally flow.

Max Eastman has expressed this difference very clearly in these words: "Some people are occupied chiefly with attaining ends, and some with seeking experience. We may name the first practical and the second poetic. Poetic people are moved by the quality of things. They are possed by the impulse to realize, the wish to experience life and the world." That is the essence of the poetic temperament, and I think that is the essence of the preacher's approach to literature—to realize an experience rather than to attain a practical end.

There is a very real danger pictured in the old nursery rhyme:
Pussy cat, pussy cat, where have you been?
I have been to London to visit the Queen.
Pussy cat, pussy cat, what did you do there?
I frightened the little mouse under a chair.

It is possible to get a cat's-eye view of life in which the chief end of man seems to be to pounce on something. It is possible for a preacher, confronted with a city, a palace, and a queen, to pounce on a little homiletical mouse that happens to be scurrying around under the furniture.

A few years ago I had occasion to go up into the State of Vermont in the early days of October. If you have been in Vermont in October, I don't need to tell you anything about it. If you haven't, I'm not enough of a poet to tell you. I can simply say that sometime if you feel your chances of heaven are getting slim, go up to Vermont in October. It is the next best thing.

After looking at the mountains, the lakes and all the color, I came back, and along the roadside I stopped and bought a can of maple syrup. Now, if you had asked the children at home what their father brought home from Vermont, they could tell you very well, because he brought home a can of maple syrup. But I also brought back something else and greater that mid-October from Vermont, something which makes the poet say, "I shall make a last song when I am old out of the shining of remembered days." It was the shining of remembered days, and not anything you can carry in your hand, that was the great thing that was brought back. That is what one brings back from literature if he brings the great thing.

Look at some of the services which literature can render first to the minister himself, and then through him, to people.

First, *literature can bring the enlargement and multiplication of life.* Carl Sandburg puts this picturesquely.

> If I had a million lives to live
> And a million deaths to die
> In a million hum drum worlds,
> I'd like to change my name,
> And have a new house number to go by
> Every time I came back
> To start life all over again.
> Wouldn't you, and you, and you?

The enlargement of experience which literature brings us by opening doors into other lives, gives us a new name and a new house number. We read *Les Misérables* and our name becomes Jean Valjean. We read Thoreau and our house number becomes Walden Pond, Concord, Mass. This vicarious enlargement of experience is the rarest form of travel. All too frequently travel is too much like a shipment of baggage by express, merely moving 175 pounds of flesh from place to place. The record for some people becomes merely a recital of "What I ate in Paris," or "What I wore in London, or California." The travel into other people's minds and lives has been well described by David Livingston as "the sovereign duty of crawling under the other man's skin." It is the exciting adventure of exploring other lives.

This was pictured in a magazine in the years of the depression in the middle of the 1930's, describing a trip a man took by bus across the continent from Los Angeles to New York. There were twelve people going all the way through. The author wrote that after you had a conversation for twenty-five miles and held the baby for fifteen more, they began to know each other, and that when he got to New York he actually *was* twelve people, five men and seven women. It was said of Robert Louis Stevenson that "he died with a thousand stories in his heart." It is a fine way to live, and much travel in the realm of gold, literature, enables us to live with a thousand stories in our hearts.

One of the high services of literature—fiction, poetry, drama—is that of jail delivery. A preacher's danger is that of living behind barricades. We speak of a church's ministry to shut-ins. But the preacher himself may be a "shut-in." He may be shut in from some of the characteristic experiences of his time. If he is steadily plugging at his parish job, he cannot possibly touch personally many wide and varied areas of life. He must be liberated by the vicarious extension of experience that comes from literature. He finds the reward promised by Jesus—"He that loseth his life will find it." If we lose it in other lives—whether it be Shaw's *Saint Joan* or in Ma Joad in the tragic odyssey in *Grapes of Wrath* going west to nowhere, or in a Negro condemned to death in Chicago—we have widened our area of awareness. There is a vivid picture of that experience, an all embracing Christ-like sympathy, in W. W. Gibson's poem, *Hands*.

> Tempest without; within the mellow glow
> Of mingling lamp and firelight over all—
> Etchings and water colors on the wall,
> Cushions and curtains of clear indigo,
> Rugs damask red and blue as Tyrian seas,
> Deep chairs, black oak settees, hammered brass,
> Transculent porcelain and sea green glass,
> Color and warmth and light and dreamy ease,
> And I sit wondering where are now the hands
> That wrought at anvil, easel, wheel and loom,
> Hands slender, swart, red, gnarled, in foreign lands,
> Or English shops to furnish this seemly room
> And all the while without the windy rain,
> Drums like dead fingers tapping at the pane.

There is a picture of brotherhood, the dead fingers of those whose hands have furnished the labor that fitted the room, drawn into an inseparable fellowship in which they were members one of another. Our task is in some way to supply the equivalent of those dead fingers, tapping at the window pane, so that men may feel their relation to all with whom they work. That is all the more important because Christianity superficially, which is the way many take it, is the most comfortable religion in the world. Of course, if you take it deeply, it is the most costly and painful in the world, but there is a great deal of comfort in Christianity. In a New Haven newspaper not long ago there was a little item of news from Branford, Connecticut, which made this announcement, which was somewhat mysterious. It said, "The Comfortable Society of the First Congregational Church will meet Wednesday afternoon at three o'clock." Now, you know what that meant. The women met together and sewed on some comfortables. But so often you can say the Comfortable Society will meet on Sunday morning at eleven o'clock and include the whole church. Much literature will keep the church from becoming too comfortable.

Second, *literature makes truth come alive.* Shakespeare said it memorably, as he said most things, when he said of the poet, that "he gives to airy nothing a local habitation and a name." Preaching tries to do that. It takes what is, to many people, the "airy nothing" of a spiritual truth and gives it an incarnation in life. Common people heard Jesus gladly, for many reasons. But one reason undoubtedly was that in his teaching truth became flesh and walked on the stage of their imagination, as in the words, "A certain man had two sons" and "A certain men went down from Jericho to Jerusalem." We get a scene which may stand for the creative imagination at work in the grave yard scene in *Hamlet*, when Hamlet picks up a skull and sighs, "Alas, poor Yorik, I knew him well . . . a fellow of infinite jest." Then as he goes on to describe him, the bones take on living flesh and Yorik, for us, becomes a living soul.

Now we are trying to do that in preaching, if we are really doing our job. We will be greatly helped in our task, if we live with that kind of creation in our reading. Jennie Lee, the young Scotch girl who was elected to Parliament at the age of twenty-four, in her autobiography, giving the story of her life up to the advanced age of thirty, tells of her experiences with the problems of her constituents, appealing to her for help, in words that bring into sharp light this process of "making truth come alive." She writes: "Cases were the bane of my life. My difficulty was that I had no gift for thinking in abstract qualities. My mind reduced everything to the personal, the immediate, the concrete. An old man's letter, though I may never have met him, telling me he has been trying yet failing to live on his old age pension, became to me my firend, John Garrity, appealing to me, John with the leonine beard that I had taken so much pleasure in looking at; John who was brave and wise and tender and so proud. The letter right under my eyes became John." She calls it "difficult," but it is one of God's most precious gifts. Jennie Lee's words give an accurate picture of what literature may do for a person. They picture also what we must do as Christian preachers if we are to make our Gospel come alive in the minds of people.

Third, *the literature of our time is an indispensable aid in helping us to understand our time.* There was only one kind of illiteracy which Jesus ever condemned. He lived among people, large numbers of whom were unable to read and write. He never mentioned it. The illiteracy he did condemn was the inability to read the signs of the times, an ignorance of what is actually happening around one. John Bright, along the same line, said cuttingly, "It is strange that people who know so much about the next world should know so little about this one." To preach without knowing the strains under which people are laboring, is like a physican's trying to diagnose and operate without a knowledge of anatomy. Current literature may be a fever thermometer. We may not like it any more than we like a thermometer that registers one-hundred and three degrees. But, if we have good sense, we do not blame the thermometer, but the condition which it records. So literature, just by its integrity and not from any propaganda purpose, often reveals a dangerous infection. So *The Late George Appley* reveals a bad infection in Massachusetts, the paralyzing poison of a dead, clammy tradition, and *Strange Fruit* reveals one just as dangerous in Georgia. A woman said of a novel the other day, in expressing her disgust with it, "It is just a bad headache." She did not know how accurately and scientifically she spoke, for a headache is just a symptom of a deeper disorder. The novel was a "headache" in that medical sense.

There is a very deep thing in a preacher's equipment for his work as a healer of souls, a healer of his time. It lies in the truth that he cannot render the largest possible service unless in his own mind and spirit he is a sensitive plate, registering the tensions of his generation. We read in the Epistle to the Hebrews, "We have not a high priest that cannot be touched with the feeling of our infirmities; but one that has been in all points tempted like as we are." That sensitive sharing of experience makes for priestly power. If the evils and sufferings and frustrations of our time are just a foreign land to us, it is impossible to establish real fellowship. It is when we are able to say truly, "I, too, have suffered; I, too, know what it means to have despair gnawing at the edges of the mind," that we can really bring help to another's pain.

There is a fine line in Thornton Wilder's, *The Angel That Troubled the Waters*, in which an angel says to a crippled man, helping another cripple, "only the wounded can serve." That is true. Pain is an unofficial sacrament, a means of communicating the grace of God. The refusal of Jesus to take a narcotic on the cross to deaden pain, is a heroic attitude, which might well find expression in our reading. We, too, by a real consecration, should refuse to deaden pain. We should say, "Whatever may be my individual taste, whether romance or detective stories, I am going to look at my world, and see it; I am going to listen to its cries of pain and hear them." By so doing, we make a consecrated use of literature.

Fourth, *much literature is an ally of the spiritual life.* John Drinkwater puts this service into memorable words in his play *Abraham Lincoln* when he says that "when the high soul we celebrate," then, when we recognize "greatness passing by, ourselves are great." Some of the enduring literature of the race is a vision of "greatness passing by." We do live by admiration, hope and love. Whenever we read literature that reminds us, that in spite of all the evil in the world, there is yet a capacity for greatness in many men and women, for heroic devotion to duty, for sacrifice, when we uncover our heads before the spark of the divine in human life, that is a genuine religious experience. To see that does not mean that we renounce the Christian conception of human nature, which recognizes clearly man's capacity for evil. It does mean that we accept the definitely Christian view of man expressed in Browning's oft quoted lines:

> Oh, we're sunk enough here, God knows,
> But not quite so sunk that moments
> Sure, though seldom, are denied us.
> When the Spirit's true endowments
> Stand out plainly from its false ones
>
> . . . .
>
> There are flashes struck from midnights.
> There are fire flames noon-days kindle.

I am quite ready to grant that there has not been enough of the stuff of greatness in the American literature of the past thrity years, not nearly as much as there has been in actual life. That is one of the sound indictments to be brought against the literature following the first World War. There has been a dearth of representations of the real servants of the time, both well-known and little-known, who have been, to indulge in understatement, as deserving of a place as heroes, as many of the hairy-chested men of Hemingway, most of them with the mind of a moron and the muscles of a baboon, or the drunks who stagger through the pages of Dreiser and O'Neill.

Nevertheless, there is a striving company which step out of the pages of fiction in our generation. The women of Willa Cather, who act out the always stirring story of the triumph of soul over circumstance; the men of Rolvaag in *Giants in the Earth*; the men and women, many of them, in Ellen Glasgow, and Dorothy Canfield; the father of *The Yearling,* who did something greater than understanding Einstein's mathematics; he understood a boy. Then there is Elizabeth Maddox Roberts, a champion of the human spirit, knowing life is from within, and saying, "One man is greater than a million blades of grass. Although flesh is but grass, man has asserted himself above the grass, and enslaved the fruits of the ground." Then, not to be left out is Francie, the young heroine of *A Tree Grows in Brooklyn.* A little tree rises in triumph above the rubble in a tenement backyard; a symbol of a mind and heart, a lovely thing, unfolding like a lily blooming in mud.

Fifth, *literature has been and can be an aid to quickening the conviction of the reality of the spiritual life.* John Masefield wrote that the chief difference between his life at sea and in the carpet mill at Yonkers was that in the mill he "missed the companionship of the sky." That is a perennial need of life. A man with whom I was walking once in New York City during a summer storm, said excitedly to me, "Listen! That's the first time I have heard thunder in New York for many years!" In great cities we hear noise of the street car and the rumble of the truck; and the voice of the sky is drowned out. Much literature can make the voice of the sky audible. Poetry is an ally of the spirit in its warfare against things. Poetry, in Emerson's words, can cause the village drudge to

> "Spy behind the village clock
> Retinues of airy kings
> Spirits of angels, starry wings
> His fathers, shining in bright fables,
> His children fed at heavenly tables."

We get this aid in Dante, in *In Memoriam*; in the *Ode on Intimations of Immortality*; in T. S. Eliot's *Ash Wednesday*; and in many a younger voice. To realize this is not to turn a blind eye to the negativism and the spirtual defeatism that have been so marked a feature of much writing of the past thirty years. Yet is is true that great literature has been emphatically on the side of life. DeQuincy has put this with restraint: "Creative literature does restore to men's minds the ideals of justice, of hope, of truth, of mercy, of retribution which else, (left to the impact of daily life in its realities) would languish for want of sufficient illustration. These ideals, were it not for this amazing power of literature would often remain among us as mere notional forms, whereas by the creative forces of man put forth in literature, they gain a vernal life and germinate into vital activities." ᴖ

A Hunger for Affirmations

Our theme is the evidence that much contemporary literature gives of the fact that we are today in the midst of a major change in the popular mood, the equal of which has not occurred for generations. That change of mood makes a favorable opportunity for the preaching of the gospel, the match for which has not been presented for a long time. Thus there rests upon the church and its ministers a compelling obligation to buy up the opportunity, to redeem the time, for the Christian faith and for evangelism in the largest sense of the great, and much-abused word.

In brief, the present mood is that of wanting, and demanding positive affirmations. I realize that that assertion demands some specific evidence from a wide range of present day literature. Its consideration demands, also, a look at the qualifications that must be made and the hazards, moral and spiritual, which lie wrapped up within that popular mood. There will be neither space nor time to allow us to look at the evidence in any minute detail or inclusive range. But I have a strong conviction that a large and significant amount of contemporary literature will furnish the documents in the case.

The mood is what has been widely, and as I think, justifiably, called *a hunger for affirmations*. Archibald MacLeish expresses it, "Poetry, which owes no man anything, has nevertheless one debt, to give an image of man in which man can believe." Van Wyck Brooks writes, "I see on all sides a hunger for affirmations, for a world without confusion, waste or groping, a world that is full of order and purpose." In more strictly theological terms, the poet, William Rose Benét, puts this hunger: "It is up to writers to show us very clearly what God we have today, as the early Christians had a God to stem the flood of evil, and to show us why we should *not* serve both God and Mammon." These words may lack much of positive theological affirmation, but, at least, they begin where religious experience begins, with a hunger and a conviction of need.

For a generation we have been living largely on a diet of criticism, of a relentless realism. It has been needed and salutary, and has had large ethical and social and religious values. But in the threat which the war years have brought to many of our treasured values, people have made the discovery that as man cannot live by bread alone, so he cannot live by criticism alone. He cannot live in a spiritual vacuum from which great faiths have been exhausted. As a character in one of George Bernard Shaw's play of the 1930's, *Too True to Be Good*, puts it: "I stand midway between youth and age like a man who has missed his train, too late for the last one and too early for the next, I have no Bible, no creed; the war has shot both out of my hands. I am ignorant, I have lost my nerve, all I know is, I must find the way of life for myself and all of us, or we shall surely perish." That man spoke for multitudes just at the outbreak of World War II. He was at least standing where the Philippian jailer stood when he cried out, "What must I do to be saved?"

We have had a hundred Goethes, running about our world, psychological, economic and social, with sharp peeping eyes and diagnostic fingers, crying as Arnold said Goethe cried, "Thou ailest here and here." In the 1930's there was piled up the greatest amount of clincial diagnosis a sick world ever saw. If man could be saved by expert diagnosis of disease he ought to be saved now. But instead, he has been increasingly imperilled, or in more adequate theological language, damned. We surely have learned, or at least a great multitude of people have learned, that we cannot be saved by diagnosis, especially when unaccompanied by any sense of absolute values. So many of the writers of the 1920's and the 1930's seemed to wallow in misery, after the pattern of Shakespeare's Richard II: "For God's sake let us sit upon the ground and tell sad stories of the death of Kings." Writers all the way from the opaque James Joyce to Hemingway, from Eugene O'Neill to James T. Farrell, were bent on proving that life is a dark little pocket. Quite inevitably, a time of national and world disaster has turned multitudes to a search for something by which the spirit can live, to positive affirmations. We would be culpably blind if we did not see in the expression of that mood in every type of literature an immense opportunity for the proclamation of an answer to man's hunger. There is a great opportunity to do what the evangelist Philip did when he met the Ethiopian Treasurer in a searching and inquiring mood. Philip began at the point which the man had reached in his experience "and preached unto him Jesus."

This mood of dissatisfaction is a point much like the conviction of sin in Christian experience in the fact that the question mark has become flesh and dwelt among us. A vivid question walks among men, a red question mark, colored with blood, "Have we been on the right road? Is a way of life which in twenty-five years has produced two world wars, with a world-wide depression sandwiched in between, the right road to anywhere except ruin?" Is a road from which God has been so largely crowded off one that leads anywhere except to the city of destruction? We have journeyed from an exclamation point over man's achievements to a question mark. Now the major problem is, Can we go on from a question mark, from a skepticism about man's glory and his optimisms, to a new exclamation point, punctuating with emphasis the affirmation, "Thou hast the words of eternal life?"

There can be no question about the extent of this revolution in feeling and mood and thinking. There has been a real revolution on the necessity for a spiritual basis of life. Will we sleep through it, as Rip Van Winkle slept through the American Revolution, or can we adjust our thinking and action to change?

Before we turn to the evidence of this revolution in specific writings it may be well to glance at the trend in general. The present catastrophe in the world has opened the eyes of many to the fact that there was something deeply diseased in the whole nineteenth century way of life, with its illusions of progress, its confidence in itself and its immoral optimism. As Rebecca West, one of the most thoughtful of British novelists, writes, "We can see what was the matter with the Victorian age which set itself to multiply the material wants of mankind (with what results we see today) and whittle down its spiritual wants to a mere ethical anxiety which was often mean." To us, looking back from today, the closing period of the nineteenth century seems to appear in the light of a golden age. It was an era of peace in Europe, an age of great technological advance, of the accumulation of wealth, of growing tolerance, and spreading imperialism. And yet, when viewed historically and critically, as we can view it today, it emerges as an age fatally sick with materialism, with smug self-confidence and uncritical assurance. To use a perhaps overworked figure of speech the escalator which men were sure would steadily ascend almost automatically to measureless progress stopped, and then went into reverse in the first world war, and has been steadily going down in reverse ever since. Herbert Spencer, the High Priest of evolutionary progress, wrote words which sounded to many like a new gospel: "Progress is not an accident but a necessity. What we call evil and immorality must disappear. It is certain that man must become perfect." And with what a bang that escalator bumped on the bottom! But yesterday the word of Herbert might have stood against the world. Now lies he low with few so poor to do him reverence!

There is a perfect picture of this bit of history in the Crystal Palace of London, that great glass Temple, erected for the London Exposition in 1851. It symbolized the widespread feeling that Britain and Europe were at the beginning of a new era when unrestricted competition would render all wars unnecessary. It was burned just on the eve of the Second World War. It was left a mass of charred ruins of twisted steel and broken glass, a symbol of the broken confidence in the pagan god Mammon, which it served as a shrine.

Take a much later expression, in American verse, of that same confidence in mechanical power. Here are some verses by Berton Braley, *A Song of Power*, written about 1930.

This is a song of the men who master
Motor, dynamo, fuse and switch,
Who lift our life to a pace that's faster
Who move the world by a finger twitch.
Men in shop and laboratory
Men who work with the thunderbolts
Who outmatch even Alladin's story
With a magic lamp—of a million volts
With vaster marvels for us to scan.
A song whose jubilant lifting chorus
Rings with the hopes and dreams of man.

Try to repeat those words, "a million volts" representing "the hopes and dreams of man" in the ruins of Coventry, of Plymouth and Warsaw, or in the fields strewn with the graves of fifteen million dead! The words turn to ashes on our lips.

All this is a twice told tale. One could multiply it for days at a time. But such words are a reminder that God and a moral order are the only sure foundation for a world's life. Let one word suffice, a terrible prophecy from the German poet Heine, who saw with X-ray eyes. A little over 100 years ago, discussing the future of Germany as he saw it, he wrote these words: "Should the divine talisman of the cross ever fail, the old stone gods will rise from the long forgotten ruins, and rub the dust of a thousand years from their eyes, and Thor, leaping to life with his giant hammer, will smash the Gothic cathedrals." Was ever a prophecy so literally and terribly fulfilled? The talisman of the cross did break and the cathedrals were smashed.

Gamaliel Bradford wrote some twenty years ago some light verses entitled *Exit God* which express the mood of today.

> Of old our fathers' God was real
> Something they almost saw
> Which kept them to a stern ideal
> And scourged them into awe.
> I sometimes wish that God were back
> In this dark world and wide.
> For though some virtues he might lack
> He had his pleasant side.

That was only a playful satire. But all through these years, in the most unexpected places, there has been the echo, "I sometimes wish that God were back." For history in the last generation has made clear that, in the language of the Old Testament prophet, Amos, when God disappears, "the sun goes down at noon."

In one simple fact of language we have seen dramatized the choice offered in the Old Testament, "Choose ye this day whom ye shall serve." The root of the word "hallowed" in "Hallowed be Thy name" is the same root as in the word "Heil" in "Heil Hitler!" We have one choice. We can either say "Hallowed" to an august God, or we can say "Heil" to a little tin pot deity. For, in the picturesque words of John A. Hutton, "We are so made that when true religion goes out at the window, something else comes up from the drains."

One bit of literary evidence which may stand for hundreds of pages is to be found in the book, written during the early years of the second world war, *A Chart for Rough Waters*, by Waldo Frank, novelist and critic. "Europe," he writes, "has been in rough waters ever since it broke with the great tradition. And by the great tradition, I mean the Hebrew-Christian tradition, the Christian tradition which had enormously enhanced the individual with pride of immortality and a God come down to earth, and the Hebrew tradition of justice and brotherhood, the great tradition in the sense that the individual has purpose and direction and worth and dignity because God is in him." In these words we find a hunger for affirmations. In like manner in another book, *Darwin, Marx and Wagner*, Prof. Jacques Barzun, of Columbia University, describes the world chaos as due, in real measure, to the denying of purpose of the universe, through the prestige of Darwin and Marx, with the result of the substitution of opportunities for morals, and the emergence of Machiavellianism in politics.

Some months ago a woman whose son was in the army, stationed in the Aleutian Islands, was asked where her son was located. "Oh," she answered, "he is in the illusions." We are all in the "illusions" if we imagine we can have a durable world structure without a spiritual plum line.

Another notable recent volume, *Puritanism and Democracy*, by Prof. Ralph Barton Perry, of Harvard, which makes a striking reevaluation of the Puritan, gives evidence of the re-examination of the spiritual elements in American history. His conclusions stand in glaring contrast to the popular misconception of the Puritan so prevalent twenty-five years ago and later, which made him a figure for scorn and caricature, a loathsome "kill joy," as depicted in Kirby's famous (and infamous) cartoons. Prof. Perry writes: "He who would reject the religious ideas of the Puritans must be prepared to accept in some degree one or more of their opposites, a frivolous disregard of moral questions, a confusion of values, a blurring of moral distinctions, a lack of principle, and an acquiescence in the meaninglessness of life."

May I impose upon your patience for one more quotation, for I am anxious to give some of the evidence, at least, that I am reporting upon a trend actually found in present day literature, and not merely spinning cobwebs out of my own wishful thinking. Here follows a quotation from Aldous Huxley's latest novel, *Time Must Have a Stop*. Mr. Huxley, whatever else one may be moved to say about him, is making one of the most interesting intellectual and spiritual pilgrimages now going on in the world of literature. He is on his way to the City of God, even though he may seem to have reached, up to the present moment, only a vague form of Buddhism. But in his religious insight into the fruit of godlessness, he is superbly on the side of the angels. In this novel, at least, in the passage quoted, through the mouth of his character, Sebastian, he speaks his own thought:

> "I used to think . . . as a strict sensualist, and aesthete, I
> had no responsibility for what was happening in the world.
> But the habit of sensuality and pure aestheticism is a
> process of God-proofing. To indulge in it is to become a
> spiritual mackintosh, shielding the little corner of time, of

which one is the center, from the least drop of eternal reality. But the only hope of the world of time, lies in being constantly drenched by that which lies beyond time. Guaranteed God-proof, we exclude from our surroundings the only influence that is able to neutralize the destructive energies and liberal churchmen, the abolition of God left a perceptible void. . . .

"True religion concerns itself with the givenness of the timeless. An idolatrous religion is one in which time is substituted for eternity, . . . either past time in the form of a rigid tradition, or future time, in the form of progress toward Utopia. And both are Molochs, both demand human sacrifice on an enormous scale, Spanish Catholicism was a typical idolatry of past time. Nationalism, Communism, Facism, all the social pseudo-religions of the twentieth century are idolatries of future time. Before or behind time can never be worshipped with impunity.

"And it is only by deliberately paying our attention and our primary allegiance to eternity that we can prevent time from turning our lives into a pointless and diabolical foolery."

That last sentence deserves the sharpest of italics. For, coming from one who was in the 1920's, the high priest of the school of cynicism, it gives sure evidence that he has been traveling toward affirmation, toward allegiance to eternity.

A part of the picture is to be found in the growing disconcernment of the limitations of science, expressed not only during this war, but in the years before. Let one quotation suffice (it could be matched by many) from a leading novelist of England, playwright, and critic, J. B. Priestly. He wrote, in *Rain on God's Hill:*

"Great scientists are nearly always wise men, sages; But, after all, there are not many of them, whereas there are multitudes of triumphant little men. It is these little men who produce the "nothing but" accounts of this life, robbing it of all mystery and wonder. Life, they tell us, is "nothing but" something or other, and if I know nothing else, I know in my very bones that these fellows are wrong. I would rather believe the wildest nonsense ever imported with the tinned fruit and films from California, than march round their tiny circle with these "nothing but" men. I would rather believe I am an ex-Babylonian Queen who has been turned into a Yorkshire author by a Great White Master in Tibet. I would rather believe that I am guided by the spirit of my late great-uncle Alfred through a dear Red Indian who speaks in the voice of a stout woman in a Brixton basement. Anything, anything, rather than this cheap, cocksure intellectuality, which despises every age but this, because we know, and they didn't know, how to fly the Atlantic or to use X-rays."

Out of the same mood and feeling a poet, Alfred Noyes, asks a deep question of science:

"Was the eye controlled by blindly moving atoms,
Or the still, listening ear fulfilled with music,
By forces without knowledge of sweet sound?"

A very extensive indication of this hunger for affirmations, is to be found in the large number of historical novels, which the last decade has produced. This is particularly true of the spate of novels dealing with America in other years and centuries. The need to "defend America" has projected the questions, "What is America? What are we defending? What are the positive values realized in the experiment of democracy in America?" So scores of fictional portraits of America in the making, and facing the crises of other days and other cennturies, have been written in answer to a definite need, and have received wide reading. There is a wide variety to this historical fiction, in which the names of Howard Fast, Esther Forbes, Marcia Davenport come readily to mind. It is realistic fiction, endeavoring sincerely to portray the actual conditions of life in the period, a vastly different type of fiction from the earlier books of historical fiction which flourished about the turn of the century, marked by such "cloak and dagger" stories as *When Knighthood was in Flower, Richard Carvel,* and *To Have and to Hold.*

But the prevalence of this mood, which furnishes such an enormous opportunity for the proclamation of Christian affirmations, brings also some very great spiritual and ethical dangers. These cannot be elaborated here, but they must at least be named, and recognized so that they can be guarded against. There is the very real danger that this mood may, in many people, extinguish entirely the capacity for ethical and moral criticism. That would be an immeasurable loss, and a strangling of the Christian criticism of our society. Such a mood might easily lead, indeed it has already done so in multitudes of people, into a sort of a holy baptism of the status quo, and the suffocation of a sense of Christian social and human values.

Again, this mood, unless tempered with a Christian vision of what the Kingdom of God on earth involves in human relations, will lead to a backward looking *nostalgia* into the lazy feeling that "whatever used to be is right."

Finally, the fact that for four years we have been living on incessant and impassioned appeals for "national unity" constitutes, in itself, a great moral and spiritual liability. National unity is a necessity in war. But we should never dare forget that a vital democracy and a vital Christianity depend on the virtues of diversity from dominate opinion in Galilee and Jerusalem. With forthright boldness he brought in a minority report, "Ye have heard it said . . . but I say unto you." As it was in the beginning of Christianity, so is it now and ever shall be. ℞

H. H. Farmer

H. H. Farmer was professor of philosophy at Westminster College, Cambridge, England when he delivered
the Mullins Lectures in 1946. His many books in the field of
Christian philosophy and theology made him known
throughout the English-speaking world. His book on
preaching, *Servant of The Word*, has become one of the
classics of modern homiletical literature. Professor Farmer
lives today in Hove, Sussex, England.

The three lectures presented here (by permission) were
first published in the *Review and Expositor*. Farmer's
theme was "The Source and Setting of the Sermon."

Preaching and Worship

In the preparation of these lectures on preaching which you have greatly honoured me by asking me to deliver before you, I have found myself confronted by the difficulty that I have already published a book on preaching. Obviously, that by itself need not necessarily cause embarrassment, for apart from the question whether anybody has read it, it was a slim volume, and —it is quite superfluous to say—was very far indeed from exhausting the subject. But the point is that in it I tried to set forth what might be called the general philosophy, or theology, of Christian preaching, as I understand it. I tried to explain, that is to say, what preaching essentially is, what distinguishes it from other types of public utterance, and why it has, and must ever have, a central and indispensable place in the Christian message and conduct of life. I tried to show that "the strange activity of preaching" rests upon and arises out of the "strange" Christian Gospel, and all that it implies concerning God's nature and purpose with mankind. (Preaching, I said, is not merely a means for conveying the content of the Gospel; it is bound up with the distinctive content of that Gospel. Preaching is part of God's saving activity in Christ—necessarily, indispensably so; and it is that because the Gospel is what it is and not something else. All this I sought to maintain in *The Servant of the Word*.) Now the difficulty is this: if, in these lectures I am to speak to you about some aspects of the practical business of being a preacher, much that I say will unavoidably presuppose, in greater or less degree, what I have said in the book referred to: for obviously we cannot have right ideas on how to preach, unless we first have some right ideas on what preaching essentially is and what it is intended to effect. The danger will, therefore, be, either that I shall repeat what is already available in print elsewhere, or that, in the endeavor to avoid such repetition, my argument will lose force because it rests on assumptions which, though they are present to my mind, are absent from yours. I can only say that I will do my best to avoid both of these pitfalls, though perhaps it is too much to hope that I shall avoid them altogether.

When your honoured president wrote and asked me to give these lectures, he said that the intention of the Mullins foundation is that the lectures should deal "with the materials of preaching, that is, the source of preaching materials, with special emphasis on literature as a source, but of course including the Bible itself." That instruction is definite enough, and I hope to fulfill it not too inadequately; but I have found as I have proceeded with the task, that my conception of the preachers work is such that I cannot fulfill it in quite the direct way that might seem to be required. I have found that I must approach the task indirectly, so indirectly that you may possibly wonder at times whether I am fulfilling it at all. I must, therefore, make plain at the outset why I feel I must make this indirect approach, and what I mean by such an approach.

The point is this: I believe that if a minister has a right understanding of his vocation as a pastor and preacher, and a right attitude to it, he will infallibly gather the right materials for his preaching, by a sort of instinct, from his whole commerce with men and with life; moreover the materials he will gather will in the nature of the case be the right materials for him and for his style of preaching—he being what he is in all his idiosyncrasy as a person. The materials I would gather would not necessarily be suitable for him, or such as he could make effective use of. On the other hand, if a preacher has not such a right understanding of, and attitude to, his task, the most careful instruction will not avail much. Indeed, it may do harm by seeming to give countenance to an attitude which can be wholly deplorable. The deliberate and continuous seeking of materials for preaching, if it be not exceptionally well disciplined and controlled, can defeat its own end, and ultimately impoverish the preacher's work rather than enrich it. For it can both express and foster a narrow, professional, second-hand attitude of mind, which lacks the power to respond sensitively and directly to the glory and the wonder, the humour and the tragedy, of human life itself. It is in its own way an attitude comparable to that of the engineer who sees, say the Niagara Falls not as a glorious work of God before which his soul is both uplifted and abased, but only as a source of energy to be piped and directed, at a profit, into the refrigerators and electic irons of a thousand back-kitchens. I remember my old teacher, Dr. Oman once telling how a young minister once came into his study and observing a complete edition of Goethe's works on the shelves, tapped it, and said "Any sermon material in 'Goath'?" "Goath," you observe, was not to be read for his own sake, but only in order to be piped into his sermons. The attitude is fundamentally wrong. And because it is wrong, not all the most assiduous and well-directed gathering of materials from 'Goath' or from anybody else will make such an one a great and effective preacher. On the other hand, as I have said, if the attitude is right, the gathering of materials will to a quite considerable degree inevitably follow.

The important thing, therefore, is to come to our preaching task in the right frame of mind. Hence it is with that right frame of mind that I must begin, and to it I must continually return in anything that I may be able to say on the gathering and use of preaching materials.

These remarks help to explain why I have chosen to speak first of preaching and worship. For indeed I cannot think of a more adequate way to describe that fundamentally right attitude to our work as pastors and preachers of which I have been speaking than to describe it as one which is informed and sustained all the time by the spirit and intention of worship. I say "the intention of worship" because it is as part of worship that most of our preaching will in fact be done, and that fact ought to govern all our preparation for preaching.

In passing I would like to say that I believe it to be a wholly right instinct which has led the Christian Church to give at least the main ministry of preaching the setting of worship. Preaching needs worship, the setting of worship, in order to keep the personality of the preacher in its proper place and proportion. The preacher needs the protection of worship against certain obvious dangers to his soul. But the congregation needs its protection against the preacher, if I may so put it. It needs its protection against his weakness, if he is weak. For him the weakness of his utterance is plainly of less account, if it be but a small part of a great act of worship wherein men are lifted in adoration and thanksgiving, in confession and intercession, into the very presence of God. But it needs its protection also against his strength, if he be strong, if he be what is known as a powerful or popular preacher whom crowds flock to hear. The *worship of the preacher*—the so-called pulpit giant or prince of the pulpit (to use the loathsome phrases of religious journalism)—has been an evil thing in certain types of Protestant Christianity. It has been a source of weakness alike to individual souls and to the corporate life and witness of the Church. There is only one thing to keep it in check, and that is another sort of worship—the true and deep worship of God. Who, standing in the presence of God, dare think of any sinful man, no matter what his gifts or how much God may be pleased to use him, as a giant or a prince? In the true worship of God such thoughts and words die. Who in that presence is not a pygmy, who is not a poverty-stricken beggar?

Eric Gill in his autobiography tells of the profound sense of something being crucially different when he was taken as a young lad for the first time to a great service of worship which was not dominated by the preacher, which was what he had been used to. He says: "Not only was the weight of the preacher lifted off (and if you have never sat under a minister—what a marvellous phrase and how descriptive of the oppression—you cannot understand how great a relief it was) but you became impersonal yourself, the weight of your own personality was lifted too, and, though not so obviously, this was an even greater relief. For the trouble with evangelical religion as commonly understood is that it is too personal altogether. There is too much emphasis on the personality of the minister and too much emphasis on the personal reactions of those who are ministered to—too exhibitionist on the one hand and too introspective on the other. There is very little conception of objective corporate praise as of the morning stars singing together."

Making every allowance for Gill's unrestrained way of putting things (not to speak of the ambiguities of words like evangelical, personal, impersonal) there is truth in this. Yet Gill himself goes on to insist on the necessity for preaching—"it is essential", he says, "to keep a balance." It is certainly true that if preaching needs worship, worship also needs preaching. For if the preaching, when it is not duly balanced by the worship, becomes too personal in the bad sense meant by Gill, it is equally true that the worship, if it be not duly balanced by the preaching, becomes not personal enough in the sense of bringing new light to the mind and new challenge to the will. Worship can so easily degenerate into a matter of vague feelings and aesthetic satisfactions, with little or nothing of deeper insight into the penetrating, cleansing, condemning, demanding, comforting truth of the Gospel, little or nothing of that personal encounter with the Holy Will of God, in its absolute demand upon our will and its final succour for all our private and individual as well as corporate needs—that personal encounter which may at any moment be a major crisis in our personal destiny.

But this has been to digress. Let us then examine the relation of the preacher to the act of worship which he conducts and of which his preaching is usually a part. Let us try to see why, and in what sense, our preaching and our preparation for preaching, must be sustained and informed by the spirit and intentions of worship.

The relation of the preacher and his preparation to the act of worship which he conducts and of which his preaching is a part is in fact a rather peculiar one. In order to understand it we must take note of what may be called the paradox of worship. I am thinking of course of the worship we engage in in Church. The paradox is this: On the one hand the worship must be in the nature of the case a withdrawal from the business of life. For worship is the conscious and deliberate turning of the whole person, along with others, towards God in and for Himself. In the act of worship God becomes for the time being the whole object of the whole man, in a way that is not possible at other times and in the course of other activities. It is therefore, and must be, as I have said, something of a withdrawal from life. That is precisely why we come apart, to a special building, on a special day, not devoted to other things, to do it. I know that there is a sense in which any activity can be pursued, and ought to be pursued, as unto God, pursued—if one may use one of those vague pietistic phrases which I fear we often use without much meaning—in a "spirit of worship." I know that it is possible even in the midst of the most absorbing activities to "throw" as it were a thought, a desire, towards God, and be the better for it. But speaking generally we do our tasks in the world more effectively if we concentrate our minds wholly upon them, not letting them wander even in the direction of God. The engineer had far better be watching the signals and the pressure gauges, than engaging in his prayers on the footplate. And, if it be said that to watch the signals and the pressure gauges is to worship God—*laborare est orare*—then that it seems to me is to use the word worship in a somewhat unnatural and misleading sense. Nevertheless, on the other hand, here is the paradox—it is quite clear that worship, according to the Christian understanding of it, though it is a withdrawal from life in so far as it is the deliberate focusing of the whole being upon God, must not be unrelated to life. A worship which is divorced from, and exercises no observable influence upon, the kind of life a man lives in the world is from the Christian point of view a scandal—it must be either dead and formal, or the worship of some other God than the God revealed in Jesus Christ. This then is the paradox—withdrawal which is nevertheless not withdrawal. The paradox is of course partially resolved, or should be, by the act of preaching; that is one reason why the Church has been wholly right in making preaching part of worship, for it is part of the functioning of preaching, in relation to worship, to bring home explicitly to the mind and the will at least some of the implications of worship for the daily life. But the paradox can never be wholly resolved by this; for worship must still be in considerable measure withdrawal from the business of life, if it is to be worship, and is to exercise its full effect upon our lives.

The truth of the matter is that in a considerable degree the paradox is resolved all the time unconsciously, and at a deeper level than that of explicit awarenesses of a man's mind. The power of true worship, Christian worship, to shape a man's personality, to govern his values and reactions to life, to give meaning and direction to his daily enterprises, is exercised unconsciously, if it is exercised at all. The act of worship, if it be truly done, affects the whole man just because it is an act of the whole man, and the whole man includes a good deal more than he himself is ever explicitly aware of at the moment. From the deliberate, conscious, withdrawing act of worship there flow, through, so to say, non-deliberate, unconscious channels, influences which reach, and make a profound difference to all that a man is and does in his daily life.

Now to return to the minister and his preparation. He is in a rather peculiar and difficult position. He has to prepare for the act of worship and the act of preaching in a way, which, in so far as it is concentrated on the preparation, can no more be an act of worship in the full sense than the driving of a locomotive can be such an act of worship. In preparing the devotional part of the service, and still more in gathering the materials for, and preparing, the sermon you cannot in the nature of the case concentrate your whole being on God. To prepare a prayer is after all not to pray; to gather materials for and to write a sermon is not to preach. Nevertheless, because the final end and aim of the activity is the whole act of worship, the relationship of the act of worship to the minister's work cannot be left quite so fully to unconscious processes as it can be in the case of others. It ought to be so left in some degree—for certainly if a minister's whole being and life are not being deepened and nourished by worship they will grow thin and poor and sterile: (that is why it is most urgently necessary that a minister should of all people have a strong and well cultivated devotional life of his own, and why ministerial conferences and retreats are so important and so necessary). But it cannot be wholly so left, inasmuch as his work is preparation for worship, he at least must understand something of the way in which worship enters into and shapes men's daily lives. He must know something of the fundamental human needs that true worship and preaching should reach and satisfy, and in his preparation bear them in mind as a criterion of his work.

I ask you to consider three such fundamental human needs to which the act of worship, including the preaching, bears, or should bear, close relationship. I will call them (1) the need for release from the finite, or to put it positively, the need for an adequate end; (2) the need for release from the instinctive, or postively, the need for a right absolute; (3) the need for release from the ego, or positively, the need for proper humility.

(1) First, the need for release from the finite, or the need for an adequate end.

Fritz Kunkel, whose books you probably know (all ministers should certainly know them) lays down the principle that there is no understanding human nature unless you realize two things: (1) first, that no important human activity is ever exclusively concerned with its own immediate goal or end; it always points to some other end lying beyond it. He calls this the principle of *infinalism*. No human end, in the sense of an object aimed at, is ever an end in the sense of a terminus, or rounded-off conclusion. (2) Second, the further end beyond itself to which every activity points need not necessarily be, and quite often is not in fact, consciously envisaged. It is an unconscious aim or goal, but its importance is not less for being unconscious. A good illustration of these two points is to be found in the play activities of children. Play to the child seems to have quite sufficient justification in itself; he does not look beyond it. The play passes the time pleasantly, and that is enough. But in point of fact the real meaning of the play activity, and that which alone makes it any other than the antics of imbecility, lies beyond the play itself; it is to be found in the maturity to which the whole being of the child is growing up, and reaching towards. It is the preliminary exercising of powers whose real purpose lies elsewhere. The child is himself unconscious of this further end which is embedded in its more immediate needs; but it is there, and it is the most important part of the whole business.

Now the important thing to realize is this, that as life goes on, the relation of these two factors to one another—the immediate end and the further end lying beyond the immediate end—tends to change. In the young person it is of no consequence that the underlying further end remains hidden, as it does, in the unconscious. In the absorbing interest of what seems an inexhaustible brave new world, he passes from activity to activity, dropping this, taking up that, finding fairly complete momentary satisfaction first here, then there. And it would be a precocious morbidity in him to do anything else; it would be a precocious morbidity for him to ask for some other reason for doing what should be, because of its own intrinsic interest, its own justification. But as the years pass—if I may paraphrase some words I have used elsewhere—and we become, as we must, more or less fixed in the routines of a settled-down middle-age; as we come under the necessity of occupying our time, and finding what satisfaction we can, in a few rather pedestrain activities, with neither the energy, nor even the opportunity, to begin anything fresh; as, with the increase of reflectiveness, and of the need for it, we find ourselves continually looking through what we do now to what we shall be doing tomorrow, next week, a year hence; as memory of the past, with all its frustrations and disappointments grows longer, and anticipation of the future grows shorter, so that with the swift approach of the end we can increasingly see our life in this world *as a whole*;—so the inconclusive infinalism of all our activity, the latent demand for a "beyond-itself-ness" inherent in all that we do, is apt to emerge from the subconscious, and make itself felt in a certain pervasive disquietude of the whole being. It is apt to make itself felt in a recurrent sense of the futility of immediately "do-able" things, of waste of effort, of a certain ultimate meaninglessness in any achievement at all. What does it all come to in the end? As we get older this question has a way of, so to say, poking its head from behind the screen of the subconscious and making an unpleasant ugly grimace at us.

How is this to be provided against, or rather provided for? For nothing can alter the fact that our human nature is as I have just described it—that is to say, under the continuous necessity to act according to purposes which cannot reach a satisfactory conclusion in terms of themselves alone, but always point beyond themselves. The only answer to the problem, the only satisfaction of the need, I believe, is in the worship of God—the regular periodical withdrawal from immediate activities in order to look beyond them to, and to concentrate the whole being upon, the eternal God. It is only in the worship of the infinite God that the radical infinalism of our nature is at one and the same time affirmed and accepted, and yet transcended so that it ceases to be the paralysing thing it otherwise is. The Infinite God is the only reality which always lies beyond the reach of man, and yet in which at the same time his soul can come completely to rest. Our hearts are restless until they find rest in Thee: yet the essential restlessness of our earthly life, its passing from task to task, its radical infinalism must remain. In God, and in God alone, can we be conscious of possessing all things, yet having nothing. We are pilgrims wending our way home, yet in worship we are already at home, though still remaining pilgrims. It is paradoxical, but all meeting of time and eternity is paradoxical. But to anybody who does worship, the truth of the paradox will be already known. I remember once returning with Principal Micklem from worship in Mansfield College Chapel, Oxford. We were silent for a little, and then he said—"Curious what a sense of settled completeness, of final rounded-off-ness, worship and worship alone gives to our life."

It might be said, why is the worship of God necessary? Why is it not enough to have the *thought* of God in the mind, to adhere to a general theistic philosophy of life, without any regular acts of adoration and worship? The answer has already been given in what I said earlier. This infinalism of our nature is something which touches our whole being (as we have seen), touches the subconscious as well as the conscious. We need to have it settled once and for all, right down to the depths of our being, that life is not meaningless and futile—settled once and for all, so that the suggestion that it is meaningless and futile never really gets a chance, either consciously in a formulated thought, or subconsciously as a vague disquietude or dissatisfaction which we dare not face lest everything should lose such savour as it has. This satisfaction of the whole being right down into the subconscious deeps cannot be accomplished merely by thought—but it can be accomplished by the act of worship. The man who worships does not need to be continually thinking about God, as he goes about his daily business, in order to be given this victory. He can forget about God, precisely because already through worship the thought of God is deeply registered in his whole being. He carries with him the whole time pervasive sense of God as the sole adequate end lying beyond and above and yet within all his activities. The relationship might be compared to the relationship of a man working in the fields: to the infinite sky which overarches him. He is not explicitly and directly aware of the sky, as he bends to his tasks—you cannot hoe a row of potatoes and look at the sky at the same time—nevertheless, the sky is there in the background of all that he does; and whenever he lifts his eyes, behold, it is there, and he would feel very different if it were not there; something of freedom and largeness would go, as though one had passed into a small, locked room. Worship puts sky into and over the life of a man.

What then does this imply with regard to our preaching? And our preparation for it? Well, I know the danger of making sweeping generalizations about so infinitely varied a task as preaching: sermons have many uses and therefore take many forms. But I am going to venture on a generalization. I venture the generalization in the belief that it is at least true enough to be a sound regulative principle of the preacher's work—that all great and effective Christian preaching has a certain "otherworldliness" in it, if not as its explicit theme, then as a persistent underlying groundtone, which the hearer feels even though he could not put into words. Of course I must now say what I mean by "otherworldliness", for there is a false and pernicious otherworldliness which has often masqueraded as Christian, but is not in fact Christian at all. What I mean by it is I hope sufficiently indicated by what I have already been saying. I mean the temper and the outlook which makes the centre of gravity of this present life something above and beyond, and more eternal than this Life. Otherworldliness says that the true meaning of our life is not to be found in this world considered in and for itself, but rather in what this world is leading on to in "the beyond" of this world. Otherworldliness says that this world is fundamentally misused, and human nature fundamentally frustrated if, whatever else of interest and delight we may do in it, there is not produced in us in the course of our transit through it, a character fit for the nearer presence of the Most High, a character in Browning's words, "far gone in readiness for God". But perhaps the best way to express the heart and essence of the matter is to use the idea of pilgrimage. The unworldly mind knows—and its whole conduct is governed, even unconsciously, by the knowledge—that it is on a pilgrimage, that though it may delight in things of this world (why not indeed, it is God's world, He made it) it is after all only passing through it to another. "Therein," says Stephen Graham, "is a Christian disconcerned, that he seeks a city, a city which hath the foundations, whose builder and maker is God. Once we have consciously known ourselves as pilgrims on the way, then all the people and the scenes about us have a new significance. They are seen in their right perspective. Upon the pilgrim's road, our imperfect eyes come into focus for all earthly phenomena."

I am sure this is so. Preaching which lacks this note will not be great preaching, deep preaching, satisfying preaching; what is more important it will not be Christian preaching, New Testament preaching. It will easily get lost in the essential triviality and superficiality of contemporary humanistic thought or in the pitiable ineffectiveness of merely moral exhortation and uplift. (Many years ago John Brierly wrote these words: Not until we have reached this stage of thought and feeling, do we even begin to understand the real significance of the message of Christ. Its central teaching is that worldliness is not so much wicked, as that it is so absurdly limited. It is a stupid and shortsighted provincialism. Christ brings us tidings from a larger world, on which he proposes to launch us. The narrow parochial view of life finds its end in gaining purely this-worldly goods. Christ proclaims this to be a pastime for emptyheads and babes, no matter how clever they may be at it, and calls them to take up pursuits worthy of the manhood God has given them. He speaks to us as the revelation of a larger universe, to whose vaster and more splendid careers he invites us, the universe of the eternal, whose aristocracy is those who serve, whose wealth is love, whose King is God.)

Every sermon, then, ought to be a word from a pilgrim to pilgrims. Every sermon ought to be on the background of "Sky," even though it does not explicitly talk about it, every sermon must be informed with the spirit of worship. I am sure you will find it worth while to test your work by this. But of course the important thing is to have something of that spirit in your own soul; indeed it will be well to recover it and intensify it by a few minutes of meditation before ever you begin to prepare what you will later on in the midst of the worship of God's people, preach.

(2) The second deep need of the soul of man which finds, or should find, its satisfaction in worship is, we said, the need for a right absolute.

Here again we are confronted by a distinctive quality of the human person, and here again we may perhaps best indicate it by referring to a characteristic of children which has always seemed to me to be of great significance. I observed in my own children, when they were young, that each, as he or she came to the age of about five or so years, quite spontaneously imposed on himself some absolute prohibitions. One would insist, when out walking, on not stepping on any of the cross lines in the sidewalk; another on never stepping on any but carpeted sections of the floor as he went about the house. Strangest of all perhaps was the announcement that certain things were "poison" and on no account whatever to be touched, still less eaten. I have always thought that this odd behaviour, which I have observed also in other children besides my own, was really of the highest significance, for be it noted, it always took place at the point where the child was beginning to be aware of himself, and to affirm himself, as an individuality, a person. It points to this profoundly important truth about a person, that it only begins a truly personal life at the point where its purely instinctive and emotional life is met and challenged and checked by an absolute demand which must be obeyed, whatever the instinctive and emotional life may say about it. That my small daughter should declare a number of harmless things to be poison and refuse to touch them, whatever her feeling and desires might be, seems on the surface a most meaningless irrationality; but from the point of view of the deepest, though unconscious, needs of her unfolding personal life it was highly meaningful. In those prohibitions she was seeking to establish herself as a person; she was seeking release from the flux of merely instinctive life in which an animal dwells; she was beginning to master both herself and her world.

There is no question that man's calling and destiny to be a person and the need for an absolute, governing his conduct, are indissolubly bound up together. It marks, I repeat, the emergence of the specifically personal and human from the sub-personal and the animal. That being so, it is of the most urgent importance not only that this deep need should be provided for, but also that it should be provided for in the right way. For if it is not rightly provided for it will seek and find perverted satisfaction, and that means a satisfaction that does not really satisfy. The world is in fact today bedevilled with false absolutes, as Reinhold Neibuhr has so frequently insisted. For men must have an absolute of some sort. As Luther said, if they have no God, they fashion an idol. For you have false absolutes when purely human finite things are turned into absolutes, such as the nation or the state or the ruler or the leader or the party, and that means that there is no real check upon the instinctive life, but rather it is given new and deadly power and sanction, in and through the very absolute which is invoked to check it. The requirements of cruel and ambitious men, instead of being brought under the judgment of God, become a substitute for it.

From our point of view, of course, there is only one right absolute for human life and that is the will of God as this has been finally disclosed to us in Jesus Christ. That God has so made human personality so that without an absolute it cannot in fact be a personality at all is but another way of saying that God has made man for himself. But our interest is in worship and its relation to preaching. Just because we are so prone to turn our own interests and activities into false absolutes (I once heard a woman say: why do I need to go to Church: my husband and my children are my religion), it is most necessary to have a set time for worship and to withdraw altogether from those interests and activities, while we lift up our whole being to the true absolute of our life, which is the will of God disclosed in all its awful purity as Holy Love in Jesus Christ. We cannot do this in the same way when we are immersed in the actual business of our life; not only have we to attend to that business with all our powers, as I have said, but also we are inevitably caught up in the adjustments and compromises, the self-deceptions and perversions, in which our sinful state continually involves us. We must get away from the business of living if we are to discern again the absolute holy will of God in Christ, the demand it makes upon us, the condemnation with which it condemns us, the riches of personal life in its service which it offers us.

As for our preaching, if that is to take its part in the worship, if it is to help by making more explicit to mind and will and conscience what is implicit in the obeisance of the whole being before God, it must have, very clear and strong within it, this note of the absolute demand of God, as disclosed in the perfect humanity of the Redeemer. I do not mean for one moment that we should always be denouncing sin and nagging at sinners; I do not mean that at all. I mean simply that we must ask ourselves this question concerning every sermon we prepare: does it so plainly set forth, (or if it does not set it forth in plain statement, is it so deeply penetrated and infused by) the vision of God's holy claim upon us in Christ, that men must surely feel again its condemnation and its call penetrating again their own soul. This is a severe test, but nothing less will do; if it is applied it will make it impossible for us ever to fall into the triviality, the sentimentality, the mere moralizing, or philosophizing, or platitudinising, which mars so much preaching.

And do not let it be said that thus to preach, thus holding up the awful absolutes of God, will merely discourage men when what they need most of all is comfort and encouragement. There are two things to be said about that. The first follows directly from what has already been said. If it be true that man, just because he is made to be a person and not an animal, needs an absolute for his will, and deep down craves one, so that in default of the true absolute, he will fashion for himself a false one—then to set up the right absolute before men cannot ever be a merely depressing and discouraging thing. It always has something of enlargement and release in it, giving a man a sense of his true dignity and of the great issues which are bound up with his life. True consolation, let it be well understood, is not to have our immediately felt wants and ambitions satisfied, but to have our deeper nature released. The only way to have our deeper nature released is to have a greater demand addressed to it, a demand in which our clamour for comfort is caught up and lost in God's absolute claim upon us to seek first, last and all the time His Kingdom.

The second thing to be said is really our third point to which for a few minutes we will now turn.

(3) It would be indeed a serious travesty of the truth to speak as though the Christian message were merely the setting up of the awful absolute of God's holy love as revealed in Christ, an absolute which none of us has the least chance of living up to, even when we acknowledge its right to rule us, an absolute which therefore must always utterly condemn us. The Christian message is a message of forgiveness, that is to say it is a message which while it casts a man down with its condemnation yet lifts him up and sets him on his feet again. It takes away his sense of personal worth , and yet at the same time gives it back to him again in a different form. The love of God, lighting upon a man, gives him a significance and a standing in the world that nothing can take from him. When God justifieth, who is he that condemneth? Yet it also, if once he sees it in its awful purity, takes from him every vestige of self-satisfaction and self-justification.

Now this is what I had in mind when I spoke of the third need of the soul of man, the need for a true humility. I will not argue the point (for I believe it is obvious enough to any who knows anything of the minds of men) that egotism is the curse of us all. The man who is not learning to be humble, not being released from his own beloved ego, is learning nothing worthwhile, is fatally handicapped and hopelessly arrested in growth of personal stature. He remains, and must remain, a small soul. Yet what a strange paradoxical thing humility is—true humility, that is to say. Its paradox is twofold: first it has to be conjoined with strength and independence of soul, a standing upright on one's own feet, a walking by one's own inward light, otherwise it is merely a weak and pliant thing. Yet a man also must be released from any mere self-assertion, must have at all times a readiness to be found wanting and at fault, a teachableness, in short a true humility difficult to define, yet such as we all recognize when we meet it. Second, such humility cannot be cultivated. You cannot say, with the least chance of success, "go to, I will be humble," for if you were to succeed, which you wouldn't, you would then have to make another resolution, namely to be humble about your humility. As Charles Bennett said: "What the self-conscious cultivation of humility for its own sake produces is a false and detestable substitute for the real thing. The truly humble are those whom something other than themselves has humbled." And I would add, "something other than themselves has humbled, yet at the same time not taken from them the significance of their own being."

It is not necessary for me to say how supremely Christian worship, if it have at its heart a vision of the Love of God which both utterly condemns yet at the same time will not let a man go, is designed to do this great work in the souls of men, releasing them from themselves and yet giving them back themselves in a new way. The man who has been deeply shaped right down to the depths of his being by Christian worship is quite unmistakable in his combined humility and strength, his quietness and steadiness and peace in the knowledge that in standing in the presence of the Love of God he has nothing and yet possesses all things.

As for our preaching, again I need not say much. Great preaching ought to search men, ought to condemn them, ought to disquiet them, but never ought it merely to search, merely to condemn, merely to disquiet, it ought also to give them peace and quietness and a new confidence that their life, for all its weakness and folly, is of great significance, because it is of infinite significance to God. That is the gospel of forgiveness, or part of it, and if it is not explicitly set forth it ought also always to underlie, and penetrate through, everything we say.

Then indeed will our sermon be part of true worship. But if it is to be that, something of that vision of God must be before our minds both as we write it and as we preach. ✑

The Preacher and Persons

I said yesterday that preaching and worship must be thought of in close relationship with one another; but it is equally true that preaching and the pastoral office must be thought of in close relationship with one another. The reason for this I have tried to set forth in my book *The Servant of the Word*: it is that in the act of preaching, if it be true preaching, a relationship is set up between the preacher and his hearers, which, within its own necessary limitations, is of a directly personal kind. It is indeed the setting up of this directly personal relationship which in part distinguishes preaching from other kinds of public utterance, such as lecturing. But it is important to realize that when I have such dealings with a human being, that relationship which is set up is with personality in the degree to which it is—not merely transient and incidental, not merely instrumental or functional —but rather is part of, and expresses, a more permanent and inclusive interest in the other man as an individual in the totality of his being and life. For example, merely to take my letters from the postman is not to have a personal relationship with him, even though it is true that he is a person. It is when I get to know him as an individual and to enter in some measure into his distinctive personal history and situation—ask him, for example, about his wife and children, his hopes and fears for them—that the relationship begins to be truly personal; and when that happens, the otherwise purely functional relationship of receiving letters itself ceases to be merely functional and becomes itself personal. Similarly, with preaching. Preaching, to be sure, is in some degree—as I have said—an inherently personal relationship in a way that receiving letters from the postman is not; nevertheless, there is no question that in proportion as it also is taken up into a wider and more permanent system of right personal relationship between the preacher and his hearers, it gains in power and effectiveness. In other words, preaching should always be part of the pastoral relationship; it should be one activity within a settled and continuous ministry to men and women in the manifold individual, intimate problems of their daily lives. "Who may lawfully preach?", asks a medieval handbook, and the answer given is: "priests, deacons, subdeacons, who have the care of souls."

This is of great importance. In the first place, the preacher who is in close and continuous pastoral contact with people, will find therein a rich source of material for his preaching. He will know their problems and perplexities, the weaknesses and failings, in a way that is not otherwise possible—problems and perplexities, weaknesses and failings, to which if his preaching does not sooner or later, at least in some measure, bring a saving and illumining word of God, it must be accounted to have been of little effect. And then in the second place, such a close relationship with people, if it be of the right sort, be itself kept in close relationship with our preaching work, will help to guard us against some of the errors which so easily beset us in our preaching. Thus it should help to keep us aware of, and so enable us the better to resist, the temptation—which besets us all—to use abstract or semi-technical religious or theological jargon which nobody who has not been trained in a theological seminary is likely to understand. A minister has no business to be above the heads of his people either in language and ideas, except perhaps in a quite incidental way which does not impair the main impact of his message. If he is, that argues more than incapacity as a preacher; my point is it reveals a pastoral defect, even something approaching a spiritual and moral defect. It argues a failure to take the trouble to visualize them as persons and to be in their world with them as persons. I am inclined to think that a man who cannot speak with at least some effectiveness to children—finding (perhaps at the cost of a good deal of trouble) the right way to put things for them—ought to give up preaching to anybody; but perhaps that is an extreme judgment. Moreover, a close personal relationship with people will help to guard the preacher against the temptation to preach on remote, abstract, general themes, which may be of interest to him as a student of theology but which, in that abstract generalized form at any rate, have little contact with, or hold upon, his hearers. It is not much use, for example, to sit down to write a sermon at large in the abstract on, say, the forgiveness of sins, or the love of God. The danger is (as Dr. Oman has said) that "starting with such a large, colourless abstraction in the void, you will never bring it down to any actual interest of men's daily life or appeal by it to any prevailing mood of the human soul." On the other hand, if the need to say something on forgiveness arises out of, or at least immediately connects itself with, the poignant, concrete, situations of men's personal lives, which you know at first hand, that will impart a pointedness and relevance, as well as something of personal concern for men and women, to your utterance which will make it an entirely different thing.

Then in the third place, the right sort of pastoral relationship will help to compensate for some of the inevitable limitations of preaching. One great difficulty for example, in preaching is that you have to bring the same message to such a variety of persons: your audience is made up of people of different ages, temperaments, mental gifts, spiritual and moral need. In spite of what I have just said of the dangers of preaching on abstract generalities as it were in the void, there has to be, nevertheless, something of a generalized approach to truth and to its applications in the lives of men and women, because, when all is said, you are publicly addressing a general body of people. Herein, indeed, is one thing which makes effective preaching so difficult an art, namely that you are bound to speak in general terms, and yet your task is to establish such a personal relationship with your hearers that each feels that he is in some degree being individually addressed. I shall return to this difficulty in a moment. Meanwhile the point I wish to make is that one important way in which this limitation can be minimized is for the necessarily more generalized approach of the pulpit to be supplemented by the more particular and individual relationships of the minister with his people. The preacher frequently does little more than bring an awakening summons—a knock on the door. But the wise pastor often is given the opportunity to take the message a good deal farther than the door. He can get right inside the house.

Now let me return to the difficulty just referred to, the difficulty that stands all the time in the way of effective preaching, namely that, in spite of the fact that your listeners are so various and that you have to address them publicly, nevertheless you have to establish such a personal relationship with them that each feels, in some measure, if he is responsive at all, that you are speaking to him personally. How may this be accomplished? Well, a number of things might be said, but there is one quite fundamental thing which I want to develop for the remainder of this lecture. I believe very strongly that our power to establish a personal relationship with men through preaching will vary with the extent to which we are learning to *love* them, in the true and deep and mature sense of that much abused word. The Apostle said: "Though I speak with tongues of men and of angels and have not love it profiteth me nothing." What I am now saying is that equally it profiteth those who listen nothing, or at any rate, if not nothing—for God can, and does use very deficient means to His own high ends—then certainly it profiteth them a good deal less than would otherwise be the case. The deep personal concern for men and women which is what we mean by love, if it informs all our preaching, will assuredly make itself felt, and, in spite of all the unavoidable limitations of public utterance, will do something and even a very great deal, to establish that personal relationship with the hearer which we have said distinguishes, or should distinguish, preaching from other forms of set public speech. We might put it like this: all effective preaching has an indefinable note of winsomeness in it. Winsomeness, as distinct from merely hypnotic power, is precisely the capacity at one and the same time to individualize and to draw. You cannot be winsome to a crowd as such; but you can hypnotize a crowd, and much that passes for powerful preaching is often hardly more than a form of crowd hypnotism—spellbinding. You can only be winsome to a crowd by making it in effect cease to be a crowd, by in fact achieving this miracle of an individual relationship to its members. You can only achieve the miracle, by having something of the spirit of love to them as men. That is why the conscious attempt to be eloquent or rhetorical in preaching is always ineffective, even if it momentarily impresses. After all, you do not indulge in eloquence when you are talking to people for whom you have a deep concern. You remember what was said of our Lord—the greatest preacher the world has ever known. "And seeing the multitudes he had compassion on them for they were as sheep having no shepherd." That was part of the secret, part at least of the reason why, as the record says, "the common people heard him gladly."

Yet having said this, I am conscious of the danger of mininterpretation. The word "love" is such an ambiguous, such a degraded word in our tongue. To many it suggests at once a weak and namby-pamby thing, so that to say that our preaching should have some of the winsomeness that springs from love sounds like saying that it must never be strong and vigorous, never sound the note of warning, or rebuke, or demand, never make our hearers feel in the least degree disquieted. The word calls up all the horrors of sentimentality and saccharine. Let us then consider what it means to love a person in the Christian sense of the term, consider it in the assurance that in so far as we can achieve such an attitude to men and women, it will indirectly but none the less profoundly affect the whole manner and matter of our preaching without our being aware of it.

Three points:

The first thing I want to say is a little difficult to express. You only really love a person when you see him in some degree as an absolutely unique individual who is not like anybody else and is not intended to be like anybody else: one whom God has made to be just his own distinctive self, yes even if it be a self you find it hard sometimes to get on with. And you not only see him as thus having his own distinctive individuality, his own idiosyncrasy, but you accept him as such, nay rejoice in him as such. Love always thus individualizes its objects, wants people to be themselves, accepts them for what they are—warts and all—in all their infinite variety, accepts them as from the creative hand of God.

All of which, I am afraid, sounds quite intolerably vague, but perhaps I can bring home its meaning by relating it to our work as ministers. I believe that one of the things which often gravely hinders us from working and preaching effectively is that all unconsciously we develop a certain narrow professional interest in men and power. And perhaps we are the more likely to do this, the more in earnest we are about our job. We come to see men and women primarily as people to be changed, as souls to be saved, brands to be plucked from the burning: and if we are not careful, we lose the way of seeing them as they are in their individual, given selves at all. And that is very serious; for although the desire to see men saved and sanctified through Christ is certainly the highest expression and manifestation of Christian love, yet if our love does not include more than that, if it does not include a relish for them and delight in them, for their own sakes as distinctive individualities, if it does not include a desire that they should be and remain just themselves even in and through that most radical and blessed change which we call conversion, then it falls short of the fullness of love. It is in fact a narrow and restricted love, narrowed and restricted by a professionalism which is not the less professionalism for being rooted in a most worthy purpose. And the tragedy is that such love tends to defeat its own purpose. People are vaguely aware that they are the objects of a merely professional interest and they vaguely resent it. They feel that the minister is always wanting *to do them good,* that he is somehow not really interested in them for their own individual sakes. Was it Thoreau who said that if he thought that anybody was coming to him in order to do him good, he would run a hundred miles as quickly as he could? No doubt people often misjudge us parsons in this respect. They just assume that we are only interested in them as salvage, so to speak, and not as persons. They quite gratuitously imagine that anything the parson does or says is always part of a scheme for getting at them—a sort of a marked battery— when it is nothing of the sort. But the barrier between ministers and laity, which seems to be almost part of the thought pattern of contemporary man, is not the less real because it is in a measure imaginary and set up by the other man. And we have to try to overcome and see that there is no justification for it, so far as our own attitudes are concerned. We must resist this ever encroaching professionalism and the way in which it grows upon us unconsciously. Or to put it positively, we must increasingly learn what it means really to love persons.

Believe me this sacred professionalism of which I speak is not easy to resist if we are in earnest about our work; it does grow upon us unconsciously. I once tried my hand at writing a novel. I did not succeed, needless to say, but I did discover a rather sad truth about myself, namely that as a minister of the gospel I had gradually lost some of the power which I am sure I once had of seeing and appreciating men and women objectively in their peculiar and total individuality. I had come to see them all primarily as sinful men and women needing to be changed, and that meant that I was no longer able to see in them that which love would not want to see changed. I caught myself once in something of the same attitude, when travelling in a train. Some men got in and immediately settled down to play cards for money. Then as they played they began to talk about their homes and children and gardens. I was horrified to notice flit across my mind a faint feeling of disappointment. My unexpressed thought had been that nobody who is so sinful as to gamble enthusiastically could have so decent and clean an interest as delight in children and gardens; if they ran true to pattern, my pattern, the pattern that is to say of one who had got into the way of thinking of men first and foremost as people to be saved, they ought really to beat their wives. Dr. Carnegie Simpson once told me of a maid in a house where he was staying who had won something like 5,000 pounds in the Irish Sweepstake. Her mistress told Dr. Simpson that she, that is, the maid, had not spent any of the money on herself, but had provided for her old father, had set up an out of work brother in a business, had paid for hospital treatment for a sister. Dr. Simpson says he felt the maid had somehow let him down. Unattended by the professional ministrations of a gospel preacher like himself, she ought plainly to have gone straight to perdition.

We might put the point theologically by saying that we parsons and preachers are always in danger of thinking too exclusively of the God who is Redeemer, and forgetting the God who is first of all Creator. We cease to see people as God has made them in all their richness and variety of their natures, a richness and variety which they still have in spite of being sinners needing to be redeemed. We see them, I repeat, only as people to be saved, which means or may mean that we do not see them and appreciate them for what they are in themselves. And that is a failure of love, and the failure will subtly affect the power of our preaching to win people.

The second thing in the Christian attitude of love to persons of which I want to speak has to do with what may be called, in the first instance, *sympathy*. I say "in the first instance" because there is a purely natural impulse of sympathy which many people have in varying degree quite *independently* of Christian faith and experience, and what I have in mind is something rather different from that, though it has kinship with it, being perhaps the purification and enlargement of it through the grace of God. Natural sympathy, even in those who have it in a high degree, is always limited in its range and direction; for it has as its inevitable correlative, as Brunner points out, natural *antipathy*, a feeling, that is to say *against* certain types of persons—their character, temperament or behaviour—so strong that other elements in their life which would otherwise draw out sympathy are incapable of doing so.

What then is distinctively Christian sympathy to be differentiated from merely natural sympathy? Well, I hardly know how to describe it. It is the power to penetrate objectively yet feelingly (not emotionally) into the individual self-awareness of any man with whom we have to deal—yes, even if it repels or revolts us because of his meanness or wickedness or dullness—so that in some measure we get inside his skin, see the world through his eyes (even though they are mean or wicked or dull eyes) hear the world through his ears, participate in his feelings, think his thoughts, get a sense of him as an individual with only one life to live, one death to die, so isolated in his interior life, a man with his own memories and regrets and frustrations and disappointments, one still perhaps with hopes and dreams of other things and gnawing, unsatisfied hungers, to feel something of the "might-have-been" which is in every human life. But words are of little avail, if we do not know already what is meant. Perhaps two instances, one positive and the other negative, will help to make clear this sympathy, this feeling-in of love.

The positive instance is that spirit which breathes through all the records of St. Francis of Assisi—The Little Flowers, the Life, the Mirror of Perfection. Whatever there may be of legendary accretion in those records, or of the idealizations of loving memory, whatever reservations we may be inclined to make as to the wisdom of this or that particular thing that the saint did or did not do, however much we might perhaps desire some admixture in him of the robuster virtues, there is no question that what shines through all the records with a realism and a power that could only have sprung from historical reality is the very quintessence of this wholly distinctive manifestation of Christian love which I have called "empathy." St. Francis had in preeminent degree what I am sure we all ought to have in some degree—the blessed faculty of imaginatively feeling his way into the personal and individual being of the other man, whoever he was and just because he was there as a man. Thus he came as near as any man could to standing in the shoes of the loathsome lepers, sitting where they sat, feeling as his own the desolate loneliness of their state as they walked the roads ringing their bell and shouting "unclean! unclean!" that all might flee from them; and knowing what such an act would mean to them he even sat down with them to eat from the same dish as that in which they dipped their rotting and bleeding fingers. And whatever we make of the strange story of the stigmata, according to which the very wounds of Christ appeared in Francis' own body, surely Arthur Shearly Cripps is right in seeing in it the symbolic expression of this same power of empathy which is distinctive of Christian love. The Saint says in Cripps' poem *The Death of St. Francis*,—"I felt as mine

> The dark distresses of my brother limbs,
> To feel it bodily and simply true,
> To feel as mine the starving of the poor,
> To feel as mine the shadow of curse on all,
> Hard words, hard looks, and savage misery,

And struggling deaths, unpitied and unwept.
To feel rich brothers' sad satieties,
The weary manner of their lives and deaths,
That went in love, and lacking love, lack all.
To feel the heavy sorrow of the world
Thicken and thicken on to future hell,
To mighty cities with their miles of streets,
Where men seek work for days, and walk, and starve,
Freezing on river banks on winter nights
And come at last to cord or stream or steel.

The horror of the things our brothers bear!
It was but nought to what came after,
The woe of things we make our brothers bear,
Our brothers and our sisters.

The negative instance is modern, indeed contemporary. Consider these dreadful moral perverts who have been responsible for the unspeakable horrors of the German concentration camps and which the whole world apparently has derived considerable satisfaction from seeing hanged. I have heard many Christian people express themselves on these men and women, both publicly and privately; I have not heard one in whose accents could be detected the least tincture of agonized concern for them as living individual persons; or, if that be asking too much, for that is indeed a very hard thing to feel when the mind dwells upon the horrible things they perpetrated on other living persons, I have not heard even an acknowledgement that a Christian ought to feel such a concern, and that failure to do so needs the pardon of God. The usual attitude has been that these perverts must be destroyed as lice or beetles are destroyed. The whole thing, that is to say, has been on the level of natural sympathy and antipathy. The depth of natural sympathy for the tortured has produced an equal passion of antipathy to the torturers. Do not misunderstand me. I am not saying that there is no place for moral revulsion and indignation. Of course there is; but then moral indignation or recoil is not, by itself, distinctively Christian reaction. It only takes on a distinctively Christian quality when there enters into it and informs it something of the "empathy" of love towards the evil-doer. That turns indignation into an agony. That brings you at least distantly in sight of the Cross.

How does this affect our preaching? I believe that in so far as something of His attitude is achieved, it will affect it deeply, for the reason I indicated earlier. It will give that strong winsomeness of mature love to our preaching without which it will lack real effectiveness. In particular it will affect our whole treatment of the theme of men's sins and weaknesses. We must indeed speak plainly and truthfully about sin, though always humbly including ourselves in the condemnation. It is no part of love *not* to do that. But the merely sledge-hammer denuciations which one sometimes hears effects little. It merely hardens, or on the other hand, ministers to people's good conceit of themselves. It is so easy to "Compound for sins we are inclined to, By damning those we have no mind to." I remember once hearing a sermon by W. R. Maltby, which searched you through and through in this matter of our sinfulness and need for forgiveness; but the searchingness of it resided not merely in its penetrating insight; it resided just as much in the manifest concern for sinful and erring men and women, the imaginative love for them in all their ways, which breathed through it. In comparison Parker's famous conclusion to his sermon denouncing the Armenian atrocities—"God damn the Sultan!" was surely as useless and ineffective as it was violent, crude, and merely natural!

The third thing which distinguishes the Christian attitude of love—and one which will affect our preaching more directly and obviously perhaps than the points already set forth—is one which has to do with our relation to other men as a *thinking* being. Speaking generally, what is required of us is a deep and continuous respect for men as beings, persons, who are called above all things else to walk by their own insight into, and apprehension of, the truth.

Now that may seem an obvious thing to say. Of course a man must follow the light within his own soul, steadfastly adhere to the judgments of his own conscience on what is right and true, not turning aside under the pressures either though the light he has is a very poor light, he must have that loyalty to it which is the indispensable prerequisite of getting more light. These are the merest rudiments you would think of any right philosophy of personality, not to speak of any sound Protestant doctrine of the rights of general truths when they are stated; it is an infinitely more difficult thing to have all one's concrete, actual dealings with men and women deeply sustained and informed by them, and most difficult of all is it, perhaps, when you are a minister and preacher who most earnestly and eagerly want them to believe as you do, and walk the same way of Christ as you have set out to walk. Then indeed it is necessary that you should love them as persons with that high, austere, mature, patient, selfless love which is, or ought to be, distinctive of the Christian soul. Let me seek to make plain what I mean by one or two illustrative points.

First, if you rightly love a person you will most deeply respect, and pay regard to, his *need for truth,* his right to truth; you will know that truth is his due, for only by coming to know more of the truth can he grow in stature and strength as a son of God. The soul needs truth as the body needs bread. This is not always deeply realized, though it may be subscribed to as an abstract proposition. In everything worth while in our life we make progress by having our eyes opened, by coming to see things which we did not see or know before. Over every step forward of any consequence, every entering upon a new stage of growth these words might be written: there fell from my eyes as it had been scales; whereas I was blind now I see.

Always spiritual growth and increase in insight, knowledge, discernment go together, and if you love people you will know that what they most deeply need, and what you must seek for them, is that increase. You remember Paul's prayer for the Philippians: My prayer is, he said, that your love may be more and more rich in knowledge and discernment of what is vital.

This means that your ministry, particularly your preaching ministry, must be in a most steady and solid way a teaching ministry, if you like, a doctrinal ministry. It ought to seek to give men and women, and build them up on the foundation of, a sound and living theology, a theology which, without losing contact with the problems of daily life, nevertheless does justice to the whole Christian faith in all its range and depth, as a deep or massive and unitary and adequate doctrine of God and man. Don't let your preaching get involved in trivialities or sentimentalities or merely passing topical themes. I want to insist on this if I may. This, after all, is a shaking and shattering world in which people are called upon to be Christians today, a world of vast seismic movements and impacts wherein almost everything that touches even their private individual lives comes out of a background of large-scale cosmic happenings. People need insights and convictions which are commensurate with these things, which in their range and depth and massive comprehensiveness can stand up to the challenge. They need to be built up in Christian truth. Vague sentimental affirmations of the fatherhood of God and the brotherhood of man, are not only not adequate to the full reach of the Christian faith as it has come to us through the centuries of Christian thought and experience, but also to men's situation today. It is like trying to put out a conflagration with a garden syringe. I am sure it will always be good for us to ask concerning any sermon we write and preach, I am sure it will be part of our love to men and women to ask, what of distinctive Christian insight and truth—I emphasize the word distinctive, for it is so easy to think that we are being Christian when we are merely echoing contemporary errors and superficialities—am I seeking to convey, am I likely to convey, by this discourse?

Second, if you rightly love a person you will deeply respect, not only his need for truth, but also his capacity for truth. I want to say only one of the many things which might be said in this connection. I believe that it is one of the surest marks of distinctive Christian love to men and women that you are ready to receive truth from them as well as to seek to impart truth to them. The preaching minister has no monopoly of truth; others beside himself have a capacity to receive it from the Holy Spirit and to impart. Does not the Scripture say that it is with all the saints that we know the love of God in Christ? I am sure that such a humble and loving readiness to learn *from* your people as well as to teach them will deeply affect the winsome power of your preaching to get past the exterior defenses of their minds to the innermost places of heart and conscience. That is why I think pulpit preaching, if it is to play its full part in a teaching ministry should always be supplemented by opportunities for the sharing of minds with one another in conference and discussion. I like to fill out in imagination the hints which the Gospel records give of our Lord's method of talking with, and not merely preaching to, his disciples. The analogy breaks down, for the disciples had nought of truth they could give to Him who was Himself the Truth; nevertheless it indicates a spirit which we perhaps have the more reason to cultivate because we need what others can give to us as much as they need what we can give to them. I remember once being in the vestry after a service with a minister who was not only a great preacher, but also a great Christian soul; nay indeed he was a great preacher precisely because he was such a great Christian soul. A man who had listened to the sermon he had just preached came into the vestry in a state of some excitement and protested against some of the things which had been said. A painful situation might easily have arisen, but the minister listened gravely to the man's protests and then said: "Thank you so much for coming to tell me your thoughts and feelings. Perhaps you are right. We must be fellow-seekers after the truth, fellow-helpers to the truth. Let us talk it over together." It was one of the finest manifestations of Christian love I have ever seen, and I am sure the spirit of it had not a little to do with the unusual effectiveness of that man's preaching work.

Third, if you rightly love men and women, you will deeply respect their freedom as persons, and in particular their freedom to refuse the truth which you are commissioned to bring them; you will respect what has been called their sacred right of rejection.

Nothing is more important than this for setting the whole tone and manner of our preaching, and saving us from peremptoriness, from denunciatory hardness, from impatience, from anxiety, and from in the end perhaps losing faith in our calling and our work.

I cannot do better I think than paraphrase here some words of John Oman in that noble and lovely work entitled *Vision and Authority*, which I do most strongly commend to you. "Though God," he says, "from a tender regard to the spirits of His children made in his own image with this power of free choice, of rejection, endures much resistance to his will and confusion in his world, his servant is not always able to escape the temptation to be peremptory when he has power and hysterical when he lacks it. The sense of responsibility in face of the sad estrangement from God of the souls he cannot by his message convince, has often led to hard antagonism and hurtful insistence. Nor has any one done more than Christ himself to place us in this danger. He so taught us to value truth and love men that it is very hard for us to admit failure. The peril is then great that we shall begin to waste our strength in mere conflict, mere denunciation, mere negation, or what is worse the energy which should have gone to the patient proclamation of the truth will be diverted to the embellishment of it in order as we think to make it more popular and palatable. Yet Christ if he has exposed us to this peril has also sought to warn us against it and to protect us from it. Nothing is plainer both from his own whole bearing in face of the rejection of men as well as from his explicit teaching than that he would have his disciples go forth to preach and to manifest the truth in plainness and humility, not striving and crying, but being strongly patient and gentle towards all men. They have not duty to embellish the truth, much less of putting anything else in its place. The responsibility for rejecting it lies between the man himself and God. And the final task of winning men's hearts for it, is not ours but God's." We must be content to leave the truth to make its own appeal, or rather we must be content, having preached it, to commit ourselves and our hearers to the Holy Spirit, to the patience and wisdom of God who unlike ourselves has interior access to the hearts and minds of men.

Have you ever thought how much of the mind and spirit of the Master (how directly and rebukingly it speaks to us who would declare His gospel) is revealed in that incident when the Samaritan villagers refused to receive him, shut their doors, in effect, in His face? James and John came back, you remember, in angry indignation at this rejection of their master. Master, they said, wilt thou that we command fire to come down from heaven and consume them, even as Elias did? And he turned and rebuked them and said: Ye know not what manner of spirit ye are of. For the son of man is not come to destroy men's lives but to save them. And they went to another village. Everything is in that simple phrase. ✒

The Preacher and Culture

That the man who will sustain for any length of time an effective preaching and teaching ministry must read and study diligently and thoughtfully goes without saying. No man can possibly "give out" continuously over a period of years matter which is in any degree adequate both to the need of the age and to the riches of our Faith, unless he is just as continuously "taking in." Here, as in less exalted spheres, imports must balance exports. Reading, said Bacon, maketh a full man; and we may add, preaching without reading soon maketh an empty man—soon (to change the metaphor) "wears thin." I am aware of the difficulties, of course. The modern minister, unlike the minister of a former generation, is apt to find his time so overfull with this, that and the other—the endless business of running a church in all its multifarious activities and connections—that anything like sustained reading gets crowded out. The reading has to be snatched in the interstices, the snippets of time, and so inevitably becomes snippety reading. It is a great pity when that happens, for in many ways the need for an informed and well-read ministry is greater today than it was when ministers had opportunity to be, and often in fact were, more cultured and well-read, as compared with their contemporaries, than they now are. And then there is the expense: ministers are ill-paid and books are costly. Difficulties, however, exist to be overcome, and I can only urge you to try to overcome them. (The late Lord Asquith, throughout all the period of his tenure of office as Prime Minister of Great Britain, including even the terrible burdensome war-years from 1914-1916 insisted—according to the testimony of Lady Asquith—on always reading for two hours before he went to bed.)

I shall ask you in a few minutes to consider the question why a well-sustained cultural life is so essential to an effective preaching and teaching ministry today. But before going on to that, I want to urge you to keep up in your ministry, the regular and assiduous study of *theology*. Herrmann says somewhere that the most distinctive function of the ministry (for it is the one which practically no one else in the Christian community can under modern conditions discharge) is to produce, preserve, and apply, a sound theology. There is great truth in that. I spoke yesterday of the need of the modern man for instruction in theology. The point now is, that you cannot meet that need effectively without continuous theological reading and study. I do suggest that you should try always to have on hand some really "meaty" theological work, which you study not primarily for sermon material (a motive which, as I said earlier, I am inclined to distrust), but because you realize the unspeakable importance to men and women of knowledge of the deep things of God. I think it requires a certain amount of faith to keep oneself to the study of some big and scholarly book—the pressure of other things is often so great that such study seems at times an insupportable irrelevance. But I am sure, if you can manage it, it yields rich dividends.

Let us now take up the general question—why is a well-sustained cultural life essential to the life and effective work of a minister and preacher today? Culture is much more of a living process than merely reading a lot; it requires the intercourse of living persons, and especially the companionship of those whose minds and experience and character are fitted to elevate, instruct, and sweeten our own. I think that some ministers sometimes allow themselves to move in far too restricted a circle of interests and persons, a world which is too much confined to parochial or ecclesiastical concerns, and to parochially or ecclesiastically minded people who are of no bigger stature, often indeed of rather less stature, than themselves. They live rather too exclusively in the world of their ministerial responsibilities. Very often this is the result of the earnestness and consecration of their lives, and is so far good. Such earnestness and consecration cuts, as it were, a very narrow channel like a mountain torrent. Yet one could desire that there were more of the amplitude of the lowland river which reflects the whole arc of heaven and fertilizes the broader acres of the countryside. Nevertheless the main source of culture must be, for the minister, his books; it is of that I am thinking particularly this morning. Why then, I ask again is a well-sustained cultural life so essential? I want, in reply to that question, to develop two main points.

First, there is, I believe, a close relationship between the cultural life of a minister and the quality of his personal life as a Christian man. The general question of the relationship of the pursuit of culture to the Christian way of life is a difficult one which has not I think been sufficiently explored by Christian thinkers. At the bottom it is the question of a Christian *hierarchy* of values—it is a question of the priorities. And it is a question which can take a very poignant form in some people's lives. I recall a boy in the congregation of a church in London of which I was once minister. He was a brilliant artist and before he was twenty had had pictures hung in the Royal Academy. Then he felt a call to give his life to the poor in the East End of London. It was a terribly difficult choice. In the end he went to the East End and surrendered his career as an artist. I think he was right. The same choice confronted Schweitzer when he felt the urge to give up his philosophical work and his music and devote himself to the disease-ridden natives in Lamborene. We need not, however, go into this general question. We are, or we are going to be ministers of religion, so that for us the question, the priorities, have been settled. Our task is to preach the gospel, to give ourselves to the pastoral care of souls, and everything else must take second or even a lower, place in our hierarchy of values. Nevertheless, subject to that overriding priority and indeed in the service of it, culture can still play a not negligible part in that self-discipline, self-purification, self-enlargement without which a minister and preacher cannot do his prime task really well. To cultivate the self merely for the sake of self-cultivation is of course no Christian motive at all, but to cultivate the self in order, if possible, to be a better and more efficient instrument of God's purposes in the contemporary world, that is another matter. Such a motive is the source of all right self-discipline, all right asceticism, in the Christian life.

I want to say two things in connection with this matter of the relation of true culture to the personal life of the minister and preacher.

First, I believe that the *effort* involved in maintaining at least as high a cultural life as opportunity and your gifts allow is a not negligible expression of, and contribution to, that dedicated and reverent life, that life in which the spiritual always rules over and controls the natural, to which all Christians are called and which the Christian minister should especially exemplify. In this connection I find it interesting and suggestive that the word culture has etymological connection in the Latin with, on the one hand, the tilling of the soil and, on the other hand, religious reverence and worship. There is I suspect a deep underlying significance in this double connection: it points to the fact that man's first major victory over his *natural* environment, namely, the cultivation of the soil, was rooted in his religious sense, his awareness that there is a sacred purpose above the merely natural to which he owes a final allegiance. Only by allegiance to that which is *above* nature is he released from the leading strings of nature, released from the merely instinctive natural life which is characteristic of the brute world. Only thus is man set upon the arduous way of mastery over his world and over himself, that way which begins in agriculture and ends in culture, ends in the finest products of the spiritual life. This deep connection between culture and the religious life I like to think still remains. The Christian man, and still more the Christian minister, who has a poor and thin cultural life, who has no desire, or will take little trouble to enter into, the great things (say) of literature and art, surely properly comes under some suspicion as to the quality of his religious life. I very much suspect that a man with a deeply worshipful spirit will inevitably fulfill the Apostle's instruction, and think upon, and take increasing delight in, all things that are true and pure and lovely and good: and on the other hand increasing delight in and concern for these things will enrich and sensitize his worship. I do not indeed wish to press this too far—for I should hate even to appear to suggest that a deep, spiritual Christian life is not possible for the ignorant and uncultivated. Yet even in the ignorant and uncultivated, I have more than once noticed a distinct change in the direction and scope of their interests and tastes, when they have been soundly converted, showing that the connection is still there. It must be there, for religion is a concern of the whole man or it is nothing. In this connection I recall the noble part played by the Christian Church in England and Scotland in promoting education for the masses: furthermore I would insist on the absolute rightness of the educational side of foreign missionary work. I remember, too, how in the days of my youth many of the Free Churches of England had what was called a literary society. That seems to have died out in recent years, which is a pity. Some of our neo-orthodox brethren have rejoiced in the disappearance of the literary society on the ground that it is not part of the Church's distinctive business to provide general culture. Well, it is certainly not its *main* business, but to suggest that it is no part of its business at all is I believe a very superficial and even dangerous view. We shall come back to this again later.

The second thing of which I would wish to speak in this matter of the cultural life of the minister is this. One of the supreme marks of the great Christian soul—and how can one hope to grow in stature as a

preacher, if one is not growing all the time in stature as a Christian?—
is that he can face quite frankly and realistically all the muck and
misery, the tragedy and heartbreak, the agony and frustration, of
human life and yet find his sensitivity to high and holy things, his faith
in their final victory—God's final victory—not only not impaired, but
also growing stronger. A mature and strong Christian soul is at once
ruthlessly frank and sincere in facing evil and corruption and yet at the
same time most sensitively responsive to what is good. Now, this
combination is by no means easy to achieve. Many ministers fail to
achieve it. One of two thing seems so often to happen to them. Either
they move in varying degree towards, become a more or less close
approximation to, the conventional picture (so frequently portrayed
in contemporary fiction and drama) of the clerical saint—one, that is,
who would be inexpressibly shocked if anyone swore a good hearty
oath in his presence, one who ought to be protected as much as
possible from any impact of this coarse and wicked world upon him; or
on the other hand they move in varying degree towards the other
extreme and become a more or less close approximation to the
minister (also not infrequently portrayed in comtemporary fiction)
who behind all his professional behaviour and duties hides a heart
which, through its traffic with life, has become empty, disappointed,
somewhat cynical, somewhat worldly. The problem of avoiding these
two extemes, the problem of being able to mix in the evil in human
life, not glossing it over or pretending it is other than it is, and yet to
grow in appreciation of and dedication to the good, is no light one; it is
the old, difficult problem of being in the world and yet not of it. Now,
among the helps that are available for solving this problem a not
unimportant one is, I believe, to keep company with great minds
through great books. That is one way in which we may cultivate what
Whitehead has called "the habitual vision of greatness", without,
however, any loss of real contact with life. For it is surely one of the
distinguishing marks of great literature that it keeps you in touch with
the realities of human existence—brings you out of the somewhat
protected and insulated ecclesiastical world of nice, well-behaved
people amongst whom it is so easy for a minister almost exclusively to
move—and yet at the same time renews and nourishes and develops
whatever sensitivity he may have to the great and mysterious
possiblities and actualities of truth and beauty and goodness which
somehow overshadow and interpenetrate it all. An outstanding

example is the novels of Dostoieffsky, with their strange power to evoke in the reader the sense of the dreadful mystery of *evil* in human life, and yet also to give him a renewed faith in God and in Christ, a renewed faith in the soul of redemptive good at the heart of things evil. I knew a minister once who worked in one of the most sordid areas of industrial England and made it his business to tackle some of the foulest spots in it. He told me that he made it a habit every night to read Wordsworth or Keats, in order to cleanse and resensitize his soul; nor was that in any sense whatever what it is now fashionable to call escapism; rather it was to keep company with great minds who themselves knew something of the "weary weight of this unintelligible world" and yet had insight into the goodness and beauty which are at the heart of the mystery, and in addition, the gift to convey it to others.

The second main reason why it is good for the minister to have a well sustained cultural life to back and inform his preaching and teaching has to do with the general cultural situation by which we are today surrounded and to which we have to bring our message. I shall have to speak here mainly in the light of the situation in my own country, but I think what I shall say will not be irrelevant to your situation and task in this country. I shall have to make some rather sweeping generalizations, yet I think not so sweeping as to lose their value, even when all necessary qualifications have been made, as important guides to us in our work.

The cultural situation seems to me to be this, that the church is today confronted by a civilization and a culture which on the one hand is becoming increasingly secular, and yet which on the other hand and at the same time is still sufficiently impregnated and permeated in its general moral tradition with Christian values for most people, both inside and outside the churches, *not* to realize what is going on, not to realize that what is going on before our eyes is nothing less than a struggle for the soul of our western civilization. Which way the struggle will go remains to be seen, but there is no question that Christian ministers and teachers have an important part to play in it. And they will not be able to play that part effectively unless they realize what is happening. Let us take in turn each of the two points just mentioned.

First the secularization, or paganization, of contemporary culture. We may best realize this by considering contemporary literature, science, art, drama (including in the latter the films), by considering, that is to say, the spheres where the cultural life and values of the community are being creatively fashioned by people in a more or less deliberate and self-conscious way. I hazard the generalization that in these spheres there has been, and is, a pretty complete departure from Christian principles, standards, presuppositions, from the Christian view of the right meaning and uses of human life. In so far as it is possible to discern at all a general viewpoint underlying it, it is a humanistic viewpoint, that is to say it rests upon the assumption, consciously or unconsciously made, that the proper ends and norms of human activity can be fully comprehended in terms of man's own mind and being. Along with this there goes as a rule a strong mixture of scientific postivism, that is, the view that human life and behaviour are merely the resultant of psychological, sociological, economic forces which only science can hope to understand or control; also there goes along with it sometimes a vaguely optimistic belief in an inscrutable and impersonal life force which may be counted upon to keep things in an upward direction. I say *sometimes,* because there is also to be discerned in contemporary culture a recurrent mood of pessimism, which is not all sure that anything worthwhile is in fact being wrought out through the flux and chaos of human history. And as for moral standards, there do not seem to be any clear and settled ones at all; how could there be when the underlying philosophy is that man, as a personal being stands utterly alone in the universe, with no reason therefore to do any other than consult the devices and desires of his own heart.

Now I do not wish to overestimate the importance of the people who write our novels, poems, plays, etc., especially such as those, who like to consider themselves among the cultured elite, read and discuss. But it would be folly to underestimate it. For the general outlook of the people who would ordinarily pass for educated and cultured does shape in all kinds of indirect ways the mind of the vast uncultured masses who throng the picture houses, patronize the dance halls, read the cheap newspapers and the shoddy books: it helps to create climate or atmosphere of the time; it soaks into people by every avenue of their being, from the very first day they go to school and are submitted to an educational process which, be it noted, takes no account of a religious interpretation of life at all. And, mark this, this is true also of those who are *in* our Churches. There are many folk in our churches whose essential culture—the standards and values by which their thoughts and purposes, their business activities, their politics, their reading and recreation, are controlled—is only partially Christian, if Christian at all. It conforms in many ways to the dechristianized secularized culture by which they are surrounded. And the mischief is, as I have said, they do not realize this. Now of course this situation, if I have correctly assessed it, is not going to be altered in a few weeks, or even years. Some may be inclined perhaps to question whether we shall ever see again a universal culture among civilized peoples resting on Christian presuppositions such as obtained in Europe in the Middle Ages. Well, only time can show that—a much longer time than any of us here will live to see. But whatever the future, in the providence of God, may hold, I am quite sure that the situation is not one we dare let go by default. We dare not surrender the rich cultural life of humanity, that cultural life which so greatly influences the whole tone and temper of civilization to the devil. I wish we could get many more vigorous Christian people, people who know where they stand, into the world of books and criticism and art and entertainment and all the rest. And we must seek to train our people more than we do in Christian discrimination, so that they may be protected by their own insight from the subtle corrupting influence of the pagan culture by which they are now surrounded. In this surely our ministers, and preachers and teachers, must play a part. I would indeed re-emphasize that the prime task of the minister is to preach the Gospel and to teach the great revealed truths of our holy religion. I would rather have that done by the most unlettered evangelist than not done at all, or done by one who though dripping culture from his finger-tips has not the fire of the gospel in his soul. But we are not in fact shut up to such a choice. The situation calls for a preaching and teaching ministry which is not outside of, not ignorant of, the cultural life of our time, rather it, knowing its way about in it so far as time, opportunity and gifts allow—is in it, I repeat, yet not of it, in it in a definitely and consciously Christian way, exercising a Christian discernment and discrimination all the time.

I do want to emphasize the importance of this, though not to over-emphasize it. I would even plead for some place to be found in our theological seminaries for some instruction in the state of contemporary culture and in the bringing to it of Christian judgment. I think that in England at any rate the divorce which came about during the last century and earlier between strong and vigorous evangelical religion and the best cultural life of the community has had something to do with the situation which has developed and which I have described. Many years ago now Matthew Arnold deplored what he called the philistinism of the Churches deriving from Puritanism or from the evangelical revivals. He granted that these churches had done much to make human life orderly, moral, serious, but he recoiled from the cultural emptiness and poverty of that life—a round, as he put it, of tea-meetings, prayer-meetings, openings of chapels, and sermons. He pictured Vergil and Shakespeare forced to sail to America in the Mayflower with the Puritan fathers and asks whether they would not have found their company intolerable. No doubt there was something of injustice in this; some failure, too, to discern the real difficulties of the problem of the relation of Christianity to culture—yet there was and there still is truth in the indictment and we must face it. The failure of the Protestant churches on the whole to provide a basis for a true and rich *Christian* humanism has surely had something to do with the rise of the false humanism of our time. I sometimes think that the Roman Church has perhaps something to teach us here. For all its errors—errors which the older I get I do not find less shocking and monstrous—it *has* preserved something of the ideal of a Christianity which claims and redeems the whole of human life; it has preserved more of the Christian humanism of which I have spoken. It was precisely this criticism of Portestantism that Roman Catholics like Von Hugel and G. K. Chesterton so frequently and so strongly urged. I do not think that in my own country the Anglican communion has fallen into the error to quite the degree some other Protestant churches have, nor have the Presbyterian churches. It is certainly not, or at least it ought not to be in the Calvinist tradition, not to give due place to the rich cultural life of humanity its due as one of the gifts of the Creator to us to be used for his glory; it is certainly not in the Calvinist tradition to place such heavy emphasis on the God of Redemption as in effect to forget the God of Creation. Calvin himself, in spite of his somber view of the perversion and weakness of human life through the Fall, could write thus in his *Institutes of the Christian Religion*: "Therefore, in reading profane authors, the admirable light of truth displayed in them should remind us, that the human mind, however much fallen and perverted from its original integrity, is still adorned and invested with admirable gifts from its Creator. If we reflect that the Spirit of God is the only fountain of truth, we will be careful, as we would avoid offering insult to Him, not to reject or condemn truth wherever it appears. In despising the gifts, we insult the giver. How then can we deny that truth must have beamed on those ancient lawgivers who arranged civil order and discipline with so much equity? Shall we say that the philosophers, in their exquisite researches and skillful description of nature, were blind? Shall we deny the possession of intellect to those who drew up rules for discourse, and taught us to speak in accordance with reason? Shall we say to those who, by the cultivation of the medical art, expended their industry on our behalf, were only raving? What shall we say of the mathematical sciences? Shall we deem them to be the dreams of madmen? Nay we cannot read the writings of the ancients on these subjects without the highest admiration; an admiration which their excellence will not allow us to withhold. But shall we deem anything to be noble and praiseworthy, without tracing it to the hand of God? Far from us be such ingratitude; and ingratitude not chargeable even to the heathen poets, who acknowledged that philosophy, and laws, and all useful arts, were the invention of the gods. Therefore, since it is manifest that men whom the Scripture term carnal, are so acute and clearsighted in the investigation of inferior things, their example should teach us how many gifts the Lord has left in the possession of human nature, notwithstanding of its having been despoiled of its true good." (Bk. II, Ch. II).

This is clearly, by implication at least, a claiming of all culture for the Christian. I like to think that that great Scotch Presbyterian theologian James Denney, than whom there has never been any more intensely and passionately evangelical in his whole outlook, was indeed well in the reformed tradition when he found delight, as he used to do, in reading, for example, the love-songs of Catullus.

Yet Calvin would have been the first to insist that in claiming culture for Christ we must bring Christian standards to bear upon it. Delight in the creativeness of man must not blind us to its aberrations. It is precisely here that so many Christian people in our day need instruction and guidance and a continual challenge to exercise Christian discrimination . Let me give just one example of what I mean. I don't know whether the works of Charles Morgan are read in this country. They have had considerable vogue among cultured people in England. Morgan has a highly refined and cultivated mind, moving easily in what might be called the more high-brow levels of English and French literature, imaginative, keenly sensitive to beauty, loving the subtle play of ideas; and he writes in a carefully wrought manner, full of allusions of a literary, philosophical and mystically religious sort which continually give an impression of profound and original insight. Some years ago he published a novel called *The Fountain* which was widely read by intelligent and cultured people, and was generally very highly thought of as a sympathetic study of the spiritual yearnings and satisfactions of two sensitive people. Many Christian people I know read it and spoke well of it. Yet in point of fact the book was built around an adulterous relationship of a man and a woman, the real nature of which was disguised and hidden by the fact that it was made with great sublety to be part of the spiritual pilgrimage of two questing and sensitive minds. This was completely overlooked by many readers, who lost sight of the real nature of the relationship in the apparent highmindedness and sensitivity of the principal actors. This was a failure in Christian discrimination and it illustrates what I have in mind in perhaps an extreme form.

Now, second, to turn to the other side of the picture, namely that the peculiar situation in which we find ourselves today is that our contemporary Anglo-Saxon culture has become increasingly un-Christian, in the way I have just illustrated, yet also at the same time it is still sufficiently impregnated and permeated with Christian values for most people not to realize what is going on. Let me now develop that for a little before I close, though I have in fact just illustrated it incidentally from the way in which some people, misled by the real Christian values which in some degree informed Charles Morgan's novel, failed to react strongly and vigorously against its subtle and even beautiful justification of adultery.

In our Anglo-Saxon civilization there has come about in the course of the years a double process of approximation between Christian values and the values which rule contemporary society. On the one hand, certain Christian values which historically derived from the Christian understanding of God and man have become the individual person, the monogamous principle in marriage, the duty of caring for the sick, the poor and the needy, the duty of service to the community and so on. Now, the effect of this partial incorporation of Christian values in the generally accepted moral tradition has been that their derivation from Christianity has been largely lost sight of. Having the support of custom and tradition (which in the nature of the case exercise their influence subconsciously) these values appear no longer to need the support of the Christian revelation at all. The effect of this is twofold. First, those who make no profession of the Christian faith, but are otherwise seriously minded, are brought under the illusion that the main Christian values spring from a natural sense of right and wrong in men and women, which natural moral sense can be relied upon to perpetuate them in human life. Second, those who *do* make a profession of Christian belief find that there is very little difference between the life they lead and the life led by the more or less decent and respectable folk by whom they are surrounded. To be a Christian does not appear ever to call for really costly decisions. A man can be a Christian for years and yet apparently live a life of complete moral smoothness and placidity, in spite of the fact that he is surrounded by unbelievers. The reason is that the latter are living in the same moral medium and tradition as himself. Any of us who have attempted to present the Gospel to lively and earnest young minds will know what a real difficulty this causes. The question is asked—so what? What real difference does it make when you get down to the brass tacks of living to be a Christian? The preacher presents a call for a great decisive, costly choice, and behold, all it seems to come to in the end is living pretty much like other decent folk in a surburban house, with the exception that the Christian goes to church on Sunday and comes away from it vaguely troubled perhaps by the disparity between the accents of tremendous crisis in the words of the preacher and the almost complete absence of any commensurate crisis alike from the preacher's life and from his own.

On the other hand, the process of approximation has also undoubtedly worked in the opposite direction also: that is to say if there has been a partial permeation of the standards of secular society with Christian values with the consequences just indicated, there has been a permeation of Christian values or at least the values which rule the lives of professing Christians, by the standards of secularized society. No doubt the sweeping criticism so frequently brought against the Church that its members live no better lives than those outside it is in its sweepingness often gravely unjust; it rests on a blindness to the many devoted and dedicated lives which are being lived by numbers of obscure and otherwise ordinary folk. Nevertheless, it has far too much justification to be ignored. Nobody could read the New Testament with a fresh mind without a mournful sense that that life of the Church is in comparison with that teaching both worldly and commonplace. The New Testament is full of ethical bombshells; yet it is hardly too much to say that, judging from the contemporary life of the Church, the fuses have been very successfully removed. Obvious examples are the New Testament teaching about the pursuit and acquirement of wealth, and the forgiveness of enemies.

It is true that there confronts us a very perplexing problem which it would be foolish to minimize or over-simplify—the problem of how the high ethical absolutes of the New Testament are to be related to the necessity laid upon the Christian to live in the midst of a non-Christian, sin-corrupted world. Some adjustment, no doubt, there has to be between the absolutes of the Gospel and life in the world. But that problem to which Reinhold Niebuhr has devoted such illuminating thought, is beside the point here. The point I am making here is that our general situation today is such that a great many Christians are just not aware that there is any problem at all. They are not aware that there is any struggle going on, any tension between the Christian absolutes of conduct and the general partly Christianized moral medium in which they live, as this manifests itself in contemporary culture and contemporary accepted standards of life. Christians so often do not seem to realize the problem and how critical it is both in relation to their own entry into the high adventure and the rich regards of Christian living and in relation to the whole future of mankind.

But, and this is my point, Christian ministers and preachers at least, ought to be aware of what is going on, and their preaching and teaching ought to be both a challenge and a guide to others, especially to our young people. That is why I have ventured to speak as I have done. I plead for a preaching and teaching ministry which takes the trouble to acquire some knowledge of the contemporary world of culture and is exercising a sound Christian discrimination in regard to it; I plead for a preaching and teaching ministry which, without ignoring the very real difficulties is nevertheless a powerful presentation of the Christian absolutes and of their indissoluble connection with the whole Christian view of God and man; I plead for a preaching and teaching ministry which in relation to the frightful problems of these times is challengingly and trenchantly ethical and doctrinal at one and the same time. Let our people, especially our young people, see the tremendous crisis which confronts the world today, and the cruciality of the part they are called to play in it. Let them recover the sense that while Christ does not call a man out of the world, he does call him to a decisive break with the world, the sense that the unconscious acquiescence in un-Christian and half-Christian values in the ends we pursue, the books we read, the political judgments we make, is a most serious treachery to God and to Christ and to mankind. St. Paul's prayer for the Philippians comes to mind again; the prayer that Christian men in these chaotic days should be more and more rich in knowledge and all manner of insight enabling them to have a sense of what is vital. ℺

John A. Mackay

Dr. John A. Mackay was for many years president of Princeton Theological Seminary. As with many of the other Mullins lecturers, Dr. Mackay was a prolific author. One of his best-known books is *A Preface To Christian Theology.* He delivered the E. Y. Mullins Lectures on Preaching in 1948 with the theme, "Our World and God's Gospel."

These lectures were wire-recorded by Pat H. Hill and Roland C. Hudlow, and later were transcribed. They therefore have a definite oral flavor. Mackay's lectures are published here for the first time.

God's Unveiled Secret

President Fuller, Ladies and Gentlemen, the topic, as has been announced, is "God's Unveiled Secret." By that I mean, God's solution of the human problem. We began yesterday by considering together certain contemporary aspects of the human problem. Before we take up the question of the "Unveiled Secret", or God's solution, we are going to look somewhat more comprehensively and also somewhat more intensively or deeply, at the human situation, by way of background for our understanding and appreciation of what it is that God has done to meet man's situation. I think to begin with a few words of recapitulation of yesterday's sermon, as our starting point. I do this for two reasons, first, because of the many who were not able to be present yesterday, and secondly, in order to establish the continuity between our thought today and our thoughts yesterday. We considered man's life, the life of man in the light of God, that is to say, the more contemporary aspects of the human problem. We found that the most characteristic mark of the human situation today is the existence of a great void, an abysmal emptiness, an eerie vacuum. This void has a physical side in the great hunger, the great want, that marks the life of millions of people in Asia and in Europe today. But the void is deeper; the void is also what we have called metaphysical in character, relating to the question of ultimates. It is essentially a spiritual void. We noted the terrible void in the German and Japanese souls following defeat. We found that there is an emptiness in the higher circles in American thought, in our higher learning. We found that our poets sensed a certain hollowness in the American spirit today, marked by three features: anonymity, finality, and loneliness. Masses of people, hosts of people, don't know who they are, where they've come from, where they are going. They are mere atoms. Hosts of people have stopped putting up any fight for the highest and noblest. They take the line of least resistance and let themselves drive, oftentimes going downward into the abyss that is finality. And hosts of people are terribly lonely. They long to establish relations with God, ultimate reality, with the cosmos, and whatever solution may be given to the human problem.

On the social or political plane, their problem, they feel, will not be solved because they want to know whether there is a God with whom they may have relations. To carry that analysis a step forward, I introduce the study of that great Harvard sociologist, Sorokin, whose book, *The Crisis of Our Time*, is one of the great prophetic books written by a contemporary sociologist. His conclusion is that purely sensate culture, by which our culture has been marred, that is to say, a culture which more than anything else has been concerned with the physical and the tangible, with objects of perception, has nothing more to give. We are confronting exhausted cisterns, empty cisterns, and exhausted wells. In other words, the kind of culture, especially scientific culture, to which we have pinned our faith, is utterly exhausted, so far as the solution of the human problem is concerned.

We pass on now to a deeper analysis of the human situation. We have considered the contemporary phase; we now look at the contemporary in the perspective of history and enter upon the historical phase; man's historical situation and the problem which it presents. Why is there such a void in our contemporary situation? Because during man's historical existence he has been in revolt against his Maker, desiring to establish his own independence, make a world after his own image, become, if he possibly can, a divinity in his own right. And that has led, as we saw to begin with, to a kind of insanity, a delirium of grandeur on man's part, in individuals, in social groups, racial and social, ending in the manifestation of unspeakable cruelty and ultimate disintegration of human personalities, and of social groups. In other words, man is being shattered against the ultimate realities of spiritual forces in God's world. That is to say, the man or the group that tries to run his life or God's world in his own way is foredoomed to ultimate disaster; and that is the witness of history.

When we examine the New Testament, and, for that matter, the Old Testament, we get a sense of lostness. When man follows idols or exalts himself to a place of deity, he becomes hollow, he becomes lost. As you have it in that great letter to the Ephesians, he becomes alienated from God by his wicked works. He becomes without God and without hope. He becomes a child of wrath, darkened in his understanding, a denizen of the abyss. And what is more, his life and history is composed by subtle and yet sinister and inexorable historical forces which he can't control, which represent a divine judgment upon his acts. When the Apostle Paul speaks about principalities and powers in the heavenly places he is not speaking merely of supernatural personal forces—the devil and his satellites—as we shall see in a moment. Principalities and powers in the heavenlies mean more. They mean those inexorable laws such as, for example, the law of heredity. When man violates the great sanctities he gets into the grip of law which takes an inexorable toll in his progeny, and there is no getting away from it. And what is more, man in revolt created ideas, principles, which are basically false, and yet which can exert an appalling, inexorable influence in history upon great masses of people. Now you get a whole nation, or a whole race, believing in the hegemony of that nation and race, its essential divinity, exalting character and what happens? You have what happened in Germany. When you get a whole people, or class of people, believing in economic determinism or historical materialism, then you get millions of people who become committed in loyalty to a principle which is false; and yet, when it dominates the mind, can wreak the most diabolical consequences on a whole civilization, and upon a belief of them.

Now part of the trouble today is that we are in the grip of some ideas which are false ideas, and are forces which are the consequence of wrong attitudes on our part, and we have to pay the consequences. As in the law of heredity, which got going because we took up wrong attitudes in the past, so the problem becomes complicated as to how to solve the human situation. But there is another phase; there's not only a rift in contemporary society, there is not only a rift in man's historical situation, but there is also a cosmic rift. What does that mean? There are rival powers in what Paul calls the heavenlies. He carries the human problem right into the supernatural realm. He believed in a personal power of evil, in a strategy of evil, in a personal devil. And you cannot take the Bible seriously and its writers seriously, and the thought and attitude of our Lord Jesus Christ, himself, without accepting as more than an hypothesis, as a tremendously grim reality, the existence of a personal, supernatural power of evil, the devil. Now it has not been popular, never been popular in the philosophy of the Western world to admit a personal power of evil, supernatural in character, as an hypothesis for thought; and it has been quite uncommon to admit this hypothesis in much Christian theology. But what happened in these last years when utter frustration has betaken man? When his whole optimistic outlook upon human nature and human history has been shattered, he has been chastened, and is ready to re-think the whole spiritual structure of reality. And one of the interesting phenomenon in the thought of our times is that leading thinkers, laymen in particular, who are fully aware of the whole history of thought, and desperately concerned about the contemporary situation, are bringing back into the picture, quite seriously, the personality of the devil. Now no more significant book has been written in recent years than the *Screwtape Letters* of that Oxford Don, C. S. Lewis. And the Swiss writer, Dennis Darousimal, a young philosopher, has written *The Devil's Share*. We have on our own faculty a very distinguished former German professor, a theologian, Otto Piper, who, in his thinking, before Lewis wrote and Darousimal wrote, took very seriously the biblical point of view of a personal power of evil. In fact, some have said that Dr. Piper brought the devil to Princeton. Not that we didn't have him there before, in thought and in life, but he did focus attention upon that reality.

And I want, in all earnestness and seriousness, to raise the question, What is the ultimate philosophical objection to the reality of a rival of deity for the soul of man in history? Now let's be perfectly clear. Christian thought, biblical thought, does not permit of the concept of an ultimate dualism in the cosmos or in history. It does not admit of what has been called a "Manichaean philosophy" of the ultimacy of evil. It does admit that the devil is the prince of the world, that he controls secular historical forces, but that God is the King of Eternity, and that the great strategist in history in the hearts of man alienated from God is foredoomed in the end. But he is desperately, as Lewis points out, desperately efficient in his strategy, and part of that strategy consists of endeavoring to secure that men shall not take him seriously, or admit as an hypothesis even his existence. And, it seems to me, that when we are considering a world strategy for evangelization or for Christianization, we ought to become permeated with a truly biblical point of view, and recognize the existence of transcendent, supernatural forces in the heavenly spheres, as part of the ultimate problem of mankind and a phase of the problem with which God had to deal in a very creative and redemptive way. Now that's the total situation: contemporary, historically, cosmically, the great rift that exists because of sin, man's alienation from God, the true source of his life and all its consequences.

Now in the course of the ages many attempts have been made on man's part to establish unity, to bring about a reconciliation in thought, or in life. And in order once again to understand and appreciate the grandeur, the splendor, the thoroughness of God's solution of the problem, let us look at man's attempts across the centuries to bridge the abyss, to create harmony, to do away with the rift. We begin with certain classical attempts in thought and in life. Now ancient thought, of the

Greek tradition, was singularly unaware of the nature and magnitude of the rift in human nature or in man's relations with the divine. They were aware of sin and its consequence, but not as a cosmic reality of producing a cosmic rift. Now consider their approach to the problem of unity. The great Ionians, the first philosophers in the Western world, were interested in discovering some one substance which might interpret the meaning of the world and as the basis of unity. The Pythagorians believed that the problem of unity was a mathematical problem, a problem of numbers, establishing harmony. The Stoics believed that there was an eminent logos who should be taken into account as throwing light upon the meaning of life and history.

And then, taking a jump into a little over a century ago, into the heart of German thought, the great philosopher, Hegel, who was so influential in many things that came out of Communism, and many things that came out of Nazism, believed that the historical and the cosmic process was a dialectical movement; now to the right and now to the left, ending up constantly in a kind of synthesis. Hegel refused to recognize the ultimate force of evil, he only admitted the rational; "Rational is real, and the real is the rational," and he spoke about the coming of the "Idea." What you had to recognize was the meaning of this "Idea" which was working itself out, moving alternately from right to left and then forming a new synthesis. The State becoming the incarnation of the absolute idea, God walking upon earth so that for him it was the all-potent State that could solve all the human problems.

These were attempted solutions in thought. There were some classical solutions in life on the political plane. The great Alexander was so impressed with Greek thought and culture that he wanted to unite mankind around the wisdom of the Greeks. And there came the great Caesar Augustus, whose dream it was to give to mankind for all times an ideal constitution and a permanently stable State, which under Roman law and buttressed by Roman arms, would give peace and security to all mankind under the aegis of the Roman eagle. And a recent writer has pointed out that Augustus actually had the illusion and desired to go down in history as the man who had given to the political life of mankind its ideal constitution and permanent stability. 'Till the Germanic hordes stormed the citadel of the Eternal City, and then the dream was punctured.

Now, when we come to our times, there are also attempts that are being made to unify mankind, to close the rift, to introduce light, to give true light, because everybody recognizes that our situation is terribly serious. We are all riddled, honeycombed with chasm life and thought, and relations have been atomized in quite an appalling way. Now what are the attempts being made to introduce harmony, to establish unity? One way is the way of power. To do it on the political plane, to do it with force of arms, to establish a Sovietic order, to establish a Democratic order, and both groups, Russian Communists and American Democrats study geo-politics. Now what does that mean? There was the great geographer, Sir Halford Mackinder, who died recently, who wrote a book when the peacemakers of the first World War were writing the treaty in Versailles. He entitled the book *Democratic Ideals and Reality*. His view was that the peace was being made under great illusion. Nobody took any notice of his book except Germans and Russians and Japanese. The Democratic world paid no attention to it whatever until the Second World War broke; and the democracies became aware that Sir Halford Mackinder had a great insight into future politics and the way of power. Here was his formulation: Who rules East Germany rules the heartland; who rules the heartland commands the world island; who rules the world island commands the world. And the course of world politics in recent years has been no more than a tremendous attempt to secure the seats of power, and Russia has got ahead of the democracies. Now Russia has East Germany.

The heartland is made up of that great area in Europe and in Russia where the snow falls in winter and which is virtually impregnable and self-contained, so far as sea power is concerned. And the world island: Asia, Europe and Africa. Now looking at the situation from the geo-politicians' point of view, you can see why a Truman plan would block Russia in Greece and in Turkey. Why? Because Russia's design is to break into East Asia, to break into the Near East, and break over into Africa, and become the dominant force in Europe, Asia, and Africa. And then the political situation, the power situation, would be the force controlling the one, the great world island. And the force controlling the other world island—the Western Hemisphere. And geo-democratic geo-politics is aimed at preventing Russia from dominating the world island; because that would create a literally tragic situation for the Western Hemisphere. Now that is a power attempt to unite man which is not poetry, which is terribly grim reality! And which, if realized, would have the most doleful consequences for the Christian religion in its immediate future, and the spiritual forces of mankind.

Then there is the way of wisdom. What is it? The way that scientists would follow, which is not too luminous. I mentioned yesterday the fact that the assumption upon which science is based in recent generations has been punctured, and its puncturing is admitted by scientists themselves. The illusion that the acquisition of knowledge, that the accumulation of scientific knowledge, would inexorably contribute to human welfare. Now that is not only false, but has produced a sinister reality—atomic energy—which, if not controlled by moral forces, spiritually inclined forces, can wreak the doom and ruin of mankind. The way of science offers no hope at the moment, because the nuclear scientists say, "If you tell us what you want we can give you means of realizing your ideals, but if you don't know what you want, if you don't know where to go, we are helpless, because we deal with the 'how' and not with the 'what'."

Another way is the way of ideas. Sorokin's solution is intensely interesting. "Sensate culture", he says, "is exhausted. The moment has come when we must pursue high and lofty ideals; and we relate ourselves to great spiritual realities." "If the day is to be won," this Harvard sociologist says, "we must recognize that people have to be divided between saints and cynics." That is to say, the saints that pin their hope, who link their destiny to great spiritual reality, idealistic, ideational, who are willing to suffer all the immediate consequences of their loyalty to those realities, and especially be willing to confront the cynics who laugh at them and ridicule them, and all the rest. But where is the force to come out of? Where is the light to break that will create your saints who are willing to rough it that way? What about the problem of the will? How can that spirit of adventure be created? Amid man's vested interests Sorokin sees the problem. Its solution, he says, can only come in this way, when men and women of our generation give themselves with joyous abandon to things that are spiritual. But how create those men and women? There's the rub! "Knowledge I need not; knowledge Thou hast given; but Lord, the will, there lies my deepest need." Another solution, very romantic, has been offered by another Harvard professor, an admirable man, a first-rate philosopher, Professor Hocking. After the laymen's inquiry which he did, he was so singularly unaware of the disintegrating forces that were operating in the world, so little aware of the subterranean, volcanic forces that were to disrupt life in the Orient, that his solution was that we should all begin to work together towards the New Testament of every existing faith.

Take all your world faiths, get them together, look beyond to the New Testament of all the existing faiths. But two things he ignores. He ignores the fact of the Communistic forces which were to belch forth; and he ignores the fact that the great world religions were disintegrating and had nothing really more to say to solve the problem in this revolutionary age.

So, if ever there was a background that made solution imperative, if ever there was a background that made God's solution magnificent, here it is. And so we come, in the last part of this hour, and in this background, to God's solution of the human problem, "His Unveiled Secret", the revelation of His will, as to what He has done, and proposes to do, to heal the rift, to create unity, to bind man to God and man to man, and man to woman, and children to parents, and masters to servants, and Jews to Gentiles, and all together as members, as citizens of God's new order, a divine commonwealth. God's great scheme of redemption, that's what we have come to now. The moment we say "God" we are taking God in the biblical sense, and a personal, all-wise, all-powerful, all-loving, aggressive force in human history. Too long has God been merely a construction of human thought. One of the great classical declarations regarding God is that of Paschal, one of the thinkers whose life and writings are beginning to tell on contemporary thought. Said Paschal in one of his great experiences, "God of Abraham, God of Isaac and God of Jacob, not of the scholars and wise people; God of Jesus Christ; thy God and my God." If there ever was a scholar, that man was Paschal. If ever there was a first-rate, scientific mind, he was that person—great inventor, great philosopher, great mystic. But for him, the God of the philosophers is a construct of the philosopher's thought, an idea, a conclusion to which the philosophic mind comes is ultimately an idol, a symbol, a cypher. God of Abraham, God of Isaac, God of Jacob, God operating in history, weaving personality into the web of his purpose. God who became fully and perfectly and absolutely manifested in Jesus Christ; God of wisdom, God of power, but wisdom and power at the service of love, or infinite compassionate love; what is called *agape*. That which characterizes the Christian revelation and Christian view of love, over against the *eros* of the Greek tradition. No longer is the divine presented as in love with loveliness; but the divine is presented as being preoccupied with the problem of the unlovely, and loveless, and the unlovable; and is presented as entering into history to love the loveless and unlovable and to make them lovely and lovable in Jesus Christ, His son, that is, with all its magnitude and repercussions and historical and cosmic bearings—the Unveiled Secret of God, what Paul calls the mystery, the mystery of God's will. Now in the New Testament thought, and especially in Pauline thought, the mystery is not something merely mysterious, something that is hidden. And often, mystery means a secret hidden with God; now and then the mystery of his reconciling will with its cosmic proportion and its historical ramifications and its redemptive thoroughness in Jesus Christ. Now that is what we are going to explore.

The moment that the thought is accepted that the ultimate spiritual reality in the universe is paternal, that he loves, loves in such a way as Jesus Christ loved, then a glint of hope and meaning enters into the human scene. Why, no longer are we committed to the idea that the cosmos and the processes of history represent mechanical, inexorable, fatalism as Marxists believe. No longer are we committed to the idea that the religious spirit of mankind, its loneliness, longing for a father's face, or a mother's love, belongs to the earlier primitive, poetical, superstitious period in human history. We are not orphans, and the cries of our loneliness are not the cries of children hopelessly orphaned in a universe that is cold, so that all ideas about God belong to the romantic, earlier period in human history. No, the Father lives. Men are not orphans; no longer are they committed to the idea that to follow the highest and best, to give oneself utterly and sacrificially to what one believes to be true is not lost in a cemetery of dead values; because God is the custodian, and the guardian of those who give their lives for truth and goodness. No, the unveiled secret of God is that the ultimate image, pattern, or symbol, is not a machine, is not an orphanage, is not a cemetery—it's a home for the God and Father of all. The Creator, and the Ruler of the cosmos, and of history, is the God and Father of our Lord Jesus Christ, who loves with an everlasting love, and who redeems, as we shall see later, to the uttermost, all who come unto God by Him, creating a new family, a new humanity, giving this old world a fresh start in those whom he calls by His name, whom he chooses in Christ, whom He predestines unto good works, whose lives must be holy and unblamable in His sight. The new humanity, out of the wreck and ruin of this atomized, anonymous, banal, lonely order—sons and daughters of the Almighty, come upon the plane of history with a spirit of the home, knowing the Father's love and being redeemed by His Son, Jesus Christ. That is the "Unveiled Secret", as one tries to interpret the New

Testament. A great reconciliation, with cosmic proportion, centering in Christ. And Paul's great category of thought is, as we shall see tomorrow, in Christ Jesus. That is where the new humanity stands in Christ, in the cosmic Christ.

What is going to be the instrument of this great unity, this great reconciliation? The people of God, that is to say, people called by God, named by God, given a sense of sonship and daughterhood by God. In the Old Testament "Israel" and in the New Testament, "the Church." One of the happy and hopeful features in the biblical thought today is the attention that is being given to the Old Testament, and to biblical theology. The Old Testament is being considered and studied in categories that are native to itself, and not in categories that are superimposed and completely alien and unilluminated. As we study the people of Israel we find two great, majestic facts. One, their sense that they are the people of the present—that there is present in their history a divine Being, their God, with whom they had entered into covenant. And the second fact, the feeling, the awareness, that they are the people of destiny—chosen by God, enjoying God's presence, entered with Him into covenant in order to bless the world, and all nations of mankind. The moment came when Israel was not willing to bless the world, not willing to lose herself in the majesty of God's purpose, wanted to keep God to herself, and keep all the blessings of the covenant, to be selfish; and Israel was dissolved, and the Church appeared. The Christian Church, the Church of Jesus Christ—all those men and women who are in Christ, constitute the new Israel of God, the new and the true humanity, the greatest society of which history has any knowledge, the instrument of God's purpose to bless mankind. What is to be the goal of it, to the praise of His glory? That is to say, the Church is to make God visible. That is what is meant in the Bible; to glorify God, to make Him visible—all the inter-potency and secret purpose, to make it known in personal historical force. And what is the last class ever to be celebrated in time, the perpetual class, the endless class? The letter of the which in that sublime thought of Saint Paul, in the tenth verse of the third chapter of the Epistle to the Ephesians: powers higher than human powers, some angelic, some diabolic, are to see in the history of the Church the manifold, the many-colored, wisdom of God. In other words, the life of the Church, the warfare of the Church in history, the great epic of the Christian Church, is to give spirit higher than human spirits their deeper insight into God, and as Paul wrote to the people in his time,

"You are the first fruits." Do you want to know who you are? You are the people whom God has chosen, the experiences that you have had are the experiences of re-birth. You are members of the new humanity. And throughout the ages, people like you are going to represent you, this new humanity, and when we consider that, my brothers and sisters, when we see the Gospel in that perspective, in that background, we see it in all its majesty and grandeur and sublimity.

The "Unveiled Secret" of God, God's revelation in Christ as the only ultimate and adequate solution of the human problem, and the Church which is his body. Men and women who are redeemed, as the instrument of his glory, to be that nuclear center of a new humanity in which God is to be glorified and his purposes in history not frustrated but achieved until He comes whose right it is to reign. Let us pray:

O God, our Father, greater art Thou than our thoughts can comprehend; deeper are Thy purposes than our plummets can reach, but Thou has grasped us in Thy love and Thou hast Thyself gone down into the depths of our misery and woe. Illumine our lives that we may see the glory of Thy purpose in Jesus Christ. Purify our hearts that He and His love may be regnant within us. And so mold us to Thy glory and the execution of Thy Holy purposes that what we hear, think, and say and do may be written forever into the annals of our lives, and the progress of Thy kingdom through Jesus Christ our Lord; and may the grace of our Lord Jesus Christ and the love of God and the communion of the Holy Spirit be with us all. Amen. ℞

The Cosmic Christ

The topic of this second lecture is "The Cosmic Christ." When one looks at the human situation, it is tragic in its meaninglessness, lifelessness, emptiness. History reveals a great rift, an alienation between heaven and earth, God and man, in which man, attempting to take over the affairs of the world, suffers disintegration and grievous loss. And part of the spiritual situation is that in what Paul describes as the "heavenly sphere." There is also a rift in the supernatural order with a positive strategy of evil being carried on by a being whom we call the Devil, or Satan. Over against that situation God expressed a redemptive purpose; light shone into human darkness; life came into human emptiness. The rift was healed in a great scheme of reconciliation, and the powers of evil were met, grappled with, overcome by a divine Redeemer, Jesus Christ, God's answer to every phase of the spiritual cosmos, both on earth, in history, and through-out the cosmos. According to what Paul calls the "mysteries" the open secret of God, the "Unveiled Secret", the new cosmic center becomes Jesus Christ.

As we approach the person, the worth, the significance of Jesus Christ the Redeemer, we do well to approach it from the viewpoint of the yearning, of the distressed, alienated, rifted human spirit for a Redeemer, for the intervention of God. Dr. Carver in his prayer [before the lecture] mentioned the "groaning of all creation" for a manifestation of the Sons of God. It is also true to history, to the human heart, and to the revelation of God, that the broken, rifted, alienated human spirit in the depths of its woe cries out for a manifestation of God. The great modern thinker, now unhappily passed away, Archibald Boehmer, professor of philosophy at the University of Glasgow, gave a great series of lectures, "Between the Two Walls," at Princeton University. (The book is called *The Sacramental Universe*.) At the close of his last lecture he said, "Man's faith today, (he was referring to the coming of the dictators, to the advent of Hitler, Mussolini and Stalin)—Man's faith today in a deified tyrant is an aberration of his true instinct for a personal manifestation of God." Now the great truth involved in that is that when the human situation becomes so bad that man not only finds himself in darkness, but at the bottom of the abyss of despair, then no idea, however luminous, will solve his problem. Only the leader with face, and hands, and feet, can solve his woes. Now that is always the case when man strikes bottom, the bottomless abyss of despair; only a face, a hand, and a voice, can solve his problem. And it was Europe's despair that sent many nations into the hands of those deified tyrants, führers, supermen. The great Danish thinker, Kierkegaard, carried the thought further. Kierkegaard, it may be remarked, is undoubtedly the greatest religious psychologist in history, outside Augustine. He said, "When the human spirit is deeply, gravely, despairingly smitten with a sense of sin, an absolute derelict, then the spirit of man cries out for a manifestation of God in the flesh as the only solution of the human problem, of the problem of sin." And upon that fact he grounds a psychological answer to the incarnation. Stricken man, conscience-smitten man, cries out for God manifest in the flesh, as the only answer.

In these last days our greatest living historian, Arnold J. Toynbee, has applied his mind to the study of history. He finds that we are now in the twenty-first civilization in a great historic series. He sees us in our time of troubles. He raises the question as to whether our civilization can survive. "Survival," he affirms, "is dependent on our capacity to become adjusted to the eternal, to God." "There's one chance," he adds, "that we may see, and take seriously, the full significance of Jesus Christ." So after scanning the pages of history in search of a personality who might offer any hope, light, leadership, he concludes with these words, "And now we stand with gaze fixed upon the further shore, the further shore of the river of death. One figure alone rises from the flood, and immediately fills the whole horizon, that is the Saviour." "And he shall see of the travail of his soul and be satisfied," says the historian.

From the viewpoint of abysmal, despairing human need, from the viewpoint of a survey of historical personalities, there appears to be but one answer; a Divine Redeemer who shall be the manifestation of God in human form upon the road of history as the Saviour of mankind. In this background we come to our concrete study of Jesus Christ, who, according to Christian faith, is God manifest in the flesh, the divine Redeemer, the center of God's scheme of reconciliation, the cosmic Christ. And so we begin with our study of the Savior. We start where He appears in history, in the pages of the Gospel. Jesus of

Nazareth, or the man Christ Jesus. It is perfectly clear that when Biblical writers describe His coming they speak about the "fullness of time," and the "fullness of the times," the time, *kairos,* which became the center of time and through this advent, the center of history. God's time, when the mystery became unveiled, the hidden secret was revealed to men's gaze, to men's thought. The Christian poet, W. H. Auden, in his *Christmas Oratorio,* has two remarkable lines. One he puts into the mouth of the wise men who came from the East, "O here and now our endless journey stops." Human wisdom, human pride, human speculation, comes to an end in Bethlehem, in the child that was born, in the Son that was given, God's wisdom, God's answer, God's "Unveiled Secret." And the line he puts into the mouth of the shepherds, "O here and now our endless journey starts." The shepherds, representatives of the poor of the earth, forlorn people, with their yearning, with their desire, get a fresh start as they look at the face in the manger. Representatives are they of humanity for whom a new springtime comes, before whom there is a new long road, under the leadership of this One. History in reverse from now on; the poor shall be something, despairing people shall have an answer to their needs, their new journeys done. Human wisdom ends, because the divine revelation has come; human progress begins, because the representative of the new humanity, the true humanity, has been born.

And so we look at him, the man Christ Jesus. What is truest about Him is that He is the supreme representative of all the parties concerned in the historical and in the cosmic human problem. Who are they? Israel, man, God. Jesus Christ, the man Christ Jesus, is in a very remarkable and vivid manner the representative of Israel, the chosen people of the earlier time, when a glimmer of the mystery was coming through, when God's purpose for mankind was becoming manifest, initiated in history, in the life of the people, the people of the present, the people with a sense of destiny. He came as their Messiah, and was so recognized by those who understood His significance. And recent study of Him in relationship to Israel, reverent, scholarly study, draws attention to the parallelism between Him and the people of Israel. "Out of Egypt have I called my son"—he comes back from an alien land when Herod is dead. Israel had its Red Sea—Jesus Christ, his Jordan River. Israel had its forty years in the wilderness—Jesus Christ, His forty days of temptation. Israel's deepest mission was to be the Suffering Servant, Jesus saw in the Suffering Servant the figure of himself in a way that Jewish thinkers never saw, and He accepted Israel's role for His own, His Messianic destiny—to see of the travail of His soul, and being satisfied, going as a lamb to the slaughter, as a sheep before her shearers being dumb. There is no doubt whatever that not only the biblical writers, but that Jesus Christ Himself, in His deepest insight, saw Himself as the representative of the new Israel, who was to carry forward into a new realm and upon a new plane what Israel was designed in the first instance to be and become.

He represented man, a true man in every sense. It is very remarkable to observe how Jewish writers in these last years are not only enthusiastic about the person of Jesus Christ as the greatest member of their race, but they are free to acknowledge that it was He, Himself, who was the unique factor, not so much the teaching that He brought, but the spirit that He brought, the atmosphere that He created; One who expressed, radiated, and incarnated love. They are free to acknowledge that never in the history of their people had there been one like Him; never in the history of mankind a personality like that. And when we look at Him as true man, the representative of true man, what do we find? We find that He is a God-centered man; no rift there; came to do the Father's will; no interest whatever except in discovering what God wanted Him to do, in living in the closest communion with God, in harmonizing His own will perfectly with the will of the Father. That is what man was supposed to be—to be God-centered, to fit into God's great scheme of things, to fulfill his destiny as God's man. But, also, in His behavior among men He expressed equally what true manhood should be, a passion for righteousness and a heart full of the everlasting mercy, one in whom righteousness— right relations—was regnant, one in whom mercy welled up. I can think of no better way of seeing the divine righteousness and the divine mercy expressed in the manhood of our Lord Jesus Christ than in the hand that was uplifted with the lash to expell those financiers, exploiters of their fellows, from the sacred precincts of the Temple. Purging the floor of the holy place, symbol of divine judgment, against all violation of God's righteous order. And the same hand that enfolded childhood, that broke the bread for the hungry, that touched the diseased and healed them, that was pierced with the nail, impaled to the cross; the everlasting righteousness and the everlasting mercy, indicative of the fact that in true manhood, in true womanhood, the two lived in holiest marriage, unity, harmony; a passion for right relations that shall express God's purpose for human life and infinite tenderness when God's order is violated and people are penitent or people are in need.

And He represented God in what way? That He was like God? More than that! He was God! God manifest in the flesh. "The Word became flesh and dwelt among us." I have already quoted Auden—I quote again from the same great poem at the end of his collected works, *The Christmas Oratorio.* He has a sense of the tragedy of life, of the mystery of life, the experience in himself, the yearning to understand and to get close to deity, and then he says, "We who must die, demand a miracle. How could the Eternal do a temporal act? The Infinite become a finite fact; nothing can save us that is possible; we who must die demand a miracle." In other words, a deep, despairing sense of the human tragedy and of human woe cries out for the Living God, cries out for the impossible which became the real when God became man. Rationally preposterous! How could the Eternal do a temporal act, the Infinite become a finite fact? But the thing happened in this new phenomenon, Jesus Christ, the God-man. Well, did the great Russian Berdyaev say that the starting point of the Christian religion is not God, or man, but the God-man, Jesus Christ? And it is no exaggeration to say that Christianity is Christ. The thing that distinguishes the Christian religion from all other religions is that it is a religion of a person, Jesus Christ. They are essentially religions of ideas—Christianity is a religion of a Person. Now that does not mean that there are not great principles in the Christian religion, no, but it is through Jesus Christ that I come to know myself. It is through Jesus Christ that I come to know God. It is in the measure in which I become acquainted with Jesus Christ that I come to understand and appreciate those great principles that are called "Christian." It is equally in the measure that I experience the power of Jesus Christ that I can in the slightest measure put into practice those same, great, Christian principles. That is to say that in the deepest, holiest things, Christianity is Christ. There is no Christianity that is not Christocentric in the most absolute sense, for this is the cosmic Christ.

We pass on from the man Christ Jesus, from his significance as the representative of Israel, of man, and of God—we pass on to Christ crucified. It is possible to give but a casual glance at Jesus Christ as a figure in history, as the victim of human hate, as a derelict, executed man. There was a famous Oxford professor who gloried in the fact that the only article in the Apostle's Creed which he could accept was "Crucified under Pontius Pilate." He accepted the historical fact of the crucifixion of Jesus Christ, but you cannot know Him as a mere phenomenon of history, crucified and derelict; you can't be an isolationist in that sense. But when you go to the Spanish-speaking world this historical isolation of the cross takes on a very grim and tragic form. In that great city of Buenos Aires, now the center of Latin culture, the best-dressed and best-fed city in the world—when an ordinary citizen of Buenos Aires wants to say about somebody that he doesn't amount to anything, that he's a poor beggar, or a poor devil, what he says is "He's a poor Christ." Now by that he means that he has associated the dereliction of the cross, the victim of hate, with the core of the Christian religion. The essentially Spanish Christ has been the crucified Christ, in isolation. As the great writer Miguel de Unamuno put it, "Death's eternity, the immortalization of death, the figure that has nothing to say to life, and nothing to say to thought, 'the poor Christ'." But that is not Christ crucified, who can only be understood in the true context of his life, in the perspective of history, and in the light of eternity and God's purpose in Him. And so we look at Him.

Now to my mind the most profitable way, the most meaningful way in which we can look at the crucified Christ and interpret the atonement made by Jesus Christ, is to regard him as the victor, as the one who deliberately assaults all the alien powers, who undertakes as the vicegerent of God, as the representative of man, and of Israel, to solve the human problem, meeting all the difficulties and alien foes that bar the way to victory and to the kingdom and to spiritual triumph. Sometimes we unduly stress and misinterpret the "blood," as if it were the blood of one who were purely passive, a victim. Sometimes we attach as it were a physical, magical significance to the blood; but what does the blood mean in the deep, biblical, Christian sense? The blood means the outpouring of life which the crusader and the victor gave in the course of his Titanic struggle. What does blood signify? Blood signifies life. For blood to be shed means for life to be given. When it is affirmed that Jesus Christ saved us by His blood, what is meant is that he saved us by laying down his life, by giving his life in all its fullness, and sanctity, and virility, in this blood.

Now, wherein did the struggle come? What were the forces that Jesus Christ had to meet before he could claim the victor's right, before he could triumph as the crucified One? He had to meet the Law; all the requirements of the divine law for man. And in the days of his flesh he showed himself to be a perfect man in his love of God, in his love of man, so that none could accuse him of sin, and when at last the arch-enemy came he could find nothing in him. In other words, here the representative of humanity, the new man, the second Adam, fulfilled perfectly God's law of righteousness for human nature. He was a true man, a perfect man ready to give manhood a fresh start. He met sin. He met it in its personal representative, in the leaders of religion who had a false view of God, and no vital interest in men. He found it in the fickleness of the multitudes, he met it in Peter, and in Judas, in the one who denied him, in the one who betrayed him. He took it all, and he never showed by a gesture, by a word or by a thought, any unworthy reaction to what human sin in personal form or through human lips, did to him. But, rather, he recognized that as the Redeemer it was his to endure the uttermost that sin, the violation of the divine law, and true manhood, could do, whether it expressed itself through human lips, or acts, or gestures, or in institutionalized form, or in the fears of the representatives of Imperial power, or in the self-interest of the men of religion. Taking God's place in holy direction, he took it all.

And the wages of sin, which is death. He gave himself to death and allowed them to wreak their uttermost upon him as he went as a lamb to the slaughter. Now there is no human thought, no category of thought that can plumb the deep abysmal depths of what took place when Jesus Christ died for human sin, as the representative of sinners, down in the dismal, eerie, abysmal depths. If you want to have light upon it, don't think of Christ as merely standing over against God, but think of God himself in Jesus Christ, giving himself. God giving himself in sufficient, sacrificial, substitutional atonement. Now, one of the objections to the whole idea of the atonement is that while Jesus Christ comes out with flying colors, an awful reflection is placed upon God the Father. Now implicit there is the conception of three very separate beings, a Tritheism, three deities. No, the Christian atonement means that in the fullest, most absolute sense, the Living God in Jesus Christ gave himself for man, to save man. So there's no block, no stigma, now; there is the incredible thing, the impossible thing, just like the incarnation was, but that is the real thing, that the divine concern led God in Christ the Son to enter into death, to lead out a new humanity. And what happened when He died? As the great Spanish Christian, Unamuno, one of the great men of letters of our times, put it, "Thou dids't make death our mother, Thou savest death," and that's what he did. So that for the Christian who believes upon Jesus Christ, death is the womb of a new life, of a new springtime, of a rebirth. Suffering and death have no more terror because they are God's appointed way whereby new life shall come to the birth. The more one suffers, the more Christians have to die, the surer will the kingdom come and the more glorious be the dawning. Now this strong Son of God entered into death to "evangelize death," and to make death the great mother and the great friend, out of whose womb He arose the third day to be the exalted Christ.

He met the law, he met sin, he met death, and he triumphed. The center of a new humanity, the divine Redeemer, the risen Christ. Now what does that mean? It means that there exists a creative, redemptive, cosmic center in whom and through whom God deals with the human problem and with individual souls. First, every creature, every human sinner, has the right to approach Jesus Christ without the mediation of any system or hierarchy or angelic being. The cosmic situation now is that the groan of an obscure, despairing sinner will be heard at God's right hand by Jesus Christ, the cosmic Christ; that there is no place for pessimism, that there is no ultimate despair. One penitent confession, one quiet despairing yearning, will bring the succor of the Strong Son of God, Immortal Love, the High Priest forever after the order of Melchizedek. And that constitutes the core of the Gospel which we proclaim across all the frontiers of human division, that there is salvation with Him in the fullest sense.

And, secondly, life is *in* Christ. That is the great truth unveiled in the letter to the Ephesians, "In Christ." It means that while we live here, if we exercise faith in Christ, give our whole personality to Him in commitment, we live in that cosmic reality, Jesus Christ, in the heavenly spheres. We may be amid the drudgery of life, in its shame, in its rough ways, in its dungeons, but our life is hid with Christ in God in heavenly places, and we are more than conquerors through Him that loved us. In other words, He is our life, our life is in Him. This life is relevant to all the problems of our earthly, historical existence, but its source, its roots, its core are all in Christ in the heavenly sphere. And this cosmic Christ is not only the everlasting Redeemer, is not only the very soil or atmosphere in which we live, but He is the Sovereign Lord of All, the head of the Church, but also the head of the State, Lord of history and of the whole secular order, King of Kings and true Lord of

Lords. Now that means that the Christian Church has a right, and even an obligation to address rulers in the name of the exalted Christ to whom all earth's rulers owe their allegiance, who must carry on government in accordance with the laws of God, and in obedience to Jesus Christ, if they are to have a stable government which God can acknowledge.

Now, in recent times in Europe that is the truth that was apprehended afresh by Christians. That is what is at the core of the great declaration of Barmen—the greatest declaration of the Christian Church in modern times, since the Reformation itself. These men who met at Barmen before the war broke out, when Hitler was bringing pressure upon the church and desiring the church to give a higher allegiance to him and to the State, they said, "We reject the false doctrine that there are spheres of life in which we are not servants of Jesus Christ but of other masters, realms where we are justified or sanctified by others than He." That is to say, we acknowledge but one sole Lord, King of Kings and Lord of Lords. And I believe, my brethren, the time has come for the Christian Church to speak in the name of the Living, Risen Christ, to rulers, to empires, and to civilizations. And it is in this sense that we Protestants have sometimes fallen behind and below Roman Catholics, who with all their weaknesses, and, in a sense, apostasies, have dared to speak in the name of Jesus Christ. We should speak in that same name, and not in the name of natural law or of any other principle, but in the principles of Jesus Christ, in the name of the Risen, Cosmic Christ, who is the supreme authority over Church and State, the Living Lord. And when we Protestants dare afresh to do that, something is going to happen, and not only in our own ranks, but in contemporary civilization, because God has appointed Him Prince and Saviour, Saviour of souls and Prince over all things, for His body, the Church. Let us pray:

> Oh God, our Father, Thou who dids't unveil Thy Son to us, reveal Thy Son in us that He may make us the instruments of His most holy will, for the salvation of souls, and the coming of His kingdom. Make us Thy truer disciples, Thy more loving children, oh Christ. We ask it in Thy name, and for Thy sake. Now may the grace of our Lord Jesus Christ, and the love of God, and the communion of the Holy Spirit, be with us all. Amen.

The Gospel of God for the Nations

This morning we intend to draw together a number of things that we've been considering. Our topic is "The Gospel of God for the Nations." Thus far we have considered the life of man, and the purpose of God, and the fact of Christ. All these have a bearing upon what we call the "Gospel." The topic breaks in a very natural way into two parts, two parts which are two questions. The first question is "What does the Gospel mean?" and the second, "How is the Gospel to be proclaimed?"

The Meaning of the Gospel—the Proclamation of the Gospel. It might be said that the Gospel is the clue to our understanding of the Bible, the core of the message of the Bible, the Gospel, which, as the word indicates, means Good News. Good News about God for man, is the clue, is the central, most luminous category for our understanding of Holy Scripture. It is not too much to say that the Bible is a book about the Gospel. And would to God that in all study of the Bible that fact had been remembered! It is of paramount importance in studying any book that we study it in terms of its central idea, or thesis; in other words, that we take up towards it as towards a picture, that perspective from which alone we can appreciate all the meaning of the book, or the picture. And how much bitterness and how many aberrations in thought would have been avoided, and, one might add, how many divisions in the Christian Church would have been prevented if the study of the Bible had been undertaken from the perspective of the Gospel, or in the light of that central, luminous, category of the Good News of God's redemption centering in Jesus Christ. And one of the encouraging things about biblical study today is that there is the recovery and the re-discovery of this central category, in terms of which, and in the light of which, the whole Bible must be read and studied. The Bible is a book about the Gospel, about God's redemptive activity.

Just as the Gospel is the clue to our understanding of the Bible it is the core of the message of the Bible. Now the Gospel as the core, or the essence of the biblical message does not express what is sometimes called "timeless truth," even about God. Very often some idea about God is taken which may be perfectly true, and the affirmation made that that is the Gospel. If I say "God is love," I am making an affirmation regarding the inmost nature of God; but to say that God is love is not the Gospel. But if I say that "God so loved the world that He gave His only begotten Son, that whosoever believeth shall not perish, but have everlasting life," that is the Gospel; because the eternal truth about the love of God, his inmost nature, took historical form and the Gospel became real. If I say that every human soul is of infinite value, I am stating a timeless truth. But that timeless truth is not the Gospel. But if I say that Jesus Christ died for those souls, for the sins of those souls, that is the Gospel. And if I say with Paul, "He loved me, my soul, and gave Himself for me," that is the Gospel. Now the importance of this is that the Gospel is not the expression of merely timeless truth about God or about man; the Gospel becomes the Gospel upon the plane of history and in relation to redemptive acts which God performed in history.

Now the significance of that is this: that the specifically Christian truth is not timeless truth, like the truth of philosophy, in which philosophy is interested; Christian truth is truth that becomes significant truth in the moment it becomes related to history and to human life. So that we might say Christian truth is truth that becomes, "The Word became flesh and dwelt among us." Now that is the difference between Christian truth and the eternally philosophical truth, those timeless truths in which philosophy is interested. And, further, that is an indication of the fact of how inextricably bound up with history and the human problem Christian truth is, and in the central place, the Gospel.

Then what is the Gospel? What is the Good News? It seems to me that the simplest way in which one can state the meaning of the Gospel is, that God wrought in Jesus Christ complete salvation for man. God wrought in Jesus Christ complete salvation—redemption—for man. The Gospel is the good news about redemption, and has in it at least four facets, or four elements, which are inseparable, the one from the other, each one of which is one aspect of the Good News, one note in the orchestral harmony of the glad tidings. First: great redemptive acts which God wrought in Christ for man's salvation—His advent, or the incarnation of the God-man; the good news that the man, Christ Jesus, was the perfect man; that He lived a perfect life; that He overcame all temptation as the representative of the new humanity as the second Adam; that He died for human sin, the just for the unjust; that He rose again from the dead, the living, victorious Christ, the head of the Church, the ruler of the nations, the Lord of history; and that He is a High Priest forever, lovingly accessible to every human soul that in penitence supplicates Him and his mercy. God News regarding great redemptive acts which center in Christ. That's the first element of the Gospel.

And the second: Good News that when a human sinner accepts this Christ as his Saviour, something happens; there takes place then an inner, a subjective experience, a complete transformation of life; the great act of redemption as related to a human spirit—that too is a part of the Good News. In other words, that it becomes the joyous privilege of a sinner saved by the grace of our Lord Jesus Christ to bear testimony to His followers that something has taken place in him, that he is a new man in Christ Jesus, that with all his failing, all his unworthiness, something happened—he was blind, he now sees; he was loveless, a flame has been kindled within him; he didn't know the way, now he sees what life means; he was before, a nameless, anonymous atom, adrift, banal in his life, without hope, he has been called by his name, he has been given significance, he's been given a vocation. And now it is his joy to bear witness of the fact of the Good News that a human life, however lost, however much adrift, however sin-stained, can be redeemed; and by the grace ofGod, he is what he is. Now you cannot separate the subjective note from the objective; both are part of the Gospel, of the Good News—personal witness to the truth of the Good News, what happens when the Good News is accepted.

But there's still something more, there's a third element, which is also Good News. That is to say, that there exists in the world a redemptive fellowship, the fellowship of all those who have been redeemed, who profess their allegiance to our Lord Jesus Christ, who become members of the Christian Church, that Christian Church being the creation of the Holy Spirit. Now the Church, let us never forget, is a part of the Good News, namely, that God has not willed that individual Christians, redeemed by His grace, should be mere atoms, that they should live in isolation, that they should be mere individualists, but that they should be members of the community of the redeemed. And it is only in this membership, in the fellowship of the redeemed, as members of the Christian Church, that they can perfectly grow up in the nurture and the admonition of the Lord. No one can be a full Christian in isolation. God provides the community, the corporate groups, in order that the individual may come into a Christian heritage, that he may be nurtured, that he may be disciplined, that he may get work to do, that he may get sympathy and advice, and a sense of strength and solidarity in his weakness. It is no exaggeration to say that part of the Good News is the fact of the Christian community, that God has provided a family for the solitary, lonely Christian, that there is no need for one to be cosmologically lonely, for one has God as one's Father, Christ as one's Redeemer, and one's brothers and sisters in Christ, who can mean more to one even than the members of one's own family, according to the flesh, that is Good News! That there is an historical, Christian community where Christian life grows, and where God's purposes are fulfilled.

And there's a fourth element, which is also inseparable from the Gospel. The Good News that those Christians who have been redeemed, that this fellowship which is the body of Christ, is going to triumph in the end. The day of full redemption is coming, the consummation of God's purpose through the Church and in and through Christ Jesus, is going to have a glorious end. We Christians can look at all of the grim realities of our time and be mercilessly realistic about it all, and admit all sorts of facts including the possibility that the twenty-first civilization of mankind may come to an end, and calmly and serenely proclaim the Good News that Jesus Christ shall triumph in history, and that the Christian Church shall continue to be the instrument for the fulfillment of the purposes of his glory within history; and that the time is coming when He shall rule; and triumph. In other words, there's no place for a note of ultimate pessimism or despair in the Christian community, because God is God, and His purposes are all "yea" and "Amen" in Christ Jesus. God shall not be baffled, He shall not be frustrated. What the church is, and stands for, if loyal to God, shall win out in the end, even though we go plunging into a darker valley than humanity has ever been through up to this time. Now that is part of the Gospel of God. The Gospel of the ultimate, eventual triumph, even in history, of the Blessed God and our Saviour, Jesus Christ. Now that's Good News for despairing, lonely, baffled, frustrated people today—that there's no need for them to be in that condition, if they take the Gospel seriously.

And so, we pass on to the second aspect of our subject, to ask, and to endeavor to answer, the second question. If that is what the Gospel means, then how is the Gospel to be proclaimed? The Gospel of God is to be proclaimed in the background of bad news. The Gospel is Good News about God, but in the background is very bad news about man. And I venture to say that the Good News about God will never be appreciated unless the bad news about man is understood and taken into account. The news about man is bad, and at the present moment it simply couldn't be worse. In what does it consist? It consists in several things that we have been finding. That when we look at human nature, we can't be merely idealists. We have got to acknowledge the fact of a great rift in human nature, the fact of sin, and of man's alienation from God. And the true source of life, the Gospel, has full meaning in the background of the terrible rift in human nature, and its consequences in alienation between God and man. And there's so much data in contemporary society, and in contemporary thought, to make that background very real and very vivid.

Another part of the good-bad news is that this rift has, in our time, produced a literally appalling void, as we considered it the first morning together. This utter emptiness, lack of light, lack of meaning, anonymity, banality, loneliness, in low places and in high places, around the globe today—this eerie emptiness, creating a problem for light and for life to illumine the abyss, and to organize the anarchy, and, as you remember, there are two great crusading forces that feel that they have the light and life necessary to do just that job—Soviet Imperialism and Roman Imperialism. All that is a background of bad news for the proclamation of God's Gospel. And the news is still worse! There's an adversary, supernatural in nature, who is capable of carrying on a marvelous strategy in the affairs of men, and most successful in not introducing too much his own presence, or even the suggestion of the thought of him, into human perception or conception. That is the cosmic rift, the strategy of evil, the personality of the devil, bad news! Man's up against it with his rift, and his loneliness, and the devil on his trail, Bad News! And it appears to me, brethren, that the more real we can be about the human situation in its contemporary, historical and cosmic aspects, the more powerfully and luminously shall we be able to proclaim the Gospel, and with the more relevance to the problems of real men and women in their life and in their thought. In other words, the Gospel of God is not going to be something superstitious, or romantic, or mythical, or unrelated to life. It is the thing that's most related to actual life and to actual thought.

How is the Gospel, then, to be proclaimed? It is to be proclaimed in the background of bad news; it is to be proclaimed to all men everywhere, where they are; to all men everywhere, in the place where they are. Well, where are the people? A good many of them are in the Church, church members. You can get them there, speaking from a pulpit like this, now, amid all the bad news. There's one thing for which we should be at least thankful, though not complacent, and that is that according to the statistics, in these United States, there is a larger proportion of people who are members of the Church than at any previous time in American history. The proportion is much larger than it is in England, or Scotland—much larger. Now that is, at least, encouraging; but, the preacher of the Gospel should not become complacent; he dare not take it for granted that all those people to whom he speaks, who are members of his church, have taken the Gospel seriously; that they know the Gospel; that they have experienced the Gospel; that they are living the Gospel; that they are inspired by the Gospel. Some of you may know, and I hope all of you will try to get a copy of that remarkable report got up by the Archbishop's Commission of the Church of England, and entitled, "Toward the Conversion of England." I don't know of any finer study of evangelism and of a concrete human situation, or Church situation, than that great report, "Toward the Conversion of England" by an Anglican commission. Now what is the viewpoint taken? It is stated that the situation is lamentable. Only a small minority of the English people are interested in the Church. Fewer go to Church, so the Commission says, and calls upon Anglican clergymen to consider that they must not regard the pastoral phase of their office as any longer the supreme phase, but states, "You must recognize the fact that many of those people, perhaps most of those people who are your parishioners are not real Christians in their hearts, that they need the Gospel and that they need to be evangelized by the Gospel." And every Christian minister has got to have that in mind, that there are lots of people who are nominally, conventionally, decently Christian, so far as their social or ecclesiastical status is concerned—they're in the church, but the Church is not in them. They render lip service to the Gospel, but they've never known the thrill in their souls or in their minds of what happens when the Gospel is taken seriously, and when Jesus Christ comes into the heart to live there. Now that means that our evangelistic task is always with us, to proclaim the Gospel to the people in the Church for their acceptance. Of course, lots of people come to church who are not church members, we've got to have them in mind, but, we've got to have in mind the hosts of people who never come to church, who've got prejudices against church, who can't be got to the church by horses or being trailed or hailed by jeeps—they won't come. If you're going to reach them you must reach them somewhere outside of church circles. In neutral places, whether in homes, whether in public places, in the open air, neutral halls, in your secular circles, through personal witness. You've got to go to them where they are. That is to say, no Christian minister, no Christian worker fulfills his function, or hers, if they are complacent about or satisfied with, their immediate orbit of activity, as ecclesiastical and within the frontiers of their church circles.

We've got to break out beyond the frontiers, bearing in mind that the majority of our American people are not connected with any church or religion. Now there's the task. Those of us who know Latin America and have been interested in the evangelization of Latin America, know that if you want to get at the people, you can't get at them in church. You speak to them in a theater, or speak to them in some place, a university auditorium, it may be, in some place where they're accustomed to going, and then, if you start with a real theme, a human problem, you can reach your solution, with God's solution in Jesus Christ, and they'll listen. If they feel that you have a grasp of the problem, they follow you, come out where you want, if you proceed logically from step to step, and give your Gospel solution, as it has been my privilege, in different times, to speak at atheneums, and university auditoriums, and theatres, in Latin America, starting from a theme which interested them and ending with the preaching of the Gospel. Now I am profoundly convinced that we've got to seek more opportunities in this country for that kind of thing, that we procure, that we try to introduce, the divine solution by starting from the human problem, and in places and environments and circles where people are interested in those problems. Now it won't be any good if we go right in and break into, or intrude ourselves in those circles with simply a jargon which we may feel is perfectly true, but unrelated to their problems, or their lives. It can't be done in that way. We've got to sit down where they sit, know what they're thinking, know what their problems are, be friendly and neighborly. Let's get them to believe in us and trust in us, and see us as men and women that they know and respect, and the way is ready to approach the secular mind with the Gospel.

And, of course, beyond the frontiers of the nation is missionary activity. And so far as the non-Christian religions today, the news is very, very bad for them, and they know it. Chinese tells us that there's nothing in Confucianism today that's offering any hope for the Chinese people. Shintoism is dead, in Japan; it's been smashed as far as any hope of new life, or new birth is concerned. And the new India is going to demand a religion which has more relevancy to life, and more tender mercy than Hinduism, or Buddhism. Because it is perfectly clear that only that love which in its Greek term *agape* means the compassionate love of God for the loveless and unlovely, is going to have any appeal or any efficacy. And India in her dire distress is confronted with this fact, that in its laws there is no place for love or mercy; and our world needs both. Hinduism may speak about the love of God, but the Hindu's love of God has no relevancy whatever to his love of his fellows. It has produced the caste system. And Buddhism, where it speaks about pity, limits pity to the absence of hostile or unkind feeling toward others, but Buddhism knows nothing of a passionate, pitying, postive concern for others. Your Buddhist won't do a nasty thing or a wrong deed; but he won't lay himself out to get down beside the unlovely and the down and out; so that never, literally never, was there such an opportunity, such a background among the nations for the Christian Gospel.

And let us thank God, brethren, that whatever happens, whether there emerge Fascist or Communist governments, there are Christians in all the representative areas of the world who know the Gospel, fruits of Christian missionary activity in the last century. They know the Gospel, and they're bearing witness to the Gospel. It's a great day for Christian missions which are now entering upon the phase of partnership between the older and the younger churches in a comradeship of faith, to proclaim Christ's Gospel amid the bad news, and in a situation which is more ready than ever to appreciate, to understand the meaning of Good News, in the environment of bad news. The Gospel is to be proclaimed. How? In a background of bad news; to all men everywhere, where they are.

And, thirdly, with passionate conviction and crystaline clarity, passionate conviction and crystaline clarity. We've come to a time when conviction has not been well regarded, especially in academic circles, rather, frowned upon. University teachers in many academic circles have not been well thought of if they appeared too dogmatic about anything. A professor of philosophy, a friend of mine, in one of our greatest universities, told me that his colleagues, when he became a professor of philosophy in that institution, told him, "Now you're going to ruin your career if you link yourself too fully with any particular point of view, particularly the Christian point of view." In other words, we've come through a period when anything that appeared to be savored with conviction or dogma was taboo. And if you look up in your dictionary, the Oxford dictionary, you'll find a rather luminous and suggestive definition of dogma, when you take that background and particular intellectual mood into account: "A dogma is an arrogant expression of opinion." Anybody who'll appear to have a dogma is arrogant. But there's a better definition: a dogma can be a settled opinion, positively expressed. You start with an opinion, you reflect on your opinion, you test your opinion, you validate your opinion in life, and then the moment comes when you're prepared to pass on your opinion in a very positive way, as something which for you begins to take on a note of ultimacy, or of absolute character.

Now I venture to say that there's nobody in academic circles, or popular circles today, who is going to make the slightest impression or the slightest impact on the thought-life or the problems of people unless those who listen to him get the impression that the man has convictions. Nobody's going to make "first base" today who does not represent a tremendous conviction. The only people who are interesting, even in student circles, in our universities, if I know anything about the situation, are those people who come, not on their tiptoes, trying to apologize for a remnant of Christian truth, and gasp lest their audience be too scared, or feel that they don't know all the difficulties that are in the way. As I sense the situation, the only people who interest students today are those who come right out with a conviction, and are prepared to validate it, unabashedly, and unashamedly, to proclaim it and proceed to give their reasons for it and its relevancy to the situation in thought and life, and they'll be listened to. Now, one can give a good illustration from the public ministry of a man like Reinhold Niebuhr. Now you may not always agree with Niebuhr, but you've got to listen to him. And I think it's only fair to say that he's made a greater contribution than any other thinker in this country to expose the fallacies of an older intellectual mood and to bring people face to face with Ultimate Reality. Now you know the academic climate of the University of Chicago—relativism, positivism, historicism, and all the rest. Well, when Niebuhr goes to the University of Chicago, all the professors who possibly can attend and listen. Now, he invariably makes them raving mad, but they come back, they listen, because they've got to recognize that though they don't accept his position, he has a position, and that position may be the solution of a very real problem. Now they regard with horror his solution, but they listen!

Now that's what I mean, and that's the only way to come, with a real conviction that is luminous and relevant to the human situation, and there'll be no lack of an audience, anywhere. And passionate conviction, the conviction of a thought that is glowing, of a mind whose imagination has been stirred, talking about something that is regarded of supreme importance, not a mere cold, icy, dogmatism, but a spirit aflame with living ardor. Now we've been tremendously scared of emotion in religious circles in these last years. And in some church circles people have gone out for a liturgical movement that is designed to keep emotion well within bounds. Now I am all for a reverent service, whether it be extemporary prayer or whether it be the prayer that somebody writes, calmly and prayerfully and offers to the Almighty there, or whether it be the Anglican edition of the liturgy. Why we have our own ways, but we have got to admit that there have been great Christians and great saints who have used different ways. Temperament, sense of propriety, heritage, and so on. But, the peril is, if it is ever thought that a well worked out liturgy with beautiful phrases, perfect diction, creating an emotional mood, offering aesthetic enjoyment and thrills, is going to solve the problem of real worship. I've quoted W. H. Auden more than once; here's another couplet. Now Auden has been terribly concerned about the intrusion of a certain asceticism into Christian circles, and he says, "Ruffles, the perfect manners of the frozen heart, and once again compel it to be awkward and alive." Now he means by this, that if it comes to a choice he'll be all in favor of uncouth life against aesthetic death. Now that's it. And that's sometimes where our Pentecostal friends come in. They may have all the uncouthness, but there's something going on there, *Life.* They've been dealing, as the Pentecostals down in Chile where I've seen them, where the Pentecostals have ten times more converts than all the other denominations together, they've got 40,000 and all the rest together about 4,000! Now that's tremendous, especially when you find that in the second generation there's a greater sanity and a little more of the aesthetic.

But the point is this, that nothing can be a substitute for life and for the living expression of religion, and I can say that as a Presbyterian, because nobody can accuse us of too much of the uncouthness, or the let-go-ness. And yet I've got to say to my Presbyterian and other friends that as you go back over Presbyterianism and Reformed history, that in times of great revival in Scotland, why people did let themselves go, because something uncontrollable happened, no way out—God got them! Human nature doesn't change, but here is the tremendous fact. It is taken for granted that emotion has a natural place except in the Christian church and in Christian meetings and in Christian circles. You can go crazy in a Democratic or Republican Convention, or a baseball game, a great opera—anything, but caution, in religious gatherings or in religious circles. Now, we can stifle things very easily. Now don't misunderstand me, I'm not in favor of a disproportionate measure of uncouthness, but I am desperately concerned about the reality of life, and that we should take into account the primitive situation of many people on the brink of misery, that need to express themselves in some kind of way; and what I'm really advocating is something from the point of view of the person presenting the Christian message, passive in conviction, linked to— and let me add another. I spoke about Auden; I might have referred to T. S. Eliot. Now T. S. Eliot, the other Christian poet, is aware of the situation that fire must confront fire. He says, "We only live, only suspire, consumed by either fire or fire." Now by that he means that our generation is going to be consumed by one fire or another, by the fire of the flesh, or depraved passion, or the fire of our anaberational crusading group. For the fires of the spirit, pure, bright, incandescent, but the issue of our civilization is going to be solved by fire, or fire; one fire or the other.

We've got to take that into account. Not by any kind of a cold ecclesiasticism or academicism, or anything of that kind, but crystaline clarity. Now here's where we often fail. The words that we use in many a sermon, and the concepts, are simply not understood by the people, or they are understood so well by the people that they have a soporific effect on the people, and they go to sleep. They are so used to certain words and phrases that they don't make the slightest impression any more. Now a new preacher appears and there may be questions here and there, but if they hear one or two classical words, "blood," "grace," etc., then "that preacher's all right." They can make up for loss of sleep the night before. "He's sound; he's orthodox, he's a worthy person to preach in our church." And the others, they simply don't know what those words mean, even the common words. Now you take the very word *love*. Preached in a sermon to a lot of people whose only concept of love they get out of the movies, or by reading our sex novels where love is dragged into the gutter, now I say that is not a good preparation for the Love of God. You have got to get under, you've got to distinguish the real Christian love from a lot of eroticism and all the rest. And there's a real task for the ministry in the background of that, to take each one of the great Christian concepts: sin (not talk about sin in general, but be awfully concrete); grace; and love; redemption; God; man, all those things about which people have the most perverse notions, and yet we drag them in, all in a bevy, together—make them do duty.

We've got to analyze every phrase and word we use, to see that we get the most out of words; and in many instances we've got to use new words that have never been used in preaching before, and in sermons which people understand and which stab them and shock them. Now it's very interesting that in Great Britain today two writers who are exerting the greatest influence in the British Isles are two lay people, C. S. Lewis, the Oxford Don, author of *The Screwtape Letters*; and Dorothy Sayres, a writer of detective stories, who is an out-and-out Christian and who has written some marvelous books on religion, using the words that people understand and introducing a whole new vocabulary for the presentation of Christian truth on those high and holy things of the incarnation and the atonement and the resurrection and the rest. Now there's a great task here for preachers and Christian workers, to understand people's problems, and the words they use and develop the finest and most forcible speech, needn't be slangy, but it can have a virility about it and a pungency about it, and a cogency such as the ordinary sermonic language does not have. And we've got to develop it with crystaline clarity.

And finally, with what object in view? In order that it may be said, "He's a great preacher?" "Oh, I enjoy his sermons." I remember I was once down in Florida on what they call the "Chain of Missions" and I think it's a grand enterprise, but how often some of those who are passing the winter down there would come up afterwards and would say, "Oh, here we do enjoy missions," but the suggestion was that it was just one more entertainment—they were there to be entertained, to be sunned, to be basked in the air, to be rid of the winter's cold and the problems of the North, and they wanted to enjoy everything that came along. And they enjoyed missions! But you felt that it didn't make any difference. Now there's so much danger in becoming professional "sermon tasters" and conoisseurs of everything homiletical, and all the rest. No, there's one great function of Christian preaching; to preach for a real verdict, for a total response of personality, for repentance and faith, so that when the Gospel is proclaimed, this Christ who demands the total allegiance of human souls, as Saviour and Lord of life—what He wants is repentance, that is to say, the re-orientation of life towards him—the re-thinking of everything; and the re-orientation of life towards him. And faith, what does Christian evangelical faith mean? Not simply a set of doctrines about Christ, but the commitment of personality in its wholeness to Christ, to this Living One who was dead and is alive forevermore. That is to say, the wholehearted commitment of one's personality in its concreteness and totality, to Jesus Christ, the Risen Son of God, Saviour and Lord of life.

I know of no more perfect symbol of what it means to respond to the Gospel and to be a Christian than John Calvin's famous crest. Now when we think of John Calvin we think of him as a very austere man and so he was, intellectually, a giant. Massive and architectonic in his thinking, but if he had any originality at all it was as the theologian of the Holy Spirit. The man had a warm heart, a deep devotional life. His interest in doctrine was not for its own sake; he was interested in the pure doctrine of Godliness. Now what did he mean by that? What is John Calvin's crest? A flaming heart in an open hand, and the words underneath in Latin, "My heart I give thee, Lord, eagerly and sincerely." A heart that is aflame, symbol of the whole of personality, given to God. And the hand, which is the symbol of action, the instrument of the self, emblem of the fact that the hand which gives the heart must serve this same Saviour and Lord; heart and hand together in the service of the Lord Christ. And preaching is successful, and only is successful when the people come to the point of being willing to say with John Calvin, "My heart I give thee Lord, eagerly and sincerely." Then the Gospel becomes Good News in the inmost recesses of the heart and of mind. ℚ

Christian Action on the Frontiers of Strife

I am most thankful, both for the kindness that has been showered upon me by President Fuller, Mrs. Fuller, members of the faculty, student body, pastors and friends. "I was a stranger and ye took me in." And I've never felt more at home in my life. I have sensed the spirit of a great institution, and I've lived in the atmosphere of a great church which will have increasingly more to give to the kingdom of Christ, the world, and our time. Amid all the expression of thankfulness, and of eulogies which have been uttered, it is very difficult for me to recognize myself, and I seem to slip back into anonymity. And I think one is safer there than when one begins to raise any kind of peacock's feathers, because one seems to be regarded as somebody in the church. I think one is always safer in the shadows and especially in the shadow of the figure of our Lord himself. If you have received anything from this ministry, thank Him whose one is and whom one tries to serve, our common Lord and Saviour Jesus Christ. So let me thank you one and all and say that I've received more by way of inspiration than anything that I've brought, and this week will linger with me long in the years ahead, not simply as a memory which has been most happy, but also as a fountain of inspiration, and as a family circle of dear friends.

Now this closing topic I have formulated as "Christian Action on the Frontiers of Strife." It is based largely upon, or inspired in, the latter part of Paul's great letter to the Ephesians. I'm not going to follow it verse by verse, offering a commentary, but the great concepts which Paul has there constitute the source of my inspiration, and also indicate the direction in which I try to make my thoughts go. Christian Action on the Frontiers of Strife—Action is the essence of life as combustion is the essence of flame. There is no true Christianity that does not express itself in action. The contemporary situation as we have studied it demands action. The eternal purpose of God is for action. The Cosmic Christ is a leader in action, and the Gospel is to be proclaimed to the nations by men of action. In other words, Christianity is not a "sitting" religion, but a moving religion—a religion that expresses itself on the road, moving onward toward the goal, and ever looking toward the frontiers.

Action is Christian when it is the action of a community of brotherly enthusiasts. Now Christian action is not action that is carried out haphazardly by those who love to do their own individual will. Christians are members of a community, whether of a local congregation, whether of a wider community. That is to say, it must be coordinated action, the action of the community, where the community serves Christ and where the individuals of the community coordinate their efforts in a great crusade. Now, the Christian community, as an active community, ought to be made up of a group of brotherly enthusiasts. Now let me stress that. The true Christian ought ever, as we have seen, to be an enthusiast. But, enthusiasm has a perennial nature, that is, that it may produce types of people who want to do the job alone, in isolation, independently of other people. That is always enthusiasm's peril. You get a host of people with different kinds of enthusiasm, all saying that they serve the Lord—the feeling that the Lord has given them different mandates. Now the solution of that is not to stifle enthusiasm. I admit that wherever enthusiasm appears in a community it can constitute a danger. It can be disruptive, it can be devisive, it can produce people who want to have the preeminence and to always allege that God is speaking to them and only to them. Toynbee, in his great work on history, has said that oftentimes enthusiasm or fanaticism has been sterilized at the cost of extinguishing faith. Now I want to say that I'm never scared over a young enthusiast who may be bordering on fanaticism. There's a chance to mellow him. The person who makes me deadly afraid is the man who enters the seminary without any enthusiasm, with a dead indifferentism, and with a blasé professional air, who is in the ministry as he would be in any other profession. Now unless he gets religion in the real sense before it's over, I think that every effort should be made to see that a young man like that does not graduate from a Christian seminary. I don't think we should perpetrate that blasé kind of professionalism on the Christian Church. But I admit, the problem of the fanatic, of the enthusiast, who is a great individualist and thinks he's the only one who is right, the only one who sees something, can constitute a danger; but the true antidote and the true safeguard is that he be a member, and recognize that he is a member of a community of brotherly enthusiasts.

Now the true Christian community is the community inspired by brotherly enthusiasm. You introduce the element of brotherliness, and what do you have? It is a unity in Christ, whereby all become submissive to the one, common Lord Jesus Christ, and whereby each person, however enthusiastic, is willing to subject himself in love to the brotherhood and be willing to obey the mandates of the group. Now it seems to me that Lenin, the great founder of the Soviet Republic, solved that problem by making all his communistic enthusiasts members of what he called "a militant, monastic order." Now that appears to me to be very near to the New Testament ideal. A group of people who know what it is to be related personally to Jesus Christ, who have a witness to give, but who are members of the community of others who have had the same experience, and who are willing to exercise a discipline and to be disciplined by their brethren in the Lord, so that the group may concentrate their efforts in a great, blazing enthusiasm in one direction. In other words, that is the harmony which we always should try to establish. Personal enthusiasm, but subject to the discipline of the group so that there may be concerted action in a given direction under the guidance of the Holy Spirit. That is what I mean by Christian action.

Now Christian action is always action upon the frontiers. The frontiers are ever moving. The place for the Christian Church is the frontier. When the Church begins to settle down complacently, enthusiasm dies, deviousness enters and a bourgeois spirit comes. Christ wants His Church to be on the moving frontier, ever crossing boundaries, ever occupying new territory, because He himself is everlastingly the Christ of the frontier, moving on, and moving on, enlarging the bounds of his kingdom. Now the frontiers of today are blazing, flaming frontiers. They are frontiers of strife, where trememdous conflicts are taking place. There is the flaming frontier, the frontier of strife in the natural order, and the frontiers of strife of the supernatural order—and I want to deal briefly with Christian action, as the Christian community of brotherly enthusiasts faces and fulfills duty on both these frontiers.

Now, in the natural order there are two frontiers, where as Christians we must always think, which are quite inescapable. One is the frontier of the home, the domestic frontier; the other is the frontier of work—of business. Both are inescapable. The relationship between husband and wife, between parent and children, the relationship of work—business between masters and servants. Read the closing part of the letter to the Ephesians and see how Paul deals with both these spheres there.

Let's begin with the frontier of the home. It ought to be the frontier of peace, of bliss, the supreme abode of love, but is it so in our time? Is it not the case that we have come to a moment in the history of our country when the home is too often a frontier of strife. Oh how painful, how lamentable, how tragic, that two human beings, one man and one woman, who, according to the Scriptures, have become one flesh, are so often suing for the breach of the nuptial relationship in the divorce courts. And how tragic that the affirmation should be made that there is marital disloyalty there, that more and more the family as a unit is becoming disrupted, that neither husband nor wife are what they should be, under God, nor parents and children what they should be. You take the sex novels, the most popular kind of novels, and it is indicative of the fact that all is not well with the relations between men and women, all is not well with the home.

Now read again what Paul says about that situation. Read what the great principles are which he would bring into operation. It seems to me that as he looks at the problem of the home, which is much more of a problem than it was in his time, the great principle which he enunciated is "Learn Christ." Learn Him in this atmosphere, who is the lover of the Church. The husband should love the wife as Christ loved the Church; the wife should reverence the husband as the Church reverences Christ. Now what is this principle, and how does it become operative, to "learn Christ"? Not simply to learn "about Him," to have all sorts of information, historical and theological. To "learn Him" as our chief lesson is to allow him to take utter possession of us, of our thinking, of our imaginations, of our sentiments, of our wills, so that He becomes identified with us in the most close spiritual relationship, so that we can't do our thinking save in his likeness. That we can't make a decision without an inquiry as to how it affects our loyalty to Him. That we cannot enter into relationships save the inquiry is raised as to how it is going to affect our more cosmic relations. "To learn."

Now there are two great problems in the home, especially in the modern home. One is the problem created by authoritarianism, and the other is the problem created by hedonism. On the one hand you get parents, you get fathers who think that they're biblical, and who think that they are what the husband and the father should be, when they consider that it is the husband's and father's role to be absolutely authoritarian, to lay down the law for the wife and for the children, to give mandates, and to expect that the edict, once gone forth, shall be obeyed, not as a result of conversation or conference give and take— until all are convinced that the truth has been established, but a patriarchial dictator, nothing more. "Ye have not so learned Christ." Because, when you learn Christ you will learn two things about Him: that while He is an Imperial Lord, He never forced anybody to be His follower, or to do His will. He always proceeded on two principles: on the principle of worth, and the principle of wooing. That is to say, He would not be followed by anyone who did not regard him as being worthy of being followed, and He would never consider that the last word was said unless he had wooed, persuaded, tried to inform. And, nobody has any right to enforce his will or her will in a home, especially in a Christian home, who is not regarded by all concerned as worthy of making a decision, and who does not go out of his way to woo and to persuade, so that the decision when taken becomes a family decision.

Now I'm thinking, of course, when people have grown up to a certain maturity. Now there are times when children are so small, authoritarianism may be the only way. But I do suggest this—that children are never too small to be amenable to reason, to be taken into their parents' confidence. And if the home is going to last, it must be, from the earliest stages, on the basis of mutual trust and confidence, so that, so far as possible, children can see the righteousness and the equity of something they've being asked to do, and when that takes place they respond in a marvelous way. And you get a bond of loyalty, and a solidarity between all concerned. And so too, of course, still more, the confidence between husband and wife, and wife and husband, that there should be no secrets, but come to a mutual understanding and an absolute trust. And that can only be done if Christ is learned, and Christ can be learned only if time is given at the family altar for Him to be studied, for His will to be known, for the Book to be opened—in other words, family worship, family prayer. That's the greatest security and foundation of the home.

Now I mentioned the other problem, the problem of Hedonism. That constitutes the problem of the relations of men and women outside and inside the home, because the individual man or woman is apt to say that they become interested in relating themselves to the other sex on the basis of pleasure, or what is vital, and the moment that the pleasure ceases the bond is disrupted and disloyalty takes place. Now pleasure, the pursuit of pleasure, can never be a Christian goal. No, where love is real, one is more interested in the pleasure of the other than in one's own. And that is the only basis upon which these relations can be creative and lasting. The person who enters into a relationship with the other sex purely on the basis of pleasure is a cad, nothing more, lower than many decent four-footed or two-footed beasts. In other words, that kind of relationship must be excluded from Paradise. And true love is always thinking more of the other than of one's self, and one's satisfaction. Now it's only upon that basis that loyalty becomes possible, and disciplined, and where people are prepared to stand the shock of differences of opinion, and so on. But here again many a time there will be problems between the sexes, between the husband and wife, between parents and children. If the home has instituted the practice of family prayers, there is a chance for the difficulty to be solved before it goes too far, in God's prescence. On their knees people have a chance to "learn Christ" and to relent and to draw back before the worst comes—that is always the solution.

Take the other frontier, the frontier of work, the frontier of business. Here the great apostle introduces another principle, the principle of the "fear of Christ." He wants masters to treat their servants in the fear of Christ, with reverence, bearing in mind that there's no partiality with Him, or as someone has translated, "There's no snobbery with Him." He treats all alike, who are His servants. Every master must treat with reverence the personality of all who serve. He would insist that the master treat every human personality, the personality of every workman, with reverence, that his dignity should never be infringed upon. Also, that the servant should not be merely eye-servants—that they do an honest job. That they need not always the eye of others upon them. Serving the Lord Christ they will put into an hour's work all that they're capable of putting into sixty minutes. And so the rest, because, whatever the situation, they're serving Christ primarily, and are under loyalty to Him, or break the bond between master and servant.

Now of course in our time the problem has become very much complicated. We're living in a technological society where there are two dangers—one, the depersonalization of master and worker—that both take on the appearance of a machine; and the other danger is, the emergence of tyranny as the result of technological advance. Now of course it is technological advance that has made totalitarianism possible, because no dictator could emerge in the modern sense who didn't have all the resources of a mechanized civilization at his disposal, or at the disposal of his group. And that's what constitues a terrible menace today, that the machine has so far advanced that it can only operate in the hands of a group that have the absolute power of control. And when it passes into the hands of some people, the masses can never get it back again, because some of the instruments of power today have not been produced by ordinary people, like in the old days when one had a stick and the other had a stick, or one had a gun and the other had a gun—now it's quite different, because things are concentrated. Now we must face that terrific problem of our civilization, in the fear of Christ. In other words, we have got to the utmost degree, to personalize relations in business, as relations are personalized between the Supreme Master, Christ, and every one of His followers. It is for us, Christian ministers and Christian workers, to see to it that our people in business relations shall be willing to look squarely at the business problem in terms of, in the light of, that personal relationship which should exist, which does exist, between Christ and the soul. And to see to it that nothing resembling de-personalizing, or tyranny, because one has the power, shall be allowed to prevail, where there is a Christian master or a Christian servant. Now the problem is difficult, beset with difficulty, but we can not reconcile ourselves to any situation in business where the supreme principle of "In the fear of Christ" does not mean something. In other words, Christian men and women in the relationship of work and business ought to give lead to all business and to all work, because they have "learned Christ," and live in the true fear, or reverence, of Jesus Christ, and as they must answer to Him.

So much for the frontiers in the natural order. Toward the end of that great letter Paul makes clear that Christian action must take place in a situation in which there are supernatural forces operating, carrying out a strategy. In other words, there has not been only an historical rift, there has been a cosmic rift, in the heavens. And so, he says, bearing in mind that we fight not against, struggle not against, flesh and blood, but against principalities and powers, against the rulers of the darkness of this world, against spiritual wickedness in high places; take to yourselves the whole armour of God. There will never be a moment in our lives when we must not be armed, equipped with the panoply of the Almighty. Now it is perfectly clear that Paul is not describing all the full armour. He selects seven pieces; three are incidental, and four are more vital. The breastplate of righteousness—one hasn't got a ghost of a chance where there is lacking integrity of character. The moment it be found out that the man who professes to be a Christian soldier, moving toward the frontier in the great struggle, is rotten inside and that his life does not bear out the profession that he makes, he's doomed, his breastplate's gone. He must be a man or woman through and through. No breach between character and creed. He must have the shield of faith, never allow doubt to have a place of power within him. Someone has said that for him who thinks, life is a comedy; for him who feels, a tragedy; for him who has faith, a victory. Now if we're going to be successful, keep our place on the frontier, cross it into new territory, it can only be on the basis of faith—men of faith whose action is inspired on the faith of our Lord Jesus Christ.

The helmet of salvation. When the soldier had the helmet on his head he was prepared to look up, look around with a certain serenity. We have the right to affirm that the essential victory has been won! That salvation is sure, that we're on the winning side, despite appearances, darkness and chaos, and all the rest. So we can look the world in the face with a calm light in our eyes, resolution in our whole being, because essential victory has been won. And the frontier becomes ours.

But I turn to the four other pieces, and principally to the first, the belt. Decisive for those guards, like Orientals, or even like Roman soldiers, the belt, the girdle, was decisive. When sitting, moving around leisurely, detached from work, relaxing, the girdle was loose, but the moment the trumpet sounds, or the march had to begin, the girdle was tightened. Moffat puts it, "Tighten the belt of truth around you." Now that is the symbol that we're ready for action, that we take our Christian life seriously, that we tighten the belt and then we're ready to go. Truth is that belt, that belt of sincerity, of downrightness, in what we do. Now for so many, truth is not a belt, but a bird. In academic circles, in philosophical circles, truth has been regarded as a bird to be pursued, and if perchance one day you should catch the bird and put it into a cage, next day, because of the exhilaration of the pursuit you let it go and start afresh. That's what Lessing said. He said that he was so devoted to truth that if he ever caught it he would want to let it go like a bird, just for the sake of the race and the quest. That's not Christian truth. Christian truth is not something you go out in quest of; it's something from which you start. And on the road you discover new glimpses of truth and you get new experiences of truth—that's the difference between Christian truth and philosophic truth—you start from Christian truth. It's the belt that girds you, and sets you out on your way, and then the other truth becomes more apparent when you take the right attitude on the right road. For others, truth is a badge which they ostentatiously wear, to show that they've got the right ideas, that they belong to the right set, a badge. But that's not what Christian truth should be, either. No, not a bird, to pursue as it flits through the air, but a banner to unfurl as you get on the road and begin the march. Not a bird, not a mere badge, but a torch to illumine the way. Not for something that you have that people come and look at, to convince themselves that you belong to the right set, or that you've got the right idea, but the torch which you hold which lightens up the way. And then there's no doubt in people's minds that the truth that you have is radiant truth, because it opens up the darkness, and darkness is dispelled. Truth as a belt leads to truth as a banner, and truth as a torch.

Shoes, of the Gospel, preparation for the Gospel, indicating mobility; shoes for all kinds of roads, the rough and the plain. When you are ready to go, be shod; and may the thing that's on your feet be the great anxiety to take the Gospel everywhere—the rough places and the plain, over the hills and down the valleys. Have that kind of mobility which comes when you're rightly shod for all sorts of conditions.

And the sword of the Spirit. So identify yourselves with the truth, relate it so to experience, and to the problems of your times, that whenever an issue is presented you'll have in your hands something that has a cutting edge, as our Lord was able to reply to the tempter. Not the Bible, detached of all life and experience, but the Bible, giving you a cutting edge of truth for the ever more costly human situation. So that almost intuitively you'll have the right answer and do the right thing.

And above all, and last of all, said Paul, prayer. For all the saints, he said, and for me. The seventh piece: All prayer and supplication at all times for all saints, and for me, the speaker. As I see it, that's our greatest need. To wait upon God, to listen to His voice, to supplicate Him, to show Him that we're in dead earnest, and in an agony, wholly concerned that we may be the right kind of people, that we may take the right road, make the right advance, worthily represent him on the frontier, hold the frontiers and advance into the unoccupied territory beyond. We're living in a tremendous time, and things are going to worsen before they're going to get better. But one is more convinced than ever by all the signs that it's the greatest kind of time for Christian living, for Christian action, for Christian thinking, and for Christian preaching. Now it may be that it shall not be the joy of our generation to cross over into the Canaan beyond the Jordan, it may be that we've got to live our lives in the wilderness. It's only in the measure in which we live out the wilderness experience upon us, and are utterly Christian, that a better day may dawn. And we shall then constitute a living heritage of memory for those who come after us. Our faith and our firmness, the quality of our Christian living and of our Christian action, are going to determine what is to happen today and tomorrow. As Christians, there's no need for a ray of doubt, no need for a streak of pessimism; the Lord Christ has won and He shall win, and we follow in His train. Let us therefore encourage one another with these words, and pray for one another, and move all together as a community of brotherly enthusiasts across all the frontiers of division until the day comes, the day breaks, and the shadows flee away, and He appears whose right it is to reign; And to this one and that one on the frontier, all belted and armed he says, "Well done, good and faithful servant, enter thou into the joy of thy Lord." Let us pray:

> Oh God, our Father, God and Father of our Lord Jesus Christ, whose we are and whom we serve, we acknowledge our unworthiness of one so glorious; but take us as we are; cleanse us of our sins; and make us more like to the image of Thy Son; Bind us into a living fellowship of love, a living tether of those who love Thee and serve Thee. Bless, we pray Thee, all these young men and women who are preparing themselves to man the frontiers; and thine older servants who are already in the ministry; and those to whom Thou hast already given the honor and the task of teaching youth. Bless the great institution under whose

asupices we are met; students and teachers and alumni. Bless the great church to which these Thy servants belong. Bless, we beseech Thee, the great Church Universal, the body of Christ. And grant, Oh Lord, that loving Thee we may love all thy people everywhere, until we all come into the unity of the faith, and in the knowledge of the Son of God unto a perfect man, unto the measure of the stature of the fullness of Christ, whom we love and serve.

And now, may the grace of our Lord Jesus Christ, and the love of God, and the communion of the Holy Spirit be with us all. Amen. ⟋

Theodore F. Adams

Theodore F. Adams was pastor of the First Baptist Church in Richmond, Virginia (1936-1968), and president of the Baptist World Alliance (1955-1960), when he presented the Mullins Lectures in 1956. Upon retirement from First Baptist Church, Dr. Adams was elected as pastor emeritus. For the next eleven years (1968-1979) he was visiting professor of preaching at Southeastern Baptist Theological Seminary in Wake Forest, North Carolina, home of the annual Theodore F. Adams Lectures on Preaching. Dr. Adams died on 27 February 1980, two weeks after attending, and presiding at, the lecture series which bears his name.

In his 1956 Mullins Lectures, under the theme, "A Preacher Looks at his Preaching," Dr. Adams presented four lectures of eminent practical value. His lectures are presented here with the original oral qualities intact.

The Preacher Looks at Himself and His People

I appreciate greatly the invitation to come and share with you in this Pastor's Conference and to give the Mullins Lectures on Preaching. I have looked forward to coming for some time with mingled feelings; with real anticipation of the fellowship and the opportunity, but with genuine concern about three words: Mullins and Lectures and Preaching.

I heard and saw Dr. Mullins just once. It was one of the memorable experiences in my life. I was attending the Baptist Young People's Union Convention in Chicago. I shall never forget the impression he made on me. I don't remember anything he said, but when I left, I said to myself, "I have certainly seen and heard a man of God. Plain enough so that I could understand; direct, authoritative, sincere; a winsome preacher of Jesus Christ." It is a privilege to speak in a series of lectures that bears the name of a man who made such an impression on me and on so many others throughout the years.

Then I was troubled about the word "lectures". I am not a lecturer. I am just trying hard to be a pastor and preacher. Now I was a little disturbed about this word lecture until last night at the Faculty Club. Dr. Albright, whom I have enjoyed so much last night and this morning, said that he found that he was over-doing it. He was giving a hundred outside lectures a year until he cut it back to fifty. Then I thought, why am I worrying about only four?

Also, lecturing on preaching disturbed me, because I am perfectly conscious of the fact that I break about all the rules there are in homiletics. And yet, I am a pastor, and there is no greater joy and privilege to me in all the world than to be a pastor, one of whose responsibilities it is to preach. I was greatly comforted when I found some words of Phillips Brooks. He said that "the preacher needs to be a pastor, that he may preach to real men. The pastor needs to be a preacher that he may keep the dignity of his work alive. The preacher who is not a pastor grows remote. The pastor who is not a preacher grows petty. Never let men truthfully say of you, 'He is a preacher but no pastor' or 'He is a pastor but no preacher.' Be both, for you cannot really be one unless also you are the other." Then Phillips Brooks goes on to say, "I am sure that many men who, if they came to preach once in a great while in the midst of other occupations, would preach with reality and fire, are deadened to their sacred work by their constant intercourse with sacred things."

Well then, how can you and I as pastors preach better without being deadened by the nearness of sacred things and by the many other responsibilities that are ours? We are going to think about that these four hours we have together, under the general theme, "A Pastor Looks at His Preaching."

First of all, we shall think of how "The Preacher Looks at His People." Then we are going to think about "The Faith of the Preacher"; then, some suggestions about "Planning, Preparing and Preaching," and last of all, "Preaching with Purpose and Power".

You see, preaching is just one of the many things that a pastor is asked to do. He has his pastoral responsibilities, his executive responsibilities in his church, his civic responsibilities that he may be a good citizen; he has his denominational responsibilities if he is to bear a worthy part of the work of Southern Baptists, or whatever his denomination may be. But with all the other things he is asked to do, he needs to know how to preach. Someone has well said that a pastor is asked to do a great many things, but if he can't preach, he'll never get a chance to do any of them.

The preacher is asked to do many things. Sometimes the preaching comes out last. This morning over at the Faculty Center, I watched some blacks washing the windows, and I thought of a time when, at our home in Richmond, we had some cleaning done. A fine black man came to finish up the job and to clean the windows. He was humming a black spiritual to himself and I soon discovered that he was pastor of a Baptist church in Richmond. We talked a while about Baptist life and work, and when I went in to lunch I said to the children, "You know, the man who was cleaning the windows is a preacher, too." My son said, "No, Daddy, he can't be a preacher?" I said, "Yes, he is." The boy looked at me with a quizzical eye and said, "But Daddy, a preacher working?"

Well, if you are going to preach, you have to work at it. It does take work, some of the hardest work you will ever do, but also some of the most rewarding.

In the background we need to look at the preacher himself. After an honest look at ourselves, we need to look at those to whom we minister as pastor and preacher. In the last analysis, we are responsible not to our people but to God. However, every pastor is responsible before God to do his best for his people and to serve them as he ought.

Let us then look at ourselves as we are and as we ought to be. Let us try to see ourselves as others see us and test ourselves by Christ's spirit and example.

It is a very humbling thing to try to be a pastor-preacher. As a rule, when you graduate from the seminary you wonder why everybody doesn't come to hear you preach. When you have been in the ministry as long as I have, you wonder why anybody does.

We can profit greatly from the self analysis of a seminary-mate of mine who has been a well beloved pastor through many years. The other day, starting a new year in his church, he sat in the quiet of his study and wrote a letter to his people that was published in his church calendar. And it gives us such a good background for our thought together that I want to read it to you. He says, "In a reflective mood I write these observations concerning my task as a minister of Jesus Christ. I do not find that the work of the Christian ministry becomes increasingly easy but rather increasingly difficult. Not that the preparation or preaching of sermons is a burden; I love that work although it is an enormous task for any man to undertake. Not that the calling and pastoral work are so hard; I love that, too.

"What makes the minister's work even more difficult is the responsiblity to embody in one's own life the ideals that he preaches. As I come to know more and more of the needs and sorrows and loneliness of men, as I come to know more and more of the charm and wonder and greatness of the message of Jesus, I find it increasingly hard to apply that message and to embody it in my own life.

"It was not hard to be a minister of religion at the time when religion did not concern itself with character, and when the priests of Greece and Rome never for a moment regarded as a part of their duties to help men to a purer life. But to be a Christian minister today is a very different matter, and is difficult chiefly for the very reason that once made it easy. Huxley once said, 'Clever men are as common as blackberries; the rare thing is to find a good one.' The rare and difficult thing for a minister is to be a good man. To be a great man means to be the kind of man he urges others to be. The subtle danger of professionalism, the relying on the conventional forms instead of seeking for the substance beneath, following the letter of the law only from the teeth out instead of incarnating its spirit. It is a danger which

I find ever ready to spoil the minister's own life, to make ineffective his message to men." He closes with this promise, "To a renewed determination to *profess* only what I *possess,* and to *express* only what I have *experienced,* I give myself in service to you." Every preacher ought to look at himself just as honestly if he expects to be a good minister of Jesus Christ.

I am suggesting that we look at ourselves in the light of the description of another preacher, John the Baptist. In this connection, an interesting thing was pointed out to me by a leading Methodist, Dr. Roy Smith. He said to me one day, "Ted, it is a constant puzzle to me why you Baptists pay so little attention to John the Baptist. As a matter of fact, I waited for years for a Baptist to write a good book about John the Baptist. No one did so I finally wrote one myself." It is a good book, but I am going to quote from the greatest Book of all. Go back, if you will, to Mark, the sixth chapter, to these words about John the Baptist. "Herod stood in awe of John, knowing he was a just and holy man, so he protected John. He was greatly exercized when he listened to him; still he was glad to listen" (Moffatt).

There is an early preacher for you. I want us to look at ourselves in the light of that description of John the Baptist, remembering as Dwight L. Moody said that "in all probability we ourselves are our own greatest problem." Moody said one time to a group of preachers, "The man that I have had the greatest trouble with in all my ministry is a fellow by the name of Dwight L. Moody."

I trust that you will take this message in the spirit in which I give it and in the spirit of one worshiper who went home one Sunday from church and wrote in his diary, "The minister preached a good sermon, and I applied it to myself."

The pastor then, has certain qualities that ought to commend him as a preacher. The first is that he is *respected and revered* just because of his position. "Herod stood in awe of John." He respected John. Men and women do expect something of you just because you are a preacher. I remember hearing a Methodist Bishop say that one of the first lessons that came home to him after he was consecrated a Bishop came when a man he had never seen before walked up to him and said, "Sir, my son is desperately ill. Will you please pray for him?" The Bishop said, "I learned right there that there were some things expected of me just because I was a Bishop."

There are some things that are expected of you just because you are a preacher. I learned that once on a train coming home from a week of preaching. The train stopped along the way and the Pullman car in which I had been the only passenger up until then filled up with a fine group of young men. At first I thought it was some sort of athletic team. All the berths were made up except one, right next to mine. Soon the crowd all gathered there and a poker game began.

Soon one of the boys reached into the berth across the aisle, brought out a bottle and said, "Let's have something to drink." As they started out to get some paper cups, one said to me, "Won't you join us and have a drink." I said, "No, thank you." They came back after a while and the bottle had evidently been well used. We stood talking for a while and then one man held out his hand and said, "My name is so and so, what is yours?" I said, "Mine's Adams." He said, "I am a tire saleman. We are on the way to a tire convention. What's your business?" I said, "I am a Baptist preacher." You could feel the atmosphere freeze. Nobody said anything for a while and finally, I broke the tension by starting for bed.

I was sitting in my bed when I heard a voice say, "Where did that Baptist preacher go?" "Oh, he got in bed." "I want to talk to him." The curtains parted; the young man sat on the edge of the berth and said, "Preacher, could I talk to you a minute?" "Surely." He pulled the curtains shut and said, "You know, I am awfully embarrassed. I am the boy who offered you the drink a while ago." I said, "Well, son, that's all right. This isn't the first time a bottle of liquor got a boy in more trouble than he figured on. That's all right." But he said, "I ought to know better. Did you know I am the president of the men's club in my church back home. I've got a wife and some children, and I ought to be a better man than I am." We sat and talked for some time about his faith and his church and his home. I am perfectly sure that he is going to be a better man. Why did it all happen? Because he expected something better of a Baptist preacher, just because he was a preacher.

"Herod stood in awe of John," as men will respect you. I would say to you what a peasant is said one day to have told Francis of Assisi. Brother Francis had stopped to ask the farmer, "Do you have any good word for me today?" The peasant said, "Yes, Brother Francis, try and be as good as men believe you are."

"Herod stood in awe of John, knowing that he was a just and holy man," but John knew he was a man of human weaknesses, and he was.

In a time of darkness and doubt he sent men to Jesus asking, "Art thou he that cometh or look we for another?" Jesus wasn't just what he had expected and he began to wonder and to doubt. John was a man of human weakness, too, as you and I are. We are subject to all of the temptations and sins that are common to man, plus some that are peculiar to ministers. How far short we fall of the Lord's words, "Be ye perfect." A boy in one of my churches was saying his prayers one night. He prayed, "Lord help me to be perfect, but not too perfect because then you don't have any fun."

The Lord Jesus set a high standard for us. I am constantly troubled by the way some ministers live and act, and by the way all of us fall short and also by the attitude of some laymen and women toward the clergy. I remember sitting on the front porch in a little town in the middle west some years ago. A layman who had seen preachers come and go through that town for years said to me, "You know, Ted, preachers used to be called to the ministry. They are not called like they used to be. They just choose it as the best way they can serve. They are not called any more." What preachers made him say that?

A man came to First Church in Richmond some years ago, walked into the church office on a Saturday morning and said, "I'm from such and such a church. I am going to be perfectly honest with you. I represent the pulpit committee, and we are interested in your pastor. We would like to know something about your church." He asked questions about the membership, about the activities, about the budget, and finally he said to our church secretary, "How much is your pastor's salary?" She told him. He closed up his book, put it in his pocket and said, "I might as well go home now." She said, "Why?" He said, "Well, we don't pay anywhere near that much. There is no use in my staying here." My loyal church secretary said, "Well, I am sure that if our pastor felt called to go to your church, he would go no matter what the salary was." The layman said, "Don't tell me stuff like that. Preachers move for more money like everybody else!" I wonder what preacher made him think that.

I think of the Baptist college president who said to me one day, "Ted, the hardest crowd of visitors to handle on our campus, the most discourteous, the hardest to please are the preachers who come each year for the pastor's conference." I remember, too, a Christian doctor who said to me, "Ted, I just can't understand it. I am going to get over it, but I don't know how long it will take me . . . ." He said, "The last pastor we had was dishonest and just a plain downright liar." What could I say to him or to the young pastor's wife who said to me, "When we were called from a church in a small town to one in a big city, my husband and I thought we would invite some of the other pastors in for an evening of fellowship so we could get acquainted." She added, "I give you my word, that night I heard the dirtiest stories and entertained the rudest and most discourteous guests that were ever in our home. When they left that night I said to my husband, 'If that is the way preachers are, I will never have them in our parsonage again'."

Now, those cases are not typical of pastors generally. Most of them are fine, upright, consecrated men, but such things should make us search our own hearts. It is a sad fact that the byword for exaggeration is "ministerially speaking." A chaplain said to me the other day, making out his report for attendance at his services, "It says at the bottom of the sheet, if this is an estimate, discount ten percent." My, what sins we preachers are prone to—exaggeration, pride, envy, jealousy, laziness, tardiness, affectation, cowardice, failure to live up to the qualities of true greatness. Indeed we are men of human weakness.

In this connection, I think often of the picture, "The Night Watch," that Rembrandt painted. I am told he was asked by the night watch in Amsterdam to paint their picture. Today it is one of the great treasures of the city of Amsterdam. You see portrayed there the teeming life of a great city. When Rembrandt had finished it, he called the officers of the night watch in to see it. They looked at it and were aghast because they were not in prominent places at all. They missed the point entirely that Rembrandt was trying to show them as the servants of the people of a great city and protectors of all that was good in their lives. They said, "Rembrandt, you can have your picture. We will get another artist to paint ours!" And they did.

When you go to Amsterdam, you will see their portrait hung in the same room with the great picture they rejected, and you will smile when you look at it. There they are, pompous, dressed in their best, proud of themselves. They got what they wanted. They forgot they were servants of others and thought only of themselves and their station in life.

We must do far better as humble servants of God and others. We cannot do it in our own strength. We do have this treasure in earthen vessels. You and I need well to pray with Paul for strength from on high lest, having preached, we ourselves should be cast aways."

It calls for much heart searching to preach the Gospel that can change men's lives. Our lives must be changed, too, and often we need to pray, "God be merciful to me a sinner." Then, a minister who is honest with himself knows all too well how right Paul was when he spoke about the war within himself. "Wretched man that I am, who shall deliver me?" And he can say, "Thank God, Jesus my Lord can." It is equally as important to strive earnestly for the positive witness, integrity, honesty, humility, and love. It is heartening to be able to say, "I can do all things in Him who strengtheneth me."

We can take heart from that great bit of sculpture of the two natures of man where you see two men wrestling with each other. Then you realize you are really seeing one man wrestling with himself. One man is low and brutal; he is doing all he can to hold the other down. The other man, with his arms pressing up and his face turned up toward God is struggling to stand erect. And you know he will. So can we, as we look up to Him whose we are and whom we serve for all the grace and strength we need.

"Herod stood in awe of John, knowing him to be a just and holy man," a man in touch with God. That is what others think about you and me and that is what they expect of those who stand in their pulpits. Dr. A. W. Bearen loved to tell of a lovely little girl who would always sit close to the pulpit and look up at him and he would always have a special smile for her., One day, she went out of church sobbing as though her heart would break. Her mother couldn't find out what the trouble was at first. Then she said, "What in the world happened?" The little girl answered through her sobs, "I looked at God all morning and he never smiled at me once!" He was God's man and more to her, called for God's work. You and I are expected to be just that.

How wonderful it is when a pastor measures up as has another seminary classmate of mine. Not long ago, his congregation paid him this tribute:

> The members of our church and congregation desire to express their thanks to Almighty God for the privilege of association with you over the past eleven years.
>
> We shall remember with pride and affection your direct, vigorous, challenging sermons and your leadership in the service of song. Your clear integrity, your radiant goodwill, your victorious courage and your humble

devotion to Christ have been vital in our hours of rejoicing, of sorrow, of sickness and of decision; in our home life and our life in the world. In public ministry and personal interview, with younger and older, in your pulpit and your study, in the hospital and our homes, *you have been God's word to us.*

"Herod stood in awe of John, knowing he was a just and holy man, so he protected John." Ministers are, in a very real sense, protected from life, and need to recognize that fact. There are some things we don't know much about and we are not authorities on every subject. We are insulated to a certain degree from some areas of life. There are some things that people will not say and some subjects they do not discuss when the preacher is around.

We are insulated, in a sense, from life, but it is our job to keep in touch with life. And we can through such things as our reading, the movies, good plays, athletic events, the social and service clubs and civic organizations. The minister ought to be a part of the scheme of life of his community so that others feel he knows and cares what is going on.

A pastor needs to learn to keep an open mind about some things. I remember reading what Dr. Barton once said about an experience when he was a young man at Berea College. He went out into the hills to teach for a time, and they invited the new young school teacher to take part in a public debate. He said, "What is the subject?" They told him, "Resolved: That the World is Flat." He said to himself, "Ha, I certainly am going to have an easy time in this debate. These poor folks don't know any better." Then he went on to say that to him it was a very humbling experience. He said, "I never knew in my life that there were so many arguments that the world is flat!" He added, "Ever since that debate in that little mountain school I have tried to keep an open mind on every subject."

There are many things we need to learn in all humility, but no minister ever needs to apologize for not knowing about life, because he knows far more than many realize. We are privileged to share with our people in the great crises of life, to be with them in their hours of joy and of sorrow, when they marry, when children come, and when loved ones die, when they celebrate their anniversaries, and when we finally put them to rest. The minister knows God's truth and the great realities and has the privilege of sharing with those to whom he ministers when their minds and hearts are most open.

When I was ordained, I wanted my father, who was a minister to Jesus Christ, to give me the charge as a minister. I'll never forget it. He stood before me, a good minister of Jesus Christ if I ever knew one. He said, "Son, I charge you with three things. First, keep close to God. Second, keep close to men. Third, bring God and men together." That is your privilege and mine.

"Herod stood in awe of John, knowing he was a just and holy man, so he protected John. He was greatly exercized when he listened to him." Does anybody ever get disturbed when you preach? Perhaps they should. I remember Mrs. Adams coming home one time and saying, "I met one of our members on the street, and he said that he enjoyed the sermon very much yesterday. It was one of the very best sermons he ever heard." She said, "I told him I was sure you would be glad to hear that." Then she added, "He went on to say, 'The sermon made me mad through and through. You know, I like a sermon that makes me mad once in a while. It stirs me up and makes me think. That's why I liked that sermon yesterday'. "

John made people mad. "Herod was greatly exercized when he listened to him." His conscience hurt him and he got stirred up. John was a man of conviction and the modern preacher must be, too. My good friend, Jesse Bader, once said, "Convictions are the beliefs that make convicts of us. We don't just hold our beliefs, our beliefs hold us." We do need great convictions. John had them. It cost him his head. It cost Jesus the cross. It cost Roger Williams his home and exile. Through the years Baptist pastors have paid a price for their convictions. How much will it cost you?

In our church in Richmond there is a window right next to the pulpit. In it you see two Baptist pastors in jail with their hands stretched through the bars preaching. Why were they there? What had they done? Just been true to their convictions. That was all.

Once when five Baptist pastors were brought to trial for preaching the Gospel without a license, the judge finally said, "I'll not put you in jail if you will promise not to preach the Gospel. If you don't make that promise, you go to jail for a year." John Waller looked him straight in the eye and said, "I say for myself and for my brethren, God forbid that any Baptist preacher should ever choose his personal liberty at the cost of his conscience. We'll go to jail."

I know that there are dangers here. You can get so far ahead of your people that you lose a chance to lead them. Then, on the other hand you can be so cautious that you lose their respect and their confidence. Sometimes it is tragically true that we get most excited over issues about which the world cares little. We go fighting on battlefields where the battle is long since done. We set up straw men and have a big time knocking them down, but nobody cares. There is so much to challenge us as preachers in this day, problems of injustice, discrimination, segregation, integration, world peace, poverty and misery, intolerance, and hate.

I remind myself often of a story told by Pierre Van Paassen. He pictures a young heretic who dies for his faith, burned at the stake! My, what ungodly things we do sometimes in the name of religion! As the flames engulfed him, his wife and son stood nearby watching, too numb to cry out. He cried out the name of his wife and the name of his boy, and died for his faith. Late in the day when the crowd had gone, the mother and son came back. The guard had compassion when he understood who she was and let her go near the charred body. She scraped some ashes from it, put them in two little sacks of black and red cloth. She tied them with a cord, put the cord around the lad's neck, and tucked the two little sacks within his blouse. Then she said solemnly, "Son, you bear on your breast the ashes of your father who died for his faith—the black for sin, the red for sacrifice. When in your life you see intolerance, or hatred, or sin, or evil, those ashes will burn on your breast and you will cry out against them." The lad looked into her eyes and said, "Mother, it shall be so!"

"Herod was greatly exercized when he listened to John. Still he was glad to listen." That is the great thing about preaching. The right kind of pastor can be a winsome messenger of the Most High God. There was something in John that touched people, that moved them. He stirred their hearts and drew them to him, and they came from all the countryside to hear him preach. They said, "There is a man sent from God whose name is John."

Do they say that of you? If they are going to, you and I need to study and really know the people to whom we minister and preach. Jesus did. He saw the multitudes and had compassion on them. To him they were as sheep without a shepherd. Like ourselves they were sinful and wayward and weak, and all too often selfish and cowardly. He saw them with their pleasures and their pains, struggling, hoping, dreaming, doubting—young and old, rich and poor—and he was moved with compassion. They knew he cared. Small wonder the common people heard him gladly. His sermons grew out of life. He talked about things they were interested in. His illustrations came out of life: the reaping, the sowing, and the fishing, and the lost coin, and the lost sheep. He talked their language, he touched their lives, he met their needs, and gave them confidence. His sermons grew out of their lives and gave them hope for better living here and opened the way to eternal life. Yes, Jesus and John were winsome messengers for the Most High. What a privilege you and I have to follow in their train, to preach the unsearchable riches of God in Christ Jesus.

God grant that you and I may do it so well that they will say of us as they did in the days of the old prophet Ezekiel, "As for you, Oh, son of man, your people are talking about you in the streets and at the doors of their houses. They are saying one to another, 'Come let us hear what is the word from the eternal today.' They come to you as usual, they sit in front of you, they hear your words but they do not obey them, their lips are full of lies, their minds are set on their selfish ends. They heed you as they would a love song beautifully rendered and well played. They hear your words but they will not obey them, yet when the hour cometh and it is coming, they shall realize that there was a prophet among them."

We follow in a wonderful succession since that day. You and I are called to preach, called to share the Gospel with those who need it. Though they sometimes cry out against us, we are called to share with them the truth that will set them free from the bondage of sin and of death. Norman Vincent Peale tells of meeting a patient in a mental hospital in New York who said, "I recognize your picture. You are a preacher, aren't you?" Dr. Peale said, "Yes, I am." This man, who was a leading educator from the midwest, said, "Tell me, Preacher, this stuff you preachers talk about, is it really true or is it just a whole lot of talk?" Peale said, "My friend, it is really true, and I will be glad to help you find it for yourself." That was the first of a number of conversations. Finally, there came the great day when that man was released from the hospital and on his way back to the middle west. He went by Marble Collegiate Church just to say, "Dr. Peale, thank you. You don't need to worry about me any more. I know where my strength lies."

What a privilege to preach, to share such life-saving truth, to be a good minister of Jesus Christ—a man called of God. It is ours to reveal the light and the knowledge and the glory of God as it is seen in the face and in the living presence of Jesus Christ.

Two deacons were going home a good many years ago from a revival meeting where they heard old Gypsy Smith. Their pastor was one of the greatest men of God I have every known. He had helped to bring Gypsy Smith to that city for a revival. As they walked home, one deacon said, "Gypsy Smith is a great man of God. I think he is more like Jesus Christ than any man I know." The other deacon said, "Yes, he is more like Jesus Christ than any man I know except our pastor." The deacon said, "You are so right. Our pastor is like his Lord."

The preacher of today needs to look honestly at himself and his people and then to pray that they may say of him as others said of John the Baptist, "Herod stood in awe of John, knowing he was a just and holy man, so he protected John. He was greatly exercized when he listened to him, still he was glad to listen."

Let us pray in the words of a hymn every pastor should often say as a prayer:

"Lord, speak to me that I may speak,
In living echoes of thy tone,
As Thou hast sought, so let me seek,
Thy erring children lost and lone.

O, teach me, Lord, that I may teach
The precious things Thou dost impart
And wing my words that they may reach
The hidden depths of many a heart.

O, strengthen me, that while I stand
Firm on the rock and strong in Thee
I may stretch out a helping hand
To wrestlers with a troubled sea.

O, fill me with Thy fullness, Lord,
Until my very heart o'erflow,
In kindling thought and glowing word
Thy love to tell, Thy praise to show.

O, use me, Lord, use even me
Just as Thou wilt and when and where
Until Thy blessed face I see
Thy rest, Thy joy, Thy glory share."

The Faith of a Preacher

We are thinking together on the general theme, "A Pastor Looks at His Preaching." Preaching is just one of the things a pastor is called upon to do, but a most important one. I have come as a pastor to share with those of you who are either pastors or going to be, some of the experiences and insights and hard-learned lessons about preaching that come to a pastor throughout the years.

I remember one time I was walking along the shore of a little mountain lake with my two boys. In front of one of the cottages we saw a little device that someone had made for his own amusement—the figure of a little man with his hand on a handle attached to a windmill. The little man kept going up and down, and the windmill kept going around and around. As we stopped to look at it, I said to the boys, "Does the windmill make the man go or does the man make the windmill go?" The younger boy said right away, "Why the man makes the windmill go! He turns the handle round and round." The older boy with more insight said, "No, it is the windmill that makes the man go." But we all knew that except as the unseen wind blew across it, neither one of them would move.

So it is with the minister. You sometimes wonder whether you are running the church or the church is running you. But we all know the futility of the whole business unless the Spirit of God moves in the hearts of pastor and people. So we are thinking about a pastor and one of his responsibilities. First we looked at ourselves and our people. On the other days we shall be thinking more directly about our preaching.

Often as I think about a pastor and his preaching, I remember a play I read some years ago which portrayed a younger pastor who came to be associated with an older one. The younger was sure that his new ideas were far better than the older man's, that his new theology was far better, and that he knew much better how to run the parish. One day he went to answer the call of a girl who was desperately ill. She wanted the old pastor but he was out and the young man went instead. He sat down beside the bed of the very ill and troubled girl and began to talk with her. After a time she turned her back to him and began to cry. He said, "Why, what in the world is the matter? What have I done?" She said, "I wanted strength but you had none to give; I wanted God but you have only words."

It is important that a preacher know how to preach, but it takes more than words. It is important that he be called and inspired and led by the Spirit of God, and that he have something to preach, a message to proclaim, a Gospel to declare, a Gospel that he can bear witness to because he has experienced it for himself. Let us think then about the faith of the preacher. It is well we do, because in the world in which you and I are called to preach, the basic war is not a war of atomic weapons or battleships or planes, but a war of beliefs, a conflict between opposing faiths and philosophies of life.

It is tremendously important then that the preacher know what he believes and in whom he believes, to be able to say with Paul, "It is no longer I who live but Christ liveth in me. The life that I live I live by faith, faith in the Son of God who loved me and who gave himself up for me."

A few years ago I was riding though West Berlin with Theron Rankin, who was then the Secretary of our Foreign Mission Board. We were riding with an American chaplain and a German Baptist pastor, Dr. Jacob Meister. Being a pastor and a preacher, from time to time Dr. Meister would stop the car and say, "Now, Dr. Adams, you are a preacher, you will be interested in this." I remember one corner at which we stopped as he said, "Do you see that house over there? That is where the professor lived who taught Hitler and his associates so many of the ideas they held about Nordic supremacy and belief in the old pagan Germanic gods. It was he who led them to reject the Jew, Jesus, for their old pagan faith." As we drove away from that corner, Dr. Rankin turned to me and said, "And there are still some people who say it doesn't make any difference what you believe!"

It does make all the difference in the world what you believe and in whom you believe, and so we are going to think today about the faith of a preacher. Of course, we are not going to discuss the whole wide range of what a preacher believes today. That is what you have professors for. I am just a pastor here to talk about some of the essential things I think a pastor must have a firm grip on if he is to be a good preacher. He must have faith in his Maker, in his Master, in his Message, in his Methods, and in his Mission.

Alliteration is a good thing sometimes. It helps you hold a message in your mind. Perhaps you remember this classic illustration of alliteration: A pastor preaching on the Prodigal Son said, "The story of the prodigal son naturally falls into three parts:

His badness
His sadness
His gladness
Of course, his badness naturally falls into three parts:

His cavilling
His travelling
His revelling
Of course, his sadness naturally also falls into three parts:

He went to the dogs
He lost all his togs
He ate with the hogs
Then, finally, very naturally his gladness was in three parts:

He received the seal
He ate the veal
He danced the reel."

With that apology for alliteration, we'll go ahead.

The preacher of today needs to have faith in his Maker and to be able to say with the old creed, "I believe in God the Father Almighty, the maker of heaven and earth." "For it is God that worketh in you both to will and to do of his good pleasure." "We are God's fellow-workers."

Here we face one of the basic divisions of mankind right now, those who believe in God and those who do not. You and I live in a day when we have seen not only individuals but whole nations turning against a belief in the living God. When I was in Russia twenty years ago I saw the place in Moscow where once stood one of the sacred shrines of the old Orthodox Church. One of the very first things Lenin did was to order that shrine removed. In its place he had carved, "Religion the opiate of the people." Just a few days ago a leading Russian said, "Our official policy is still 'Religion is the opiate of the people'. "

You and I live in a day when, on the one hand we have a crisis theology that says there is nothing we can do; it is all in the hands of God; and on the other hand, those who say that there is no God at all. It is important, then, that the pastor who wants to be a preacher know what he believes and why he believes it, that he has a faith, an unshakeable faith in the God and Father of our Lord Jesus Christ.

Yet we live in an inhospitable world and preach in a day and generation when that faith is denied and rejected around the world. It is an appalling fact. I was riding in the Crimea last summer with a professional photographer, a young Russian. As we went along I asked about his faith. He said, "I am an atheist." Then he went on to say, "Our communist code of morals is just as good as your Christian code of morals." Instead of arguing about a comparative code of morals, I said, "What is the source of your communist code of morality?" He replied, "I'll have to think about that a little." After a long silence he said, "The source of our communist code of morals is in our communist hopes and dreams. It doesn't root in any mythical Jesus like you talk about!" Such is the world the preacher fails. In past generations it may have been possible to be sincerely Christian and fit easily into civilization. The world once seemed a fairly hospitable place for developing a Christian faith and realizing our Christian ideals, but that is hardly true now.

The preacher, then, needs to be sure that he knows God, not just knows about God. He needs to know the theories about God but he must know God at first hand so that he can say to a skeptical student or a cynical businessman or a doubting world, "I know whom I have believed." What a glorious faith that is.

Some years ago in China, communist bandits seized two Christian missionaries and held them for a ransom. They carried them about for weeks as prisoners. One morning the two awoke bound and gagged in a little shed with some straw on the floor on which they slept. The bandits were making merry in a nearby house. One of the missionaries remembered that it was Christmas morning. It was a dull, dark day, and they were cold and hungry and lonely, wondering if they would ever see their loved ones again. But he took his bound hands and swept the straw to one side until he had a clear spot on the hard earth floor. Then he picked up some straw and shaped one word, the word "Immanuel"—"God with us". Telling about it months later after they were released, he said, "My companion looked at me and saw the word and smiled, though he couldn't speak. After that the day seemed brighter and our hope was stronger, for we knew that God was with us." Yes, the pastor who wants to be a preacher needs to have a faith like that in his Maker.

He also needs faith in his Master. He needs to be able to say with Paul, "It is no longer I who lives but Christ liveth in me." As he faces the stress and temptations in his own life and the crises in his congregation's life, he needs to be able to say, "I can do all things through Him who strengthens me." Christ must be to the modern pastor who wants to preach, not just a Jesus who lived long ago, but a Christ who lives here and now. You can illustrate it very simply with the story of a town bully who used to go around saying that he would cut off little boys' ears. One day he came up to one lad who always ran every time he saw the bully coming. This time the little fellow didn't run, and the bully said, "You better get going or I'm going to cut both your ears off this time!" The boy just stood there. The bully said, "You had better get going! I've got my knife." The little fellow just stood there and laughed. The bully said, "What is the matter with you? You are not running away." The little fellow said, "I'm not scared of you. My big brother is right around the corner." So it is with the man who knows he has an Elder Brother who gives him the grace and strength he needs when of himself he would be all too weak and inadequate.

Our people look to us—these folks in our congregation—to make Jesus real. Christ is the answer, but it isn't enough just to say that. They have so many questions, these members of ours. They want you to make Christ real and to show how He is the answer to their many needs in personal life, in home life, in family life, and in business life.

You must begin, if you are to meet those needs, with a sense of the sufficiency of Jesus Christ. We have the promise, "My grace is sufficient for thee, for my strength is made perfect in weakness." One of our poets expresses this beautifully as he first portrays other religious leaders of the world and then shows their shortcomings and their failures. Then he says of Jesus:

"But thee, but thee, oh, Sovereign seer of time
But thee, Oh, Poet's poet, wisdom's tongue
But thee, oh, man's best man
Oh, love's best love
Oh, perfect life in perfect labor writ.
Oh, what amiss may I forgive in Thee,
Jesus, good paragon, thou Crystal Christ."

When you have that faith, then you can have the faith in your message, not just your own, but His message through you. I learned that long ago in one of those humbling experiences that you never forget. Up near this same little mountain lake where we used to go when I was a boy and where I later took my children, there was a little village church. The pastor was one of the noblest old Christians I have ever known. He would hunt with his people, fish with them, marry them and bury their dead. He was a godly man, and he and my preacher father were very good friends. Every summer it was a great day in that little community when my father would preach. People would come from miles around. Father would open his Bible, hold it in his hand and preach the word of life he loved.

The year my father died we went to the mountains again, and I must confess I rather expected they would ask me to preach, and they did. I could not help but feel how fortunate they were because someone was still coming from the outside to bring them the light and truth they needed. How fortunate it was that I had been attending one of our leading seminaries and had all of the new ideas, a good deal that they had not heard yet. When the great day came in that little mountain church, frankly I had been wondering what the pastor would say to introduce me. The dear old man gave a beautiful tribute to my father, so well deserved. He expressed the regret of the congregation to my mother that my father was no longer with us. Then he just turned and looked at me and said, "Now, Ted will preach to us from the Word." Very humbly I took three or four steps from that chair to the pulpit. They hadn't come to hear me and my new ideas. There was the Book. It was my privilege to preach to them from the Word. I don't know whether they learned anything that day or not, but I learned a lot and have tried ever since to live up to what was expected of me that day.

We do have a message, and it must come to us by the Spirit of God and through us from the Word of God. The Word was made flesh to dwell among us and from his Word we study and teach and preach. What a message is there, a message for personal life and for social life, and for eternal life. How desperately the world needs that message today.

What a privilege it is to be able to stand in the pulpit and say I have faith in the Son of God who loves me and gave himself up for me. And what a responsibility to say, "Ye must be born again." "Christ Jesus came into the world to save sinners of whom I am chief." "Whosoever shall call upon the name of the Lord shall be saved."

What a life-changing gospel that is. I remember hearing a traveller tell of his journeys in the Pacific. On one island girls from a Christian school stood along side the walk singing. Their parents had been cannibals, but now their children sang, "What a Wonderful Change in My Life Has Been Wrought, Since Jesus Came Into My Heart." You and I can also bear witness to the power of the Gospel to change lives and change the homes.

One night a soldier came to my study after the evening service. He was stationed in Richmond and was troubled about the way he had been living. He came again and again, Sunday after Sunday, and began to understand what the Gospel could mean to him. Then he began to sit with one of our lovely Christian girls. In due time they came together with that light in their eyes which says even before they say the words, "Doctor, we want to get married."

After we talked about the wedding, I said to him, "What are you going to do about your church membership?" "Oh," he said, "before I marry her, I'm going to join the church." The next Sunday, he publicly accepted Christ as his Saviour and a little later, I baptized him. On his wedding day he asked his best man to put an envelope in my hand. In it was a note I still have in my desk. The note said, "Doctor, here is some money. Take it and use it in your work. I have found a peace in my heart that I never thought was possible and I never can thank you enough."

That is the message we have to preach, a message of personal righteousness and of social righteousness. We believe that changed men will change the world and that Jesus didn't teach us to pray for an impossibility when he said, "Pray thy kingdom come, thy will be done."

A young mother told me one day, "I'm having a hard time teaching my children to say the Lord's Prayer right." I said, "Well, what's wrong about it?" She said, "Well, they persist in saying, 'Thy Kingdom *will* come, Thy will be done'."

The children were right. His Kingdom *will* come and you and I are privileged to share in the realization of that hope and that dream, if we are willing to preach all the gospel and to sound out the same social and ethical notes that the old prophets did. Amos said, "Let justice roll down as waters and righteousness as a mighty stream." When John the Baptist, that man of human weakness, sent messengers to Jesus asking, "Art Thou He that cometh or look we for another?", do you remember what Jesus said? "The lame walk, the lepers are cleansed, the deaf hear, the blind receive their sight, the poor have the gospel preached to them." Jesus was willing to have his Messiahship judged by what happened in the lives of people, because of Him.

You say, "Well, it seems hopeless now. What can we do?" All God asked you to do is to do what you can in your generation. Some of these age old problems aren't going to be fully solved in our day and generation. I was in high school in the days when we were adopting prohibition and arguing about woman's suffrage and just finishing the war to make the world safe for democracy, and it looked like a whole new era was just about to be ushered in. I remember I used to pray very sincerely in my high school days, "Lord, don't let all the problems of the world be solved before I get old enough to help solve them." That's one prayer the Lord certainly did answer.

But he does expect us to do our part. I think often in this connection of the vision and faith of the Curies in their long search for radium. They had to distill out of tons of pitchblende hoping in the end to find radium. They dreamed of it, talked of it, of what it would be like, what it would do, of the people it would heal and the lives it would save. Then they came to the great day in the laboratory. It should be there, but they couldn't see it. Thinking they had failed, and heart-broken, they closed the laboratory and walked out. As the shadows fell, the husband finally said, "My dear, it is no use. It will be a hundred years before anybody finds it." That was just the challenging word she needed and she replied, "My dear, it may take a hundred years, but I'm going to see how far I can advance the search for it in my lifetime. Let's go back to the laboratory."

When they went back in the darkness to the laboratory they saw a gleam, a radiance, and knew they had found it after all. But even if not, they were pledged to see how far they could advance the search in their lifetime. That is all God asks of you, but He does ask that. You can be God's prophet for your flock in a day and generation with challenging social problems that call for the best that you and all of us together can give.

We also have a message that sees beyond the years with the perspective of eternity. How people long for that and need it, though sometimes they can teach us as much as we can teach them, that if we die with Him we shall also live with Him. What a privilege it is to be able to stand with a sorrowing family and remind them of the promise of Jesus, "I am the resurrection and the life. He that believeth on Me, though he were dead, yet shall he live, and whosoever liveth and believeth in Me shall never die."

I learned that truth as a young pastor from one of my parishoners, an old man. I had been through all the studies in the seminary and had faced the questions about immortality and eternity. I felt there was a whole lot I didn't know. Two old men in this congregation were very close friends. One of them died and the other was left alone. I remember standing by the casket as this one old man came by to pay his last respects to the body of the friend he had loved through the years. I began to say to myself, "What can I say to that old man? What shall I tell him?" As I wondered, he came up and stood very reverently by the casket a few moments. Then he smiled, waved his hand and walked away, saying very quietly, "Good-bye, old friend. I'll see you again." I didn't say a word to him—he helped me.

Yes, we have the message but how are we going to get it across to people. The preacher and pastor must have faith in his methods as well as in his message, and he has many he can use effectively. He has the privilege of personal work, dealing with boys and girls and other individuals and of counseling with families and those in trouble. He has the responsibility for an educational program and recreational and social and welfare activities. Through his preaching and in other ways, he shares in building up the church, the fellowship of believers. This is basic because it is an appalling fact that Christianity is always within one generation of extinction and only as we build up the church will the gospel be passed on to succeeding generations.

Above all else the pastor is privileged to preach, to sow the seed that beareth fruit for all eternity. I know there are a lot of doubts about preaching and its value and you hear prophets of doom about preaching from time to time. I remember some years ago in a convention of one of our great religious bodies, one preacher began his message in a very dramatic way by saying to all the preachers gathered there, "Preaching is doomed." He went on to say that in a few years there would be just a few great radio and television preachers and the rest of the pastors would not need to do preaching any more. He is wrong. There is no substitute for the personal contact of the preacher with his people when they know him and he knows them and they all love each other.

There are others who say as did one professor of preaching in a moment of cynicism, "Preaching is just pouring out familiar words to sermon-saturated pagans." Someone else has said pessimistically, "Preaching is like pouring water out of a second story window, trying to fill narrow-necked bottles on the ground below." One homiletics professor is reported to have heard a sermon in class and when asked to criticize at the end, said, "The sermon was too long by half and it doesn't make any difference which half you leave out."

So often, too, our sermons are hurt by our own lives. People when they come on Sunday, come out of a sense of duty, not because they expect much of us, because our witness hasn't led them to expect too much. I think every preacher ought to be reminded over and over again of another priceless word from Francis of Assisi. One day he asked one of the younger brethren to go with him into the city to preach. They went in and walked through the streets of the city and Francis stopped to chat with the shopkeepers and play with the children, went in to see the mothers with their babies, to minister to the sick and to see the dying. As they were on their way back out of the city again, the younger brother said, "Brother Francis, haven't you forgotten something?" "What's that?" "Why, Brother Francis, you said you were going into the city to preach today." The saintly old man said, "Brother, it's no use going anywhere to preach unless you preach everywhere you go."

But it does please God "by the foolishness of the preaching to save them that believe," and every once in a while we can be encouraged by what someone says or learns. In one of our eastern cities a woman came for a couple of months to be with her mother in a great medical center. She was very much disturbed herself and she didn't have too much faith. But when she left the city she left this letter to the pastor whose church she had attended. "In bringing about my spiritual growth, I believe God intended that I should work out my own comfort, without direct contact with a minister. He did guide me to your services and your sermons made me realize that an individual does not need to talk face to face with the minister to be helped. The minister through his sermons can point the way, but we have to work out our own salvation and everyone is equally precious in God's sight. He gave me the mind and the will to find my own comfort in the knowledge that God is love and that if we love him, we are never alone. But the inspiration of your sermons these two months will go with me all through life."

That is the privilege you and I have. And in the providence of God, it works, if we give preaching its rightful place in our life and thought.

The importance of the privilege of preaching for God from the Word is beautifully stated in some words a dear friend of mine used in the ordination of his own son. The boy had been called back to the college town where his father had grown up and where the son had gone to college. It was a very moving and dramatic scene when the father stood in the church where he had been a boy to install his son as pastor of the church where both had worshiped as students. The father said to his son, "May you ever live in your early high passion to mediate the love and compassions and mercy and forgiveness of the eternal, to bring to all the affairs and issues of life the saving salt and redeeming grace of abiding spiritual faith. As a minister of Christ you are a specialist in life's ultimate and abiding values, an interpreter of life in the terms of spiritual realities which are the only things that endure. The whole of life, everything that affects the life of man, personal and social, in the field of religion is your concern. It is yours to preach and to teach. The minister is not a parrot to repeat in attractive fashion the views and opinions held by his listerners. He is a prophet of the eternal God, to interpret all of life in terms of ultimate values. Not infrequently he must say what is contrary to opinions held by those who listen to him or that will cut across the comfortable mores by which his people live. Some won't like it.

"The comment was made by a friend concerning Dr. McCracken's sermon at Riverside Church one Sunday, 'He certainly made us sizzle and fry this morning.' That must have been real preaching. It was said of Peter and John when they came to a certain territory, 'Those who turn the world upside-down are come here.'

"You remember your first preaching? The summer when you were 18? Do you remember what you wrote to me after your second Sunday of preaching? You wrote, 'I was disturbed the first Sunday because I didn't feel I was reaching the peak.' Today you said it was different. 'I felt as though it were not I preaching, but that God was preaching through me.' May you ever be so spiritually prepared that you can always feel it was God preaching through you."

Yes, the minister can have faith in his method because he knows it works. For example, a man came up to me on a little street in a town in Virginia and said, "Dr. Adams, you don't know me, but I know you. I was in your church one Sunday night," and he named the night. He said, "Liquor had ruined my life. I had lost my family, my job, everything." He said, "I walked down the street that Sunday night in

Richmond and I saw your church open and went in. I hadn't been in church for years. When the congregation sang, I sang hymns I hadn't sung since I was a boy. When you read the Scriptures, it was the first time I had heard God's Word in years. When you prayed, I prayed, for the first time in a long while. When you preached, something happened inside me. When the service was done, I got up and walked on down the street and looked up at the stars and found God again. That very week, almost miraculously, I was offered a job as editor of the paper in this town." And I remember how he reached up and took hold of the lapels of my coat and he was so intense, he almost shook me as he said, "Dr. Adams, this Gospel that you preach, it works. I tell you, it works." Thank God for the privilege of preaching such a Gospel as that.

The minister also has faith in his mission because he has a divine commission that has never been repeated, "Go ye into all the world and preach the gospel." What a privilege it is to give men a new vision of what they are and what they can be under God. Dr. George Buttrick pictures this as he tells of some shipwrecked men slowly working their small boat toward shore. As they did, their water gave out and in dismay and despair one of them dipped his hand into the sea, expecting to find salt water but to his joy and amazement found it fresh. They knew then that they were in the estuary of a great river. As they toiled on toward the shore, in high hopes, they began to speculate on what a great river it must be to send its fresh water so far out to the sea, and what a great continent it must be and what mighty mountains, to supply such a stream. So it is with us as in our preaching we are able to give to mankind a vision of the greatness of the Kingdom of our Lord.

So the minister has faith in his Maker, his Master, his Message, his Method, and his Mission. Because of all that he can have faith in himself, as a pastor and as a preacher. God grant that your experience may be akin to that of a young minister of another generation who wrote in his diary in his seminary days—"Tonight I promised God that I would do anything, if only He would give me a chance to serve Him, that I would work hard, that I would stay poor, that I would make any sacrifice, if only He would guide me and help me and give me an opportunity to serve Him." At the end of a long and useful ministry, he closed his diary with these priceless words, "Led by His spirit, all the way."

No, the Christian preacher is not a little man futilely beating the air, but a preacher of the Word of Life if he is led by His Spirit all the way. ꙮ

Planning, Preparing, and Preaching

We have been talking as pastors about the kind of person a preacher ought to be and the faith the preacher has to share with others. This morning and tomorrow we are to think about planning and preparing and preaching with purpose and with power.

Preaching does take planning and preparing. I remember one time in the seminary I was in the library, working mighty hard on a sermon for the next Sunday. One of my classmates came up and said, "Ted, you do work on your sermons, don't you." I said, "Yes, I certainly do." "Well," he said, "I knew I had to work awfully hard on mine, but you speak so easily I thought you just got up and talked and didn't have to work." But any man who wants to preach has to plan, prepare, and work, if he thinks at all of what the congregation expects and has a right to expect Sunday after Sunday.

But how in the world can one man prepare two sermons and a prayer meeting talk and a lot of other talks, week after week after week, and each one supposed to be worthy in thought. Some years ago I went fishing with Dr. Roy Angell in Miami. As we were coming back from that fishing trip, I talked with our fishing partner for the day and discovered that he was a high-diver. He was a man whose one feat was to get up on a pole 120 feet in the air and dive through a ring of fire into a little pool of water, eight feet deep, and come out alive. As he told me about what he did and how he did it, he said, "You know, another preacher talked with me one day about this, and asked, 'You dive once each night?' 'Yes.' The preacher said, 'I suppose you practice then in the morning.' The diver said, 'Preacher, every dive has to be perfect. There ain't no use to practice'." Well, that's the situation you and I face on Sunday morning.

I got a letter from a young preacher a few months ago about another subject. The letter was written on Saturday and closed with these thoughtful words, "Well, I must go to work on my sermon again. Tomorrow will be a big day for somebody." Now, there are two things about that. The young man had the right idea. Tomorrow would be a great day for somebody. Somebody who would make a Christian decision. Someone who perhaps would experience a complete change in life because of what that preacher would say. I couldn't help but hope that he had started to work on the sermon before that Saturday night. As one of the illustrious graduates of this seminary says, "The greatest fault of most sermon delivery is there isn't much to deliver." We do need to stop and think about what we are going to say and how we are going to say it.

This morning, just as another pastor, let me tell you how I do it. It may not be the best way, but it is the way that works for me and it may suggest something for you. I take a good deal of heart from some words attributed to Horace Bushnell, who said, "There can't be much preaching worthy of the name where there is no thinking. Preaching is nothing but the bursting out of light which has first burst in or out from where God is, among the soul's foundations." Dr. Blackwood, in writing about the soul of Frederick Robertson, said, and this will help, too, "He discovered early in his ministry that he must not gamble on the inspiration of the moment. He must read, plan, write, tear up, rewrite, struggle, agonize, pray, and then he would be ready to preach."

In trying to measure up to that ideal, I suggest that you try planning a year's preaching. I do just that. I plan my preaching in the summer to go from September to the next July. It is not a hard and fast outline. I have never been one of those men who could publish in September the title and text of every sermon to be preached every Sunday morning and evening from then until the next July. I don't mean a hard and fast plan like that, with every sermon finished and prepared and ready months in advance. I don't mean that at all. That can be a deadly thing.

I remember some years ago I visited a preacher who took me into his study and proudly said, "Here are my sermon files." He pulled them out, drawer after drawer, sermon after sermon, all typed out. He said, "When I get called to my next pastorate, I'll have every sermon for every Sunday for several years all ready." I don't even know if that man is preaching now at all. I have lost track of him. That isn't preaching. Rather I like the definition of the G. I. who was going out of the chapel one day and said, "Chaplain, that was a good sermon today." The chaplain said, "Well, son, what makes a good sermon." The soldier said, "When you take something out of your heart and put it into mine."

How can we preach that way? Well, I have to plan mine ahead and having a year-round plan helps me in a number of ways. First of all, it gives me a little peace of mind. I don't have to wake up on Monday morning and say, "What in the world am I going to preach about next Sunday?" I have that planned ahead. It assures my congregation of a well-rounded diet because every sermon is a part of a program of preaching that feeds them through the year. The great things that should be in a preaching program are all included. Then it becomes not only a planning program but a filing program. Much that I read and experience and think fits naturally into some part of the preaching program for that year.

When I take my vacation one of the first things I do is to sit down and go over the diary I have kept of the past year's preaching week by week. I sit down with a big book and I write in that book the title of every sermon I have preached, every talk I have given. That brings back the full year's preaching and the high points and the low points, and I can look it over and see what was included and what was left out. Then I make a file folder for each month of the year again. In that monthly folder is a folder for every sermon or for any series that will come in that month.

Then I go over the sermon ballot of the congregation. We have a sermon ballot in the church, and it is a very humbling and illuminating experience, believe me. We publish the themes of all the sermons that I have preached that year, and I tell the congregation, "You choose the most helpful morning sermons and the most helpful evening sermons." I think that twice in all these twenty years the congregation and I agreed on which were the best sermons. As a rule, they don't choose the ones I choose. All this helps me to know the kind of sermons that have been most helpful. Now to be sure, I don't always give them just what they want. Sometimes I give them what I think they need, as a pastor should. But it helps to know their reactions and the kind of sermons which struck home and the sermons they don't respond to or appreciate. Next, I go over the material I have accumulated in those monthly files in the past year and see if it is still fresh and vital or should be thrown out or put somewhere else.

Then I am ready to plan for the year ahead. First, I note all the things that rightly belong in each month. In September, we have homecoming services and promotion day or a rally day when we suggest a theme for the year, some challenging theme for the congregation's further action. You will want to share with them some of your vacation experiences, though I have learned that the congregation soon gets tired of hearing what you did when you traveled around and they didn't. After the first sermon or two they want to hear about something else besides your trip to Europe.

October starts with World Communion Sunday. This is also a good month for a series of sermons. You don't have too many specials days coming in to break it up. I usually plan a series of sermons in the morning and another in the evening. Then in November comes Thanksgiving and the preparations for the Every Member Canvass and so I preach about missions and stewardship and tithing. In December you are thinking about Christmas and the advent message and about the New Year with the beginning of a new life and forgiveness for the past and hope for the future.

January is another good month for a series of sermons. In the morning I usually have an expository series or a doctrinal series, and the people have come to look forward to it. In the evening I plan an annual series of sermons for homemakers, sermons on love, courtship, marriage, and the Christian home.

In February there are a number of special days. The first one in February is Baptist World Alliance Sunday. I hope you won't forget that. On that Sunday when you gather at the Lord's Table, you can remind your people that they are part of a world fellowship. You naturally speak about our great Baptist distinctives and Baptist history and the principles for which our fathers stood and suffered. You also have Washington's birthday and, if you happen to be in some parts of the country, Lincoln's birthday. In another part of the country in January you observe Lee and Jackson's birthdays. February is also a fitting time to preach on brotherhood and race relations. In March you will seek to quicken the evangelistic spirit, though evangelism should be a year-round emphasis. Preach on what it means to be a Christian and a church member. Perhaps you will plan a series on the words from the cross or the events leading up to the crucifixion as you look toward Easter. In April, usually you will have your Palm Sunday and Easter messages and something about the significance of church membership for those who have united with the church.

May brings Mother's Day, Rural Life Sunday, and commencement messages. In June comes Children's Day and Father's Day. We also have our sermon ballot then and preach again the morning and evening sermons the congregation chooses as the most helpful. In July, you can sound a patriotic note. I like also in July to preach about favorite Bible passages or characters or a series on a favorite book in the Bible.

Now you can see how, when you get your monthly file worked out, you have nearly organized the preaching program for the year. Then you set up some files for special messages, other files for your expository series, and begin to accumulate material on various topics. That is the value of this sort of planning. You can file things away in the appropriate place according to the way they are going to be used in this year-round scheme. Along with your expository and your biblical files plan sermons on the books of the Bible or on the Ten Commandments, or the Beatitudes or the Lord's Prayer or sermons on the prophets.

You can have another file where you deal with the great doctrines of the church, about God and Christ and immortality and prayer. By and large the most appreciated and helpful sermons I have preached through the years have been sermons on prayer. You will find your congregation hungry for messages that will help their prayer and devotional life.

There is a constant need for sermons on marriage and the home and you should be constantly on the alert for useful material in this important field. There are some things you can say over and over again. Other subjects call for a new and a fresh point of view, so the people feel you are keeping up with their problems and with the times.

Shortly after my book, *Making Your Marriage Succeed*, was published, I was coming home from an evangelistic conference. On the train one of the preachers across the aisle said, "Ted, do you have a copy of your book with you?" Well, you can't imagine an author without a copy of his book, so I handed him a copy. As he was reading it, the train stopped at a station and a young lady came and sat next to him. She looked at the book he was reading and said, "That book has an interesting title." The young preacher said, "Yes, it is. Would you like to look at it?" "No," she said, "The people who write books like that never know what they are talking about anyway." He whispered, "The man who wrote it is sitting right across the aisle." She never looked across the aisle the rest of the trip.

Well, we try and know a little something about it anyway. This is a subject our people are keenly interested in and I think any minister is failing his congregation if sometime during the year, either in January, or May when you have Mother's Day, or in June, the month of brides, at some appropriate time he does not preach a series of sermons on the Christian home.

Other sermons or series should deal with the problems your people are facing, fear, anxiety, worry, pain. Sermons like that I like to call Lessons in Living. In the year's program you will want some sermons on the church, our world mission, world peace, and on our responsibility to win the world to Christ. I combined those two series once. I gave a series of sermons in the morning on missions and world problems and a series at night on personal problems—fear, anxiety, etc. I came around the corner one morning and saw announced on the bulletin board that I would preach Sunday morning on "Who Will Convert the World?" and Sunday night on "Why Worry?" One thing you learn in the ministry, you had better keep your sense of humor and be able to laugh at yourself.

Have special files in the proper months for sermons for special days—Christmas, Easter, and patriotic occasions. Each such season should produce some good ideas you can file away for use the next year.

You always want to be on the alert for timely topics and matters of special interest—books and movies and plays, as well as current events that call for special attention. I remember a certain editor some years ago who deplored the fact that "the pulpit in the great old First Baptist Church in Richmond had certainly degenerated." The pastor was preaching on, of all things, "What Has Become of Little Boy Blue." The editor went on to say, "I doubt not that soon he will be preaching "Little Bo Peep Has Lost Her Sheep." Well, that is the first time I ever knew it was wrong to preach about lost sheep, but the sermon on Little Boy Blue did not come from any nursery rhyme. It came from that beautiful verse of Eugene Fields about a little boy and his toy soldiers and the eternal question, "What has become of Little Boy Blue since he kissed them and put them there?" The theme, of course, was the Christian doctrine of immortality, and Little Boy Blue helped introduce it.

You will find that you can render a real service when you take things of current interest that your people are thinking and talking about and relate them to the work of the Kingdom or show what the Gospel means in such a situation. You start with people where they are and bring a message they will never forget as you lead them where they ought to go. Of course, you will deal with the great social issues as occasion offers or on special days, or as they come in your expository preaching. One good reason for expository preaching is that it does bring you and your congregation face to face with great moral and social issues. You can preach about such subjects then without seeming to "drag them in." Don't neglect that part of your preaching.

"Dreams are they—but they are God's dreams!
Shall we decry them and scorn them?

That men shall love one another,
That white shall call black man brother,
That greed shall pass from the market-place,
That lust shall yield to love for the race,
That man shall meet with God face to face—
Dreams are they all,
>But shall we despise them—
>God's dreams!
Dreams are they—to become man's dreams!
Can we say nay as they claim us?
That men shall cease from their hating,
That war shall soon be abating,
That the glory of kings and lords shall pale,
That the pride of dominion and power shall fail,
That the love of humanity shall prevail—
Dreams are they all,
>But shall we despise them—
>God's dreams!"

If you are a man of God you won't despise or scorn or dodge them. Rather, in a spirit of love and good will, you will come to grips with them in your preaching.

As you look ahead and plan your preaching for the future you must never forget that you have to be ready for next Sunday morning. It takes time to prepare a sermon. To be sure sometimes a sermon has been percolating for a long time and all of a sudden comes to full boil and you see it and there it is. You could get up and preach it right then. Through a lot of long thought, conscious and subconscious, it is ready.

There are other times when you just agonize and struggle with a sermon. You get up and walk around the block and try again. Sometimes we have to get quiet and let the still small voice come in. There are times when we are so tense that God himself has a hard time getting through. But it takes time. After all, if a hundred people are going to give you a hundred hours of human time for a service on Sunday morning—how many hours should the preacher spend getting ready? But it isn't just a matter of hours. Someone may ask, how long does it take you to prepare a sermon? One preacher answered very truly, "All of my life up to now."

It does take time, and it takes prayer. As one noted preacher says, "The whole experience with me is one that begins and proceeds and ends with prayer." We are to be God's prophets, foretelling and carrying forth what God has given and we need time for prayer and meditation, that God may speak to our hearts and minds and through us to others.

We must say just a word about all the other things we are going to be asked to talk about. The minister is asked to speak in a great many places and on a great many occasions and you had better be ready. In your planning, you want to be setting aside something that will be especially good for the Rotary Club. I've got an awfully good speech for our Richmond Rotary Club all fixed up just till they ask me to give it. You want to be ready.

When you go to a meeting always say to yourself, "If I were called on, what would I say?" That's mighty good exercise. A whole lot of good speeches have gone to waste because they never were called for, but it was good for me to sit down and think about them anyway. You ought to think ahead about these special things because you will be asked to do them. The temptation is, of course, to do too many. But there is a real service you can render. You have a message to give and it also helps your church and your relationships within your church. I cannot go to all the P.T.A.'s but certainly make it a point to go if one of my members is the president of her P.T.A. or chairman of the program committee and it is a point of honor to her to get her pastor. So her pastor goes.

When you go there are some things to remember. You go as a minister of Jesus Christ. Now you aren't going to take advantage of it always to preach a sermon to them. But don't say anything or tell any stories that would be unworthy of a minister. Say something in the field that you know something about. There are so many such things—religion and life, how religion is related to business, or the home, or matters of civil righteousness or adult and juvenile delinquency. You may center your message around the basic institutions with which you are concerned, the home, the church, and the public school. In other messages deal with some of the basic principles of life Christianity teaches, like managing yourself, or getting along with other people, or giving yourself away. If you haven't read the book, *Giving Yourself Away* by David Dunn, that is certainly one you ought to read. If you don't get a sermon out of it, read it again because there is one there.

When I make such addresses or speak on special occasions, I remember something my mother said to me long ago (and she was quoting someone else). She said, "Ted, wherever you go, always remember to say a good word for Jesus Christ." I like the words of Bishop Cushman:

I do not ask that throngs may crowd the temple,
That standing room be priced.
I only ask that as I sound the message,
They may see Christ!

I do not ask for churchly pomp or pageant,
Or music such as wealth along can buy
I only pray that as I voice the message
He might be nigh!

I do not ask that men may sound my praises,
Or headlines spread my name abroad!
I only ask that as I voice the message,
Hearts may find God!

What kind of preaching does that? It's preaching that grows out of life. Some of the things that have helped me most have been things I learned from individuals among my congregations, as well as from professors of homiletics. Dr. Clarence Barbour taught me a great deal about preaching. I remember the first time I took a sermon manuscript to him. It was my first written sermon. I had worked long and hard and I was proud of it. We sat down, and he looked at me over his glasses and said, "Well, now Theodore, let's see what we can do with this." I'll never forget that blue pencil as long as I live. He would look at a paragraph and say, "Now, couldn't we say that better if we left out this and just used this." I never knew you could leave so many words out of a sermon and still make it better. He taught me to put the truth simply and directly and to leave out unnecessary words. He also taught me how to read effectively. I wished I had learned that lesson better.

I think, too, of another professor who taught me how to use a text. He assigned us each a text arbitrarily. Mine to me was just dry wood. I couldn't do anything with it. I finally made an outline, but it wasn't on that text. When I put that on the board for him and the class, he said, "Ted, you just didn't know what that was all about, did you?" I said, "No, sir, I didn't." It was from a little book tucked way back in the Old Testament by a prophet by the name of Amos. The text was, "Let justice roll down as waters and righteousness as a mighty stream." My, what a lot I had to learn. The prophets have been friends of mine ever since because that one man opened that text and book to me and taught me how to use it.

My father, who was a good minister of Jesus Christ, impressed on me the importance of every occasion when I was called on to preach. Billy Sunday was holding a revival in Chicago at the time. Father arranged for one of his evangelistic party to come to our city nearby to speak to a great union Sunday night evangelistic service. The preacher who came just stood there and told a lot of trivial stories. Father was heartsick at the thought of a wasted opportunity. I can see the landing now on the steps of that old church as my father looked me in the eye and said, "Son, if you ever get a chance like that fellow had tonight and do what he did, wherever you are and wherever I am, I'll be ashamed of you." You can't take lightly any opportunity to preach when you recall an experience like that.

He taught me about illustrations, too. He said, "Son, the illustrations are just a basket for the people to take the truth home in." Well, where do you get those illustrations. An English teacher helped teach me that. I was in her class as a freshman. She was a sister of Dr. John McNeil of Canada, a former president of the Baptist World Alliance. She was a remarkable English teacher. The first day in class she said two things that scared me nearly to death, green freshman that I was. She said, "You are to hand in a daily theme—every single day. It doesn't have to be a long one, but you must write a theme every day." Then she added, "If there's a split infinitive in it, I'll give a zero." I didn't even know what a split infinitive was. She saw we were a little aghast and said, "I know you are wondering what in the world you are going to write about, so you must cultivate the daily theme eye. You must be seeking every day something worth writing about." I can never repay Annie McNeil for that, because she taught me always to be looking for something I can use. Of course, there is a danger in that. If you are thinking only in terms of the worth of a thing as to whether you can use it or not in next Sunday's sermon, that is wrong. But illustrations out of life are popping up all around us, if we cultivate that daily theme eye.

Be sure the illustrations are yours, if you say they are. Now you mustn't judge, because the same thing may happen to two people, you know. But they must illustrate the point you are trying to make. You can ruin a sermon by telling a good story just for the sake of telling it. Above all—and this I learned from a fine teacher of children—after you tell the story don't spoil it by trying to tell what it means. If you didn't tell it well enough so they know what it means, then practice telling it right.

Learn from your own congregation what your people think makes a good sermon. I asked my people one prayer meeting night what makes a sermon good, and the next prayer meeting night what makes a sermon bad. We'll take the second question in the next lecture. But what makes a sermon good? Here are some of the answers I got. Short, not too long; it must give me inspiration to live better; give me comfort; bring me something to live by; make me think; it must not just be negative but positive; it should make me feel good and tell me how to be good; I want to feel that the Lord is speaking to me; it should be simple enough for anyone to understand and yet deep enough for the most learned (that's a hard job); it should exalt Jesus Christ and make Him real. I want a message that has the human appeal that I can use in meeting my daily problems. I want a message that helps me do what is Christian. It should charge my battery. It should be theological, factual, honest, and life centered (there was a keen observer). It should be Bible centered and preached with sincerity and conviction. The good sermon has something for the sinners and something for the saints. It should deal with current problems and needs in a Christian spirit. One good woman wrote me a letter and said, "My boy came home from school the other day and said, 'Mommy, that was one of the best lunches I ever had. I was real hungry, and it filled me up.' That's what I mean about a good sermon. I have a hunger in my heart and the sermon fills my need."

Let's sum it all up in twelve qualities in good pastoral preaching. Let me give them briefly and we shall discuss some of them more fully in the closing message. First, it must be timely, geared to the time in which you live and in which your people live. Not like that chaplain on the front line who preached to the soldiers on the problems of the Pentateuch. What did they care about those problems, important as they are to scholars? Yes, your sermon should be timely, related to the life and times and problems of those to whom you preach.

Then, it must be timeless, rooted in the Gospel, those eternal truths that you and I are privileged to proclaim. "These are written (and spoken) that believing, you may have life in His name."

It should be spoken with authority. That is one reason why Southern Baptists are one of the most rapidly growing bodies in our major Protestant denominations; because the word is preached with authority from the Book. You may remember that priceless phrase in Lloyd Douglas' story about Dean Harcourt. The Dean was so crippled he couldn't go out and do preaching and pastoral work but people came to him by the score. Lloyd Douglas tells how every morning he would go into the sanctuary for morning prayer. Then he stayed there for his own private meditation. When he went to his study and people came, Lloyd Douglas says, "Because of that early morning hour with God, those who came to see the Dean during the day felt that somehow they had been very close to headquarters." They should feel that same way when they hear you preach.

We must be compassionate and sympathetic. There should be such a feeling of understanding between pastor and people that some can come and say, "You were preaching to me this morning." Or even better, "I felt like you were not just preaching at me but talking with me about my problem."

Our preaching must be understandable, in a language and with words that people understand that can mean something to them. To be sure you sometimes have to help them understand the meaning of great words, but all you say should be in language that they understand. I think one of the finest compliments I ever received was from a little boy who went home from church with his mother one day and said, "You know, Mommy, I don't think Dr. Adams even knows any big words." It must be understandable.

Good preaching must be interesting. God forgive us for our failures here. It should be of interest to people because we are talking about their interests in a way that is popular and attractive and related to life. For example, when it was a best seller, I preached on "One Foot in Heaven." When Bing Crosby came out with a movie called "Going My Way," I preached on "Going My Way." When "The Robe" was published, I preached about "The Robe." Many who had read those books and seen the movies came to hear the sermons and heard the gospel. I got their interest by preaching on what they were interested in and had a chance to interest them in the gospel and the church.

Our messages must be convincing because they are spoken with sincerity and with conviction. Like those who heard John the Baptist, people don't go to hear a reed tossed in the wind. He was convincing because he was convicted and believed what he was preaching. Remember the word of the actor who said, "Actors talk of imaginary things as though they are real, and the trouble with preaching is that too many preachers talk about real things as though they were imaginary."

Pastoral preaching must be prophetic in the best sense of the word, challenging, concrete, speaking out for God, cost what it may. Dr. W. A. Hatcher in his lovely old book, *The Trail of the Friendly Years*, tells how as a boy he was taken to the funeral of one of those early Baptist pastors in Virginia who was put in jail for preaching the Gospel. They held the lad up so he could look in the casket and see the folded hands of that old man of God who had been in jail for his faith. There were scars on those hands, for when he preached through the barred windows, evil men had gone up and slashed at the hands that were holding forth the Word of Life. He said, "I never forgot those hands for that man bore on his body the marks of the Lord Jesus." Our preaching must be worthy of that tradition and heritage.

Preaching today should be challenging. It must call for action. It may be a call to come forward for a confession of faith. It may be to go out and do something or be something. Jesus said, "Come, follow me." The disciples early said, "Repent, be baptized." Ours is a gospel that calls for action. Not long ago a Methodist minister when he was installed in his pulpit said to his people, "Preaching is meant to instruct, inspire, move and stir the will and often to accuse. It is not to be enjoyed." So he warned his people not to expect always to enjoy his preaching. His state paper spoke about that in the next issue and said that it frequently happens that the congregation asks for a change of preachers for the very reason that the pastor is preaching exactly the kind of sermons they ought to hear, for good sermons and good preaching is something not to be enjoyed, but to produce Christian conscience and Christian character. There are times, of course, when a sermon should be comforting but rare is the occasion when it should be comfortable. "So here is a fair test of good preaching," the paper says. "Does it pry open any minds or produce Christian conduct? Is it aimed at enlarging the sympathies of the congregation? Do the people who listen have to think in order to follow? Is any sinner made restless about his sin? For, says this editor, "A truly Christian sermon makes as heavy a demand upon the listeners as it does upon the preacher, both to think and to act."

Our sermons should be evangelistic, for we preach "good news" of salvation to sinful men. Sometimes the message will be directed primarily to sinners, but always in the sermon should be the good news of forgiveness and redemption through faith in the Living Christ. There should always be something in the sermon to call a sinner to repentance and to remind the saint of how great is his salvation. There should always be the note of concern for the lost that will win the lost and send the saved out in turn to win others because they have found for themselves that precious truth in Christ that changes all of life. Your own preaching should always be evangelistic, as it leads the lost to the Saviour and enlists the saved in the continuing work of the church and the Kingdom.

The sermon must be backed by the preacher's life, else our preaching is in vain. We may not be able to say with Paul, "The things you have seen and heard in me, these things do," but certainly we should strive with God's help to be worthy witnesses of the Gospel we are privileged to proclaim. You know that old verse that says,

I had rather see a sermon than hear one any day.
I had rather one would walk with me than merely point the way
The eyes are better pupils and more willing than the ear
Fine counsel is confusing but example, always clear.
The best of all the preachers are the men who live their creeds,
For to see the good in action is what everybody needs.
I'll soon learn to do it if you'll let me see it done.
I can watch your hands in action, but your tongue too fast may run.
While the sermons you deliver may be very wise and true,
Yet, I'd rather learn my lesson by observing what you do.
For I may not understand you and the fine advice you give,
But there's no misunderstanding how you act and how you live.

Last, but far from least, all of our sermons should be Christ centered. We are called to preach Christ, to reveal Christ with all his meaning for each life and for the life of our day, and to lead men to accept Christ as Saviour and Lord, Saviour meaning what he can do for them, and Lord meaning what they can do for him. Do you remember the tribute paid to one great man of God? Two men heard him preach and afterward one said to the other, "What do you think of him?" The other answered, "I'm not sure yet what I think of him, but I think a whole lot more of his Lord since I heard him preach." God grant that may be true when we preach. Of course, we cannot do all these things by ourselves. Thank God the same one who said, "Go ye into all the world and preach," also said, "Lo, I am with you always." I hope some day you can be in Boston and stand before the statue of Phillips Brooks. To me it is the most meaningful of all the statues of a preacher that I have ever seen. Phillips Brooks, great preacher, is portrayed there for all the city to see. He stands preaching in his pulpit. Behind him is another figure with his hand on Brooks' shoulder. It is the figure of the Christ he preached and you can almost hear him speaking, sometimes to say, "Easy now," and sometimes, "Go on, go on," but always to say, "I am with you." God grant that may be true of your preaching and mine as we stand before the people God has entrusted to our care. ✒

Preaching with Purpose and Power

It has been a joy and a privilege for me to be with you this week. I certainly want to thank Dr. McCall, Dr. Barnette, Dr. Weatherspoon, and the faculty committee that gave me this privilege. I want to thank you students and faculty who have made it so easy for me this week just to stand and talk with you out of my heart about the things that concern us as pastors, especially as they relate to our preaching.

It is good to think about our preaching as pastors, and how it can be more effective. Sometimes I am afraid that it isn't as effective as it might be. I know one time I was riding in a club car on a train to Chicago. Next to me was a gentleman who had been drinking in the club car and for some time. On the other side of him was an Army officer. This rather inebriated gentleman turned to the Army officer first and said, "I wonder who in the world would ever marry that old battle-ax over there," and pointed to a WAC officer. The Army officer said, "Sir, that's my wife." Well, he didn't get anywhere on that side so he turned to me. He said, "Have you ever seen the movie, 'Going My Way'?" I said, "Yes, I saw it." He said, "You know that movie has done me more good than any ten sermons I ever heard." I laughed and told him I was a preacher and had enjoyed the movie, too. Now that he had failed on both sides, he went back to his drink in silence.

I told you that I asked my congregation at prayer meeting on two different Wednesday nights what makes a sermon good and what makes a sermon bad. We had an interesting time when we talked about what makes a sermon good, but when we talked about what makes a sermon bad it was interesting how all said rather apologetically, "Now, of course, this doesn't apply to the preaching in our church." They gave some very interesting comments, and I'm afraid that too many of them did apply to the preaching in our church, and now I want to share them with you.

When we got them started, they just poured out—almost faster than I could write them down. The first one said that the preaching is too long, over our heads.

A woman said, "It is too 'booky'." I said, "What do you mean by that?" She said, "It isn't illustrated; it isn't full of life."

Too much preaching lacks sincerity, rambles and doesn't follow a theme.

The preacher puts on airs and has too many mannerisms, uses too many big words.

Delivery is poor, not distinct; he doesn't speak loud enough—and immediately some of them spoke up and said that some preachers talk too loud.

He repeats his poems and his illustrations too often.

He doesn't fill my spiritual hunger; I go away unfilled.

Not challenging to my thinking; doesn't challenge me to action. It isn't prophetic.

The preacher has too many prejudices that are evident in his preaching.

He is too wordy, too fluent—more length than depth. (You can think about that for a long time.)

He is just too nice; people want fearless preaching.

Too much entertainment.

Preacher doesn't practice what he preaches.

One good lady went on and wrote me a letter, a very thoughtful one. She said, "The sermons I like best are the ones that give me some definite truth to think about as I eat my solitary Sunday dinner and perhaps sometimes to argue about mentally. I like to find a personal lesson I can remember and try to apply to my life, that is a message for me. I like facts; I like to be informed. A sermon is good if it sticks to one's heart, if it deepens and enriches one's faith. The hearer must be listening and alert for that sentence, that illustration that is just for him or her." That is, the preacher and the listener must work together to make the sermon good.

Now, how can we help the preacher and the listener to work together? I think sometimes our preaching is ineffective because we lack purpose. We don't know just what our purpose is in that particular sermon. I remember in Seminary we had a very plain-spoken gentleman who taught us speech. One day one of the boys was giving a practice sermon. When he finished, he just stood at the pulpit and the professor said not a word. Finally, the silence was almost unbearable. The boy finally leaned over the pulpit and said to the professor, "Will it do?" The old professor said, "Do what?"

Now in those two words were the very basic philosophy of preaching. What is the purpose of your sermons? Many a time when I have been struggling to get the sermon outline, I stop and say to myself, "What is my purpose? What is the point of this sermon?" If I write that down I find I have the outline for the message. But if you don't have a definite purpose and are not clear as to the point you are trying to make, how in the world will the congregation ever get it. If we are to preach with purpose and with power then, we have to remember that you and I must know the purpose and then remember that it is "Not by might nor by power, but by my Spirit, saith the Lord."

Our churches make preaching central in our services. We know that we have a message that will save those that believe. "Christ, the power of God and the wisdom of God." "The word of the cross"—to them that perish, foolishness, but unto us who are saved, the power of God to change life and make it vital and worthwhile. It is the difference between life and death.

Once in Florida I went to Silver Springs and remembering that daily theme we were talking about, I came away with an unforgettable experience. I went down in the bottom of a little boat on the crystal clear water and looked out through a window in the side. There I saw the beautiful world in which a fish lives—sparkling water and light above, gleaming sand at the bottom, lacy bits of green floating about, a beautiful sight as the sun reflects on the water. It is a beautiful world. I came away knowing the difference between fishing for fish and fishing for men. When you fish for fish you take them from a beautiful life to death. When you fish for men, you take them from death to a beautiful life.

That is the gospel we preach; let us never forget it. It is a life-saving, life-changing message, the assurance that Christ is the Savior of the world and the hope of mankind; the message of the church as a fellowship of believers; God's call to righteousness in life and service; the message of a kingdom that will come, backed by the power of the eternal God.

All through the Old Testament and the New, and on down through the centuries, you see men defy that power of the eternal God and lose. You have seen other men stand by it and trust it and win! Dr. J. H. Rushbrooke, secretary and later president of the Baptist World Alliance, used to love to tell of one Estaonian pastor who, when the Russians came in and took over his country, steadfastly refused to cooperate with them. They sent for him time after time and tried to get him to betray his people and work with their conquerors. He steadfastly refused. Finally one day they gave him an ultimatum and said, "Now you are going to cooperate with us or else. What is your answer?" He refused again in the words of Martin Luther, "God help me. I can do no other." Very scornfully, the Communist leader said, "God can't help you." But God did—miraculously he was delivered from the hands of the Communists and today he still ministers to his congregation in another land where all were saved.

God can help you and me if our purpose is to save those for whom Christ died and advance His kingdom and glorify His name. As Paul told the Corinthians, "It pleased God by the foolishness of the preaching to save them that believe." It is your responsibility and mine to see that it isn't any more foolish than necessary. As we try to sum up today, I want to enlarge on what was said yesterday and give some factors that are essential if our preaching is to be not foolish but fruitful and compelling.

I am not going to tell you how many today. I made that mistake yesterday. I told you I was going to give you twelve qualities of good preaching, and when I got to the twelfth you jotted it down and closed your books and closed your minds. Just remember that rarely ever say, "In conclusion," or "Finally, Brethren." Stop while your listeners' minds are still open but don't go past too many good stopping places. I'll try and practice what I preach about that today. You keep an open mind, and I'll keep my eye on my watch because my plane goes at 12:30 and I am not going to miss it.

First, if our preaching is not to be foolish, it must be inspired by the Spirit of God and given by men who are called of God. Otherwise, it may be beautiful, talented and polished, but it will be mechanical, lifeless, and futile. Over and over again you and I need to say, "Lord, speak to me, that I may speak in living echoes of Thy tone."

Second, our preaching is going to be largely foolishness unless it is rooted in the Word of God. Remember, we are to preach from the Word. We are to say, "Thus saith the Lord." One of the secrets of Billy Graham's power in preaching is his constant use of one phrase, "The Bible says." Ours will be the voice of authority only as it is backed with an authority greater than our own. Our listeners must feel that when they hear us they have heard "A man sent from God." You will remember that was the way they felt about Charles Wesley. Once in one of the villages where he was to preach some rowdies organized a little riot in advance. They were going to throw him out of town. Some of those who were going to share in it worked their way up through the crowd toward Wesley with their stones and their clubs in their hands. Then, one by one, they dropped them as Wesley preached. When it was all over one turned to another and said, "You know, there's a man, a man like God." It is foolish to preach unless somehow people feel that they have heard the word of God and been in the presence of God.

But how can we bring about that result? How can we help people feel that we are really bringing God's message to them?

Something happened to me more than a quarter of a century ago that I want to share with you today. It illustrates this fact that it is foolish to preach unless your preaching grows out of life, out of the problems and needs and the desperate concerns of those to whom we preach. Remember, there is no real learning except in answer to a question that is already recognized. My youngest son, home from college one time, listened to his father preach once again. He said one night when we got home, "You know Dad, one of the troubles with your preaching is that you don't ask enough questions." I wasn't practicing what I am preaching now. Before you have been preaching very long people in the congregation should be saying to themselves, "You know, that troubles me, that puzzles me. I'm glad he is talking about that. I wonder what the answer to that is." If the question isn't there, you must state it for them until they realize that it is a real problem. When they are asking the question or facing up to a problem that was already real, then you bring all the resources of God's Word and Christian experience to bear on the problem or answer the question. That is true whether it is topical preaching or expository preaching. You begin with people where they are and then you bring to them all the resources and truth you can muster.

I learned that from Harry Emerson Fosdick more than twenty-five years ago. It may not be the approach for every sermon, but it will color all your preaching, so far as method is concerned. In my early days I came across a little pamphlet by Dr. Fosdick, a reprint of a magazine article on "What Is Wrong With Preaching." I have kept it all through the years and still read it from time to time. It is all marked up and some of those marked paragraphs I want to share with you this morning. "No body of tricks," he says, "can make a preacher. But if I were to pick out one simple method that would come nearer to making a preacher than any other, it would be this: Every sermon should have for its main business the solving of some problem, a vital important problem, puzzling minds, burdening consciences, distracting lives. Within a paragraph or two after a sermon is started, wide areas of any congregation ought to be recognizing that the preacher is tackling something of vital concern to them. He is handling a subject they are troubled about, or a way of living they have dangerously experimented with, or an experience that has bewildered them, or a sin that has come perilously near to wrecking them, or an ideal they have been trying to make real, or a need they have not known how to meet. One way or another, they should see that he is engaged in a serious and practical endeavor to state fairly a problem which actually deals with their lives and then to throw what light on it he can."

"What all the great writers of Scripture were interested in was human living, and the modern preacher who honors them should start with that, should clearly visualize some real need, perplexity, sin, or desire in his auditors and then should throw on the problem all the light he can find in the Scripture or anywhere else. No matter what one's theory about the Bible is, this is the effective approach to preaching. The Bible is a search light, not so much intended to be looked at as to be thrown upon a shadowed spot."

"That insight into contemporary human problems which almost all preachers use in thinking about the practical applications at the end of their sermons might do some good if it were used instead at the beginning of their sermons. Let them not end but start with thinking of their auditors' vital needs, and then let the whole sermon be organized about their constructive endeavor to meet those needs."

You know so often in our preaching you and I will preach along and then at the end we will say, "and now for the practical application," but by that time your congregation is already gone, mentally. If you begin with the practical problem and apply to it all the resources you can muster, you will have them thinking with you all the way.

Dr. Fosdick goes on to say, "The future, I think, belongs to a type of sermon which can best be described as an adventure in cooperative thinking between the preacher and his congregation. The impression made by such preaching is felt by anyone who runs into it. The preacher takes hold of a real problem in our lives, and, stating it better than we could state it, goes on to deal with it fairly, frankly, helpfully. The result is inevitable—he makes us think. We may agree with him or disagree with him, but we must follow him. He is dealing with something vital to us and so he makes us think with him even though we may have planned a far more somnolent use of the sermon time.

"Every problem that the preacher faces thus leads back to one basic question: How well does he understand the thoughts and lives of his people? That he should know his Gospel goes without saying, but he may know it ever so well and yet fail to get it within reaching distance of anybody unless he intimately understands people and cares more than he cares for anything else what is happening inside of them. Preaching is wrestling with individuals over questions of life and death and until that idea of it commands a preacher's mind and method, eloquence will avail him little and theology not at all."

How well do you know your people? This is one reason why a good pastor can be a good preacher—because he knows people. He shares their joys and their sorrows, he has been in their homes in times of happiness and times of pain and agony. His young people have come and shared with him their questions and their desires and their problems. The older people come to talk about their loneliness and their fears. He brings to the congregation that he knows so well the comforting and challenging Gospel of Jesus Christ. As they face their day and time he faces it with them and his preaching comes to grips with their lives and their needs. Preaching is foolish unless it comes to grips with life today as people have to face it.

I remember a bishop one time speaking with the utmost scorn of a chaplain he met on a preaching mission who, while men were literally going to hell all around him, was sitting in his tent writing a monograph on the folklore of Borneo.

Jesus came preaching a gospel for life. He said, "The Spirit of the Lord is upon me. He has anointed me to preach the gospel to the poor, to heal the brokenhearted, to preach deliverance to the captives and recovery of sight to the blind, to set at liberty them that are bruised and to proclaim the acceptable year of the Lord." No wonder the common people heard him gladly because he faced life as they faced it but with all the power of the eternal God and the assurance that power could be their strength and stay.

As James Russell Lowell has written:

Men! whose boast it is that ye
Come of fathers brave and free,

If there breathe on earth a slave,
Are ye truly free and brave?
If ye do not feel the chain
When it works a brother's pain,
Are ye not base slaves indeed,
Slaves unworthy to be freed!

Is true freedom but to break
Fetters for our own dear sake,
And, with leathern hearts, forget
That we owe mankind a debt?
No! True freedom is to share
All the chains our brothers wear,
And, with heart and hand, to be
Earnest to make others free!

They are slaves who fear to speak
For the fallen and the weak;
They are slaves who will not choose
Hatred, scoffing and abuse,
Rather than in silence shrink
From the truth they needs must think:
They are slaves who dare not be
In the right with two or three.

What then is the purpose of your preaching? Does your preaching issue an action? Is it not "foolishness" to preach unless something happens? It may be to bring a sinner to the front or to send the saints out to serve, but you should be preaching for a verdict.

My father came home one time from a trial. He was trying to win a certain lawyer to Christ and so he spent the day with him in a courtroom. Father came home telling how the lawyer won his case, but how, at noon as they ate lunch Father said, "How are you coming?" The lawyer said, "Well, I've got ten of them. There are still two on the jury I have to win over. I am going to work on those two this afternoon." He did and won a unanimous verdict. He was working for a verdict.

You and I have to preach with a purpose and power that will move men to decision and action. Someone has well said, "It isn't our job just to be always talking about doctrine, but to do something grand and hard" and to lead others to want to do it, too.

What a challenge we face. In one of our midwestern cities a friend of mine stood on the street corner talking to a young communist leader in that community. This young communist leader said to my friend, "We American Communists are going to lick you American Christians yet." He challenged him to win that city. The victory will go to those who really care and who come to grips with the needs of the people and the life of their day with all the power of the living God.

I once had the privilege of having tea with a group of people at the home of Lord and Lady Astor in England. As we talked to Lady Astor about the reforms she had made possible for her constituency, she said, "You know, social changes do not come because the mass of people want them, but because a few people have a vision and care enough to pay the price to make their dreams come true." Is such a spirit and purpose evident in your preaching?

It is foolishness then to preach unless lives are changed because it is changed people that are going to change the world. And you and I have the gospel that will change them as we preach the Christ who can save the lost and use them in his church and kingdom. That word *lost* is one we perhaps do not use as much as we should. Yet the lost are all around us. I remember one time sitting with a group of preachers listening to Dr. F. P. Taylor of Indiana. He said, "There is a lost word in our vocabulary." We said, "What in the world is that?" He said, "It is the old Quaker word 'concern'." Then he explained what he meant. "We are so involved in the mechanics of running a church and in denominational promotion that we have lost the concern that Jesus had for the souls and lives of men, a moving concern for the lost. When you stand in your pulpit, let your hearers sense your concern and they will respond to it."

Do you remember the story of the young minister who spoke to an older one and said, "Sir, I am greatly troubled because not many people come forward when I preach. I would like to have someone coming to Christ at every service, but they don't." The older preacher said, "Well, do you expect them to come at every service?" The boy said, "Oh, no." "Well," he said, "that's why they don't come." Let them sense your concern.

Such a concern was felt by one of our missionaries in Japan when she wrote home and said, "I am troubled because there are no shoes at my door." That meant she had no visitors coming as inquirers, who would leave their shoes at the door as they entered. She looked at herself and asked why. A few months later she wrote home a happy note to say, "There are shoes at my door." People came because they knew she cared. They will sense the concern in your preaching and respond if and when you really care.

Dr. J. J. Wicker is one of the grand old men of Virginia Baptists. He tells about one time he was conducting a tour to Europe for two or three months. He had arranged to preach in a church in Brooklyn before he sailed and to preach there on the way back. When John Wicker preached, he really preached, and always with a concern for the lost. At the close of the service he extended an invitation to anyone to come forward who wanted to accept Christ as Savior and Lord and to begin a new life. One man came down the aisle. As Dr. Wicker grasped his hand, one of the leaders of the church came to say, "Dr. Wicker, don't take that man in the church." "Why not?" "He is a hopeless drunkard; there is nothing you can do about him. He will be drunk before the day is over. As a matter of fact, this is the first time I have seen him sober in a long time." So Dr. Wicker dismissed the congregation and called a meeting of the deacons. Dr. Wicker was convinced of the sincerity of the conversion and he said to the deacons, "Well, if he stays sober until next Sunday, will you take him in?" "No, by some miracle he might stay sober a week." "Well, if he stays sober a month, will you take him in?" "No, he would surely get drunk again and that would hurt the church." Dr. Wicker said, "Well, I'm going to Europe, and I'll be back to preach for you nearly three months from now. If he stays sober that length of time, will you take him in?" They thought they were safe on that basis, and they said, "Yes, if he stays sober until you get back, we'll take him in." Dr Wicker tells how he came walking up the street to that church on that Sunday months later and the first man he saw was the convert. He held out his hand and said, "Preacher, today I get in." Because the preacher cared, God could speak through him the message that can change lives, change the life of the world around them.

It is foolish to preach unless you build up the church. If you preach just to build yourself up it is foolish indeed. If that is the case, people will join the preacher instead of joining the church. But you are to build up the fellowship of believers as they come to believe because of your preaching. In your ministry build the believers into the life of the church and send them out to share in the world mission the Lord Christ has entrusted to us.

Thank goodness we send them out, not in our own strength but backed by the power of the living God. My father taught me that when he was a pastor in Worcester, Massachusetts. The church was in the center of the city, and you could see it from all the hills around about. It was in the day when it was the style to put a lighted, revolving cross on the tower of the church. They did this there and that lighted cross could be seen from all over the city. One night all the lights in Worcester went out, but the cross kept on burning and turning. Some crossed themselves and others scratched their heads and wondered why. Father talked to the electrician that erected the cross the next day and said, "How on earth did that happen, that when all other lights were out, the cross was still lighted and moving?" The electrician said, "That's easy. In downtown Worcester we have two kinds of electric lines. One is the light line and the other is the power line for motors. Because the cross was run by a motor we put it on the power line and it had both light and power when the light line failed."

Thank God the cross is on the power line. There is light, radiance, power enough for all. When folks find a new life at the foot of the cross, they go out with the assurance, "My grace is sufficient for thee for my strength is made perfect in weakness." "I can do all things through Christ who strengthens me."

Preaching is foolishness, too, unless it is backed by the lives of the believers. Your congregation can cancel out much of what you say unless it is backed by their lives. They can go out as living epistles known and read of men to take the message far beyond those who can hear your voice. They, too, are preaching a gospel and writing one day after day by the things they do and the words they say.

It is foolishness, too, unless it is demonstrated in the life of the preacher. It made me sad to hear someone say about a preacher the other day, "It doesn't make any difference what that fellow says, it doesn't carry any weight because of the way he lives." Rather I like the tribute of the man who having heard John Erskine preach said, "Forever after he never thought of God but that the thought of John Erskine was not far away."

> Not only in the words you say,
> Nor in the deeds expressed
> But in the most unconscious way
> Is Christ by you confessed.

For 'twas not the truth you taught,
To you so clear, to me so dim,
But when you came to me, you brought
A deeper sense of Him.

And from your eyes He beckons me,
And from your heart His love is shed.
Until I lose all sight of you,
And see the Christ instead.

We preach then to save the lost; we preach to change men; we preach to build up the church, to advance the kingdom, to strengthen our world mission, and to challenge the powers of evil and unrighteousness anywhere in the world in the name and by the power of the living God. Your congregation will catch that spirit, that sense of the power of the Eternal, and that sense of devotion to duty if it is in you, not just in your words, nor in your voice, but in spirit and in truth.

I once went as a student to speak in a little church for a Sunday afternoon service. As I got off the train and walked up to the village church that morning I could hear the pastor preaching a block away. I went in and sat on the back row and my ears literally rang. I said, "I'll never do it like that." That is not the kind of power I am talking about.

Rather it is the power you find in the life of Lucius Cursius, who was sent by the Romans as an ambassador to their enemies at Carthage. After he had delivered an ultimatum, to the horror of the Carthaginians, he walked over and held his right hand in a burning fire until the hand was gone. Then he turned to an amazed crowd and said, "I did that so you would know we mean what we say. There is not a man among us who would not give both his hands gladly rather than submit to your tyranny."

Ah, but who is sufficient for these things. "Not by might, nor by power, but by my Spirit, saith the Lord." We go not by ourselves but with Him who promised, "Lo, I am with you always."

I once heard Dr. George Buttrick tell of a man who came to his study one day very much excited. He said, "Pastor, I have just had a horrible experience. You know I am called to witness against those gangsters who are coming up to trial next week. Two men came to my place of business today and said, 'Come with us. We are going to take you for a ride.' They took me out to a lonely spot and said, 'Now either you are going to promise to leave town or not testify or you die right here. What have you got to say?' He thought and prayed a minute and said, 'Well, all I have to say is, whatever you are going to do, make it quick'. " Dr. Buttrick said, "Well, what happened?" He answered, "They talked among themselves a while and then said, 'Get back in the car.' To my amazement they dropped me right near the church and I just came in to ask you to have a prayer with me to thank God that I am alive." The pastor said, "Well, tell me, how do you account for that. When your very life was at stake you did what you knew was right." He said, "I guess it was because I couldn't fail the Lord Christ." The pastor said, "That's only half of it. You couldn't fail the Lord Jesus Christ and He couldn't fail you." May that always be true of your preaching and your ministry as you are privileged to preach the Word in His name, by His power, for His glory. ✑

Henry Grady Davis

When Henry Grady Davis delivered the Mullins Lectures in 1962, he was professor of homiletics at Chicago Lutheran Seminary. Dr. Davis was known through his widely-used book, *Design For Preaching.* The theme of his Mullins Lectures was "Reappraisals of Preaching." The oral qualities of Professor Davis's lectures are preserved here. This is the first publication of the 1961-1962 Mullins Lectures.

The Personal Word

As I rise to speak to you about the work of preaching in our day, I hope that you share with me in believing that the minister of the gospel is a man under the call of God to preach the word of God. That is what every serious writer about the work of preaching is saying today in one way or another: that genuine preaching, Christian preaching, is a form of the work of God. They do not all mean the same thing by those words, certainly, but they are all saying them. And, in fact, there is a great deal of theological realism once more in the doctrine of the word of God, as it is affirmed by biblical scholars and developed by systematic theologians.

It will be my purpose to take this doctrine seriously, and try to see what difference it makes to the preacher, if it is God's word he has to preach. That appears to be what we believe, or try to believe, or think we ought to believe. Is it what we actually believe and act on when we preach? Or is it what we try to make other people think we believe? This phrase, "the word" or even "the word of God" is always on our lips, especially when we talk about preaching. There is a danger that we may speak it much too often and much too casually. It may become a pious cliché, a kind of slang which we speak without thinking whether we mean it or not.

What do we mean when we speak of the word of God? Let me put that question in another way, a way that may test us more severely. What does God mean when he says "my word"? Perhaps I offend you when I suggest that we may be using such words without meaning them or really thinking about them. Perhaps I shock you still more when I suggest that possibly we do not believe them.

Since our concern is with preaching, let me put this question in still another way. Does the preaching that we do from week to week unmistakably reflect our conviction that what we are dealing with is God's word and not our own? Did last Sunday's sermon reflect that conviction, and if so how? Did the people who heard it get that impression?

I ask this question, first, because I am really concerned but a little skeptical about the answer. A merely verbal answer is no good. If we pay lip service to a high doctrine of the word but belie it by using the pulpit to advance our own ideas and purposes, we are hypocrites, and we are taking the holy name of God in vain.

But, secondly, I ask the question because as a student and teacher of preaching I have to ask it. If preaching is the word of man it is one thing; if it is the word of God it is something entirely different. If preaching is the best knowledge and wisdom, the highest hopes and aspirations of mankind, it can be done in certain ways. But if it is the judgment and promise of God, the wisdom and love of God, then it has to be done in other ways appropriate to its own nature. And if preaching is a thing of such transcendent nature, then its study should begin with this almost incredible fact, and not with lesser concerns.

Let us put ourselves reverently before this biblical concept of the word of God, take it seriously, and consider what it implies. It means that God is not something but Somebody, somebody who is himself and not a projection of ourselves. That first. If there is no personal God, it is absurd to talk about a word of God. Only a person can speak a word, and there can be no true word that is not a personal word. It means that God has a mind of his own which is not my mind and not the collective mind of mankind, but is face to face with each of us and all of us together, as one person is face to face with another. It means that he has a selfhood, a character and integrity of his own, a will, an intention, a purpose of his own, not the same as ours, with which we can be in conflict even when we think we are in the right.

The concept of God's word means that God is sufficiently unlike us to have something to say to us that only he can say, that we cannot say for ourselves or for him. It means also that we are enough like him that he can express his mind to us, and that he wishes to do so. The speaking of a word is the act of a person towards another person. A word requires a hearer as well as a speaker. A word pronounced in solitude where there is no ear to hear is not a word in the true sense. The act of hearing is also necessary to make it a genuine word, that is an expression and commitment of one person to another. A true word, the word of a person of integrity, is a faithful expression of his mind and will and a commitment of himself and all he is. But a word does not become that kind of communication of person with person until it is heard for what it is, and believed because of what the speaker is.

If this is true in our dealings with one another, how much more is it true of God's word! The word of God, if that is not an empty phrase, is nothing less than God's commitment of himself to those to whom he speaks. But it does not fulfill its purpose as a word to any man until it is heard as God himself so speaking and so committing himself. The preacher of the word must take this into account. However earnestly God may be wishing to speak to his creature, however the Holy Spirit may be striving, however Christ may be pleading by his blood, the creature, be he preacher or listener, is not compelled against his will to hear God speaking to him, or to identify the word as God's word. Yet the purpose of preaching is that both preacher and listener may so hear, so identify the word, and rely on it in faith. And the preaching is good or bad to the degree that it is or is not conducive to that kind of hearing, not some other kind. If we take seriously the biblical language about the word of God, we must always re-examine our work and ourselves. We must constantly reappraise our calling and our task.

To call it God's word is to say that it belongs to him alone and not to us, that it is his word and not ours, that we may hear him speak but cannot make him speak, that we may by the gift of his Spirit hear what he has to say to us, but cannot by any gift whatsoever make him say what we think he ought to say. God's word is personal. It is the word of creative power, the word of redemptive and re-creative power. It is this because it is his word, his power. But this can be said only of a word that God himself is heard speaking. Therefore, in the deepest sense, only God can speak his word, the word that breaks the power of sin, and cancels fear and fruit, and conquers death and hell, and unites men with Christ in his death and resurrection, and bestows on men the life eternal that is in Christ. And anything that does less than this ought not to be called the word of God.

I am not afraid that we shall stop talking about a personal God, or even about a personal word of God, for that matter. I am afraid we may fall into the habit of talking all too easily and chummily and glibly about God and his word, without feeling the awesome implications of what we say, and then go about our lives and work, and especially about our preaching, as if the whole thing were just so much pious talk.

In both the Old and the New Testaments, the word of God is God speaking; it is not some man talking about God. It is God speaking and acting, for in him there is no contradiction and no division between what he says and what he does. His acting and speaking are one. He speaks in his acts, and he explains his acts in human words through human beings. His deed is his word and his word is his deed, from his feeding of the birds of the air, all the way up to his deed in Jesus Christ his Son, and back to his present deed in the believer. It is all one, and it is all his word.

It is necessary that we get this before us with the utmost clarity to begin with, if we are to be faithful to our calling to preach his word. It is necessary that we discipline ourselves by keeping the reality constantly before us, doing our work in its light, appraising our motives and results according to it alone. It is necessary because we are prone to trust ourselves and our accomplishments more than we trust his word. It is necessary because of the ambiguity of the human condition to which God speaks his deed and acts his word in Jesus Christ.

To show what I mean, let me go into some particulars which have to do with the way we think of preaching. I have said, for example, that the word of God is not a man talking about God, but God talking for himself. I do not think we can safely ignore that distinction for a single minute, or minimize it in the least. I think it is disregarded by many preachers, even in conservative churches like yours and mine. For this means that talking about God, however correctly and devoutly, is not necessarily preaching the word of God. Much less is there any certainty that when we talk about religion we are preaching the word. Religion is what we think and how we feel and what we do about God, but God's word is what he thinks and how he feels and what he does about us.

The human situation is such that of course we have to talk about God to preach at all. But woe to us, if there is not in our preaching something else besides talk about God. It is in this dilemma between the necessity of human speech and the greater necessity of letting God speak, that we have to preach and think about preaching.

Human speech is necessary, for there is no other. We are finite creatures in a material world. We know nothing except what is learned by interpreting the data derived through our five senses. We have to learn from what we see and hear. We have no faculty or instrument for picking up thought-waves directly from the mind of God. If we are to hear him, he must needs condescend in mercy to disclose his mind and heart to us through persons and things we can see and hear. And we on our part, if we are to hear him, must needs hear and recognize his voice and his mind and heart as they come to us through persons and things we can see and hear.

Thus, if any human being is to hear God speaking to him, he must hear through another human being, or many others, speaking the language of men, which is the only channel of communication open to us. This is just as true when one reads the Bible as when one hears the voice of a living person. We have the words of Isaiah in our eyes and ears. We hear him saying, "Thus saith the Lord." But Isaiah's saying "Thus says the Lord" is not what makes it God's word, is it? That too is Isaiah's word. It neither makes his message God's word nor proves that it is in fact God's word.

Thus we affirm that the Bible is God's written word. But that affirmation is our word about the Bible. Man's affirmation does not make the Bible God's word, does not prove it to be God's word. If it is God's word, it is that whether we say so or not. If it were not God's word, our saying so would not make it so.

We have Isaiah's words, and we have the words of the Christian community, in our eyes and ears. Without these human words we could not have the word of God. But we do not have God's word in our eyes and ears. Our eyes and ears cannot prove it God's word and not man's word. The personal word God speaks to us can come through human words, but it can be heard as God speaking to us only by faith and in faith. And this faith in which we hear God speaking personally to us is not something of which we are capable in ourselves at will. When we do not hear him, it is because we do not believe that it is he who speaks. We can at will refuse to believe. But when we do hear him speaking to us we know at once that the hearing of faith as well as the speaking is by his gracious gift—not without us, certainly, not by overriding our will, but not without him either.

Can we agree about this? If we can agree, even in general, let us try to see how this applies to preaching. The human situation seems to call for something like the pattern which we reproduce Sunday after Sunday in our churches, namely, a man in a pulpit speaking and the people in the pews looking to us and listening. How shall we understand this ritual or liturgical practice? Not that the act of getting into a pulpit and delivering a sermon is the only way in which the Christian community fulfills its calling to preach and teach God's word. But it is an important way, and it is the way with which we are concerned in our hours together.

One thing is certain: the people are going to hear a man speaking. They are going to hear their minister's words, thoughts, hopes and fears, ideals and prejudices. There can be no preaching without that. It is to be hoped that he will always be a good man, well educated, wise, understanding, compassionate, sincere in his faith, blameless in his life, loving in his ways with people, for these qualities can illumine and reinforce his words, while their lack can vitiate them.

But that is not the question. The primary question is whether the people will hear anybody besides the preacher, or will hear only a man talking. If Somebody other than he is the really important speaker, that sets an entirely new standard and furnishes quite different criteria for the value of the sermon. In that case, the decisive thing is not the sermon's quality as the self-expression of a good, religious man. The decisive thing is the sermon's quality as a medium through which the voice of that Other may be heard.

Now, I do not think there ever was a time when the deep instinct of the Christian church would not have said "Amen" to what I am now saying. But I think there has been a period in church history, including America in the nineteenth century and up to about 1930, when homiletical literature, for the most part but with a few notable exceptions, did treat of preaching primarily as the self-expression of a good man, and shaped its theory and practice accordingly.

That theory of preaching centered almost exclusively in the man in the pulpit, the individual preacher, as man, as scholar and teacher, as believer, as man of personal charm and power, as prophet and man of vision, and so on. It looked at him ideally, saw him as a paragon, a hero fighting the Lord's battle singlehanded. It saw him as a religious virtuoso, who had overcome all difficulties and solved all problems, and could from his wealth of wisdom and experience meet the needs of those who heard him. He was to be like a Moses to the people around him.

The most conspicuous exponents of this school of preaching were indeed great individuals. They were prima donnas of the pulpit. Thousands flocked to hear a man. They built up tremendous followings, disciples of their own. But when they died, most of their work vanished with them, because it had centered in the man.

Such a view of the work of preaching and of the functions of the preacher has to be critically reappraised in our day. The trouble is not that it emphasized too much the importance of the man in the pulpit, for it would be hard indeed to do that. The trouble is that it centered too exclusively in the preacher as an individual. This ideal view of the preacher, whatever it may have been in days gone by, is unrealistic in our situation for several reasons. It is unrealistic sociologically. The minister no longer plays or can play such an unique role in his community either outside or inside the church. Nor can he deserve to play it. He is no longer the most highly educated man in his immediate group. And he is not the infallible repository of knowledge and wisdom he would have to be to play that role. Not even Moses was that.

The theory is theologically wrong in two respects. First, it practically ignores the church, the Christian community which produced the preacher, from within which only can he speak. His work is not grounded in the church but in himself, and so it does not last. Secondly, and more to the point of this lecture, this concentration of attention on the man in the pulpit as a person is not appropriate, if the personal word is not his but from beyond him, if he is only its servant and not its master, if it is a word to him also and not from him, if before that word both he and we must bow together, if the transaction here is not merely a transaction between him and the people. The preacher is not God, and if we hear nothing but a preacher, we are not hearing God's personal word to us.

The situation is similar with respect to the church. If we are to hear the personal word of God at all, we must hear it through the church. We must hear it as the Christian community's word, but not simply the community's word. When we speak of the community of believers, we have to think not only of the people who make up this or that organized church or all the churches of our time. We have to think of the continuous tradition of faith through all the centuries, the countless thousands who have borne their witness, from the time of Jesus down to our own fathers and mothers. If we cannot or will not hear God speaking to us in the voice of the community of faith, we shall never hear him at all. Moreover, without the voice of the church we have no dependable assurance that what we think we hear is indeed the word.

Yet the word of God must never be thought of as strictly identical with the word of the institutional church. It is hardly possible to avoid hearing the voice of the community. Indeed, the minister is always in danger of being only an organization man. Then his preaching will be essentially sales talk, propaganda, the company line about its product, as it were. The danger is so great as to call for deep and continuous soul-searching by both the man in the pulpit and the people in the pews. For the word of God is greater than the church. It is not subject to the church's judgment, but the church is under its judgment. It is not subservient to the community's interests, but is the command and promise of him in whose will alone lies the church's peace and the world's peace too.

One thing more must be mentioned. If we are to hear God speaking a personal word to us, we must hear him speaking in the Bible. But the Bible is not God, and if we hear nothing but an ancient, venerable, holy book speaking, we are not hearing God's personal word to us.

We must hear the Bible, because the Bible is given by him who gives all good things. It is not only a message from heaven; it is also a messenger in the biblical sense, and *aggelos*, an angel. We must not worship the Bible any more than we should worship any other angel. But we must hear the Bible, because without it we have no reliable attestation to God's word, no dependable record of his deed in Christ, no standard of judgment by which to test the scattered imaginations of our proud hearts.

But it is not enough to praise the Bible, or to defend it against its detractors, or to study it as if it were a divinely authoritative encyclopedia of historical and scientific information—which it never claimed to be.

It is not enough to praise the Bible. We must hear it, and when we preach we must let Christ's people hear it. And we must hear it not as the voice of antiquity, but as a voice saying not only what is old but what is new as well. We must hear it freshly. We must listen to it, expecting to hear the voice of One who has a mind of his own which is not our mind, a purpose that is not our purpose, who is actively and earnestly engaged in the desperate struggles and agonies of our time.

Then and only then, when we listen this way, shall we hear the word as a personal word and also as a contemporary word. But that is tomorrow's concern. Sufficient unto this day must be the evil or the good of what I have tried to say. ᘰ

The Contemporary Word

> God who at many times and in various ways spoke of old to
> our fathers by the prophets, has in these last days spoken to
> us by a Son, whom he appointed the heir of all things,
> through whom also he created the world. He reflects the
> glory of God and bears the stamp of his nature, upholding
> the universe by the word of power (Hebrews 1:1-3,
> translation composite).

I begin with these opening sentences of the Epistle to the Hebrews
because they so vividly express and so exultantly celebrate the good
news that the personal word of God is also a contemporary word, that
the God who spoke of old and far away speaks here and now as well,
that he who spoke to the fathers speaks to us, and that his speaking
then and now is one speaking, one word. It is indeed a personal word,
spelled out in the flesh of a man, but a man who "reflects the glory of
God and bears the very stamp of his nature." And it is indeed the
always present word which created the world and still upholds the
universe by its power. There are so many other glorious things in this
passage that we are in danger of overlooking this here-and-now-ness
of the gospel. But if we miss that, we miss the gospel too.

Many New Testament scholars believe that this Epistle to the
Hebrews is itself a specimen of the preaching done by Christ's
witnesses in the first century of the church's life. Surely there could be
no better lesson in homiletics than to note how this preacher heard the
word of God speaking in his immediate time and place and let it speak
also by his voice and brain. This is what the preacher of God's word is
called to do at any time and in any place, namely, to hear God's
contemporary word speaking in the very middle of his time and place
and give it his brain and voice.

At this point you may possibly be finding fault with my exegesis.
Ah, you say, but it was easy for this preacher. He spoke at a time when
the deed of God in Christ was contemporary in fact, chronologically. If
he had not himself seen the face and heard the voice of Jesus and
witnessed the resurrected presence with his own eyes, he had most
probably met some other person who had. You may argue that since
this is not the case with us, we cannot possibly hear God speaking in

the present tense as he did. You may also point out that this preacher was mistaken when he called his time "these last days," that the centuries of chance and change change all that, raise doubts about his whole point of view, and make it impossible for us to preach as he preached.

Yes, I think we can argue ourselves out from under the pressure of this early preacher's example, if we want to. But I think we shall be using very doubtful theology when we do so. We affirm that God did verily speak to men and through men of old, a long, long time ago. We can believe that. We have to believe that, if we believe in the word of God in any real sense. And we confidently expect that at the last day (if it ever gets here) God will again speak to men, to all men and all angels this time, so as to be heard and recognized. Yes, we can believe that, and to believe that he is God we *must* believe that he will finally speak for himself and be heard. These are articles of the Christian faith and we can give them our intellectual assent.

Moreover, as Christians we believe, teach, and confess that once, at a time datable on any earthly calendar, between a Thursday and a Monday, at one particular place of all earth's places, God performed his given word and spoke his redemptive deed in Jesus Christ once for all, that is, at one time for every time, in one man for every man, in one only Son to make all men his sons.

This we confess in the church and with the church of Jesus Christ. We cannot take in its mystery with our imaginations, of course. We cannot explain it. We cannot prove it. That's not the question. The question is, can we trust it? And after that the question is, can we preach it? Can we trust it enough to preach it, believing that it is what we have to preach and all we have to preach? It *is* the gospel, the Christian kerygma, is it not? Can we trust that it is enough to preach this gospel? Or must we now, in these our own last times, have some other gospel alongside of this one, if not instead of this gospel?

I do not think that these are rhetorical questions or impertinent questions by any means. The answers are not automatic, like a tape recording always ready to play back. I am a teacher of homiletics, and I have genuine sympathy with students who say that surely preaching the gospel must be something besides an endless and monotonous repetition of the verbal formulas of the kerygma. They are right, of course. Preaching is not that simple or that easy. It has to be faithful to the written word to be preaching at all. But the preaching of the gospel never was a dutiful or slavish repetition of theological formulations of any kind, however orthodox or biblically correct. Sometimes a man can be so careful to square everything he says with the right authorities that he never gets anything of his own said at all. And whatever else preaching is, it is also the personal and full-hearted utterance of a sincere man. Unless it is that, preaching is not an honest act, much less a personal one.

One thing is certain, however. The New Testament never confuses the act of preaching with the word preached. We sometimes do confuse them, partly because of an ambiguity in the King James translation of 1 Corinthians 1:21. "The foolishness of preaching" is not the foolishness of the act of preaching. It is the apparent foolishness and weakness of what we preach, namely, Christ and him crucified.

But the New Testament never asserts that the act of preaching has power to redeem and save mankind, or that the man who preaches well will have that power. It says that such power belongs to the gospel itself, not to the man who preaches it, and certainly these two things, but Paul kept the distinction between them straight and clear.

The power belongs to the gospel. And the gospel is not an impersonal something, say a body of doctrines, something abstract, something that comes from God but is not God. The gospel is not a system of formulated propositions to which we subscribe and for which we argue, such as the incarnation, plus the virgin birth, plus the resurrection, and so on. I hope you will not misunderstand me at this point, and I dare to believe you will not. I am not saying that we can have the gospel without these doctrines, for I do not believe with Bultmann that we can. What I am trying to say is that these doctrines are not Christ, but are confessional assertions about Christ, assertions that we make. But our confession does not make Christ, and the gospel is Christ himself, and what God does in Christ today as in every day. That and that only—not what we believe but what God does—that and that only is "the power of God unto salvation to everyone who believes."

Let me put it as simply as I can, and even then it will not be simple, for it is the mystery of God in Christ. We are creatures of time, of the past and its memories, of history. Being what we are, we cannot step out of time to see God in his eternity that knows no time. For our sakes he put his redemptive deed in time, that we might see it and live. That is why it happened between a certain Thursday and Monday.

But the deed of God is not confined to a time and place. The dying love of Christ and the power of his resurrection are here today in this place where we are sitting, exactly as much as they were there on Calvary that Good Friday and in the garden on that first Easter. That is what the once-for-all-ness of God's deed means. It is only our limitations as children of time that require us to speak of that event as long ago and far away. It is as close to us as God the Holy Spirit.

Thus it is that the gospel is contemporary in every age and in every place. The personal word of the Lord speaks always in the present tense. It is the business of the preacher to be aware of this fact and to do his own speaking accordingly. But it seems to me that preachers in our time are not passionately concerned about this fact, for they too seldom preach as if they counted on it.

Am I wrong? If so, why do we think we have to put up such a heroic struggle to make the gospel relevant to the people of our modern age? That's the way the saying goes, is it not? "We have to make the gospel relevant." *We* have to?—we have to *make?*—we have to make the *gospel?—relevant?*

Is that a Christian theory of preaching? What do we mean when we say that we have to make the gospel relevant? What we imply is clear enough. We imply that of course the gospel is not relevant until we experts do something to it. And what is it we have to do to the gospel to make it relevant? The gospel as God makes it is either relevant to modern people or it is not relevant, is either the wisdom and power of God or it is not. If it is not relevant, you and I are not going to make it relevant. Let's get that straight. We can't do better than God; we just think we can.

What can we possibly do to the gospel? We can of course fail to see its relevance, because we fail to see the facts of the human condition, the sin and guilt that make it relevant, the folly and peril that make it our only hope. We can fail to see the gospel's relevance. Or we can try to refit the gospel to the world's wisdom, the world's preferences, to reshape God's foolishness and weakness to the wisdom and power of men. Thus we shall make the gospel irrelevant. We can do that.

We can by God's Spirit do something else instead. We can *see* the gospel's relevance to ourselves, the people in the pews, in the towns and suburbs of America, and in all areas of this frightened world. Once we have seen its relevance for ourselves, we can learn how to spell it out in the concrete particulars of contemporary human existence. The agonizing details are not new. They still come in the same old categories between birth and death: "the cares and riches and pleasures of life, and the lusts of other things." It is to these that the word still speaks. Our call is to let it speak pointedly and plainly, not to improve its accent. If this is what we mean when we talk about making the gospel relevant, the words make sense. But I am skeptical.

All this I have said about the gospel must be said concerning the Bible whose center is the gospel. We are loud in our insistence that the Bible is God's written word, but we sometimes talk and act as if we were afraid it may not be. Why are we so sensitive about the honor and good name of holy scripture, so quick to bristle at the faintest hint of question, so smug and flattered when some important outsider condescends to speak a good word for the poor old Bible? Why are we so defensive and apologetic about it? Why do we suppose that we have to make it relevant, too, have to make it presentable, perform some sort of facelifting operation upon scripture so as to make it respectable and acceptable to the people of our time? All this does not indicate that we trust it very much. If we were this hyper-sensitive about our wives, they would not believe that we either trusted or loved them.

What is it we are afraid of? Are we, after all, afraid that God spoke in the scriptures only once, or long ago and far away, but does not speak in them to people any more? But how, then, do you and I hear his word? Are we not also modern people, children of a scientific age? Are we afraid that God is an ancient deity, but not our contemporary? What do we mean when we speak of getting "back to God"? Back where? To some previous period in intellectual and cultural history, perhaps? And we have to go back there to get to God?

What is it we suppose? Why are we so determined, when we get in the pulpit, to do all the talking and explaining. and so reluctant to let the text speak for itself? Do we think that God *will* not speak for himself in the words of this text? Or is it that we fear he *cannot*, cannot speak to the smart men and women out there, that only we can speak to them?

Let us look at that a moment. Can *we* speak to them? That's the most doubtful assumption of all. All our anxious concern over the frustrating problems of communication, the treacherous character of language, semantics—all this shows that we can *not* speak to our contemporaries in general. We cannot speak to them in terms of our own religious ideas and beliefs, which do not make sense to them. Do we think that since we cannot talk to them, God certainly cannot? Is it possible that the Holy Spirit really does speak only in an outmoded language, and that he too is ignorant of semantics? Maybe he needs to go to some good up to date school of communications and learn how to talk to sophisticated folks like us!

I have made the questions sound as absurd as I could, in the hope that their very absurdity might expose the deep unconscious mistrust of God that often lurks below the surface of our profession of faith, our congenital trust in ourselves, and the way we project on him our own pitiful futility and frustrations. I hope you can pardon the absurdity and profit by the disclosure.

However, it is the preaching that I hear, from both students and ministers, that raises the questions in my mind. What I have to say is not an indictment of the men who preach, but of a *way* of preaching, a kind of preaching that is based on an untenable theory of what preaching is and how it is to be done. The theory and practice have become traditional, especially in America. We were brought up in it.

What is this way of preaching? It is a speech about religious ideas and practices, about some theological question perhaps, maybe even about the Bible of God or Jesus, certainly about us, some ethical or moral issue, some personal problem or possibility. It is a man talking about such things.

He may take a text, or rather quote a text more or less remotely connected with the thing he has in mind. Then he either drops it or makes it mean what he wants it to mean, or what he thinks it ought to mean, or what he thinks it would be good for us to think that it means. If he makes any real use of the text at all, he tries his best to make it seem to say what he wants to say. He will not discipline himself to listen to what the text actually says. He has not studied it hard enough or closely enough to know what it is saying. Too often he does not know how to study it, and he resists all efforts of exegetes and biblical scholars to show him how to study it. He is too busy. Besides, he thinks he already knows what he has to say, or knows where he can get it secondhand, cheaply.

The method makes it unlikely that the man will ever speak a word that is not his or some others man's word. If God ever speaks his own mind through this kind of preaching, it will have to be done in spite of the man. That happens, too, of course. If it did not, the church would have perished from the earth long ago.

But if, as we believe, God in Christ is present here in the church service, if he is now speaking to us for himself by his Spirit, giving his own command and making his personal promise, and if he is doing this in the text of holy scripture, then preaching is a different thing entirely, and it has to be done in a very different way. We have to reconsider the whole theory and practice of preaching. We have to find a way of preaching that is more compatible with the belief that, though God's speaking is mediated by scripture, the church's witness, and the audible voice of a man in the pulpit, it is still he who speaks the word of life, and speaks it personally to very human ear that will hear.

The difference this must make with regard to the sermon's text is clear enough. The text is not simply a striking quotation from an ancient and holy book. It is not just a piece of wisdom or prudence. It is not an impersonal truth in the abstract. The text is not merely a general principle or proposition that can be grasped and used with profit. That's what the text is in the other kind of preaching.

The preacher's function is not to validate the text and then draw from it timely lessons and admonitions. It is the preacher's business to put the text in the middle of life, where he and his people are living, and let it speak for itself to both him and them together. He is to hear what it is saying to him and them alike in the total complex of their lives, not just their experience in church. As he hears, he is to translate what it says into the language and experience of common life, language and experience familiar to everybody, and let it do its proper work, in the people to whom God speaks it.

Where this kind of preaching is done faithfully, surprising things happen in our age exactly as in all others. The text validates itself. It proves that it can speak relevantly even if we cannot. The personal word gets heard. Of course it gets heard by many who have ears but will not hear, but that is nothing new, is it? It gets despised and rejected of men, but that's not a particularly modern phenomenon either, if I read my Bible correctly. But God's word gets heard in faith, too, and yields its harvest.

The most wonderful thing ever said about preaching can be said about this kind of preaching, and about no other kind. You probably have read or heard it. It is this: that the preaching of the gospel is itself part of God's deed in Christ, an event in the redeeming work of God in

Christ. That is to say, that the death and resurrection of Jesus Christ and their being preached next Sunday in your pulpit, are parts of the same act of that love with which God so loved the world.

It means that he "who died and, behold, he lives," the Son to whom it is given "to have life in himself," the Word who was with God and was God, the Word that still upholds the universe—it means that he is not only the word here and now, but also, himself, the preacher of that word today.

It is to serve this inconceivable mystery, nothing less, that the man in the pulpit is called. ℞

The Individual and Community

Today we must reconsider the individual and community. It is a very hackneyed subject. Everybody is talking about the community. Everybody is saying that we simply must do something about it. Nobody seems to be doing much about it that is constructive or promising. I propose that today we refrain from talking about what we should do and can do about the problem of community, and try to listen seriously and freshly, as if we had never heard it before, to some of the biblical speech about it.

We should be forewarned that it will not be easy either to hear and understand what the biblical word is saying, or to see what it implies as to the character of our existence. In all our traditional ways of thinking, the individual is a self-existent and self-contained being, apart from every other self, over against every other person, and also over against his community.

But that is simply not the way the Bible sees him. We do not get this idea of man from the Bible. We get it from the philosophy and psychology that have developed in the Western world since the Renaissance. The biblical word is that "No one of us lives to himself, and no man dies to himself." John Donne had it right in that much quoted passage of his "Devotions," that "No man is an island," and so on. It sounds very wonderful and we quote it? And why do we quote it? Is it because we feel intuitively that it is saying something true and important about us, which we ought to feel and wish we could feel, something we have lost?

But John Donne is a good way back in time, closer to the Renaissance than to us. And I think we do not feel this way about ourselves, either the way the Bible talks about us, or the way John Donne felt and talked, at least sometimes. I think that, on the contrary, we feel that every one of us lives and dies in the solitude of his estrangement, in the loneliness and lostness of his private anguish or ecstasy. That is, of course, a neurotic delusion, if the biblical word about us is true. But I think we live in it just the same.

Let us begin with the highest thing, therefore the most exacting and difficult thing. Let us begin with the New Testament's picture of the mystery of our existence as Christians. The phrase, which we all know how to repeat, is "Life in Christ." It sounds good, very pious, and we all say it. But what do we mean by it? When a very intelligent high school student asks, "How can I live in Christ?", what can we say to him? There is hardly any point of reference anywhere in our ordinary thinking about ourselves to which we can connect the concept of one person living in another.

Yet such phrases are everywhere in the New Testament, especially in the letters of Paul. "It is no longer I who live, but Christ who lives in me" (Galatians 2:20). "For me to live is Christ" (Phil. 1:21). Does this mean only that Paul was a very religious man? Does he mean what he says, or does he not know how to say what he means? Inability to express himself was not one of Paul's conspicuous failings! What had become of this determined Jew from Tarsus?

One way to dodge the issue raised by these words is to say that they are highly figurative words, that this is just a metaphor Paul is using, a symbol of the reality and closeness of his faith relation to Christ, not to be taken in any literal sense. They are rhetoric, hyperbole, poetic exaggeration. But this is dodging the issue, is it not? If this is only a figure pointing to an inexpressible reality, can we suppose that the reality is less than the figure? Must we not suppose that the reality of Paul's existence in Christ and Christ's life in Paul is greater and more real than the figure he used to describe it, and not something less than the figure?

Another way to account for this fantastic language is to suppose that the idea of life in union with Christ is special with Paul. It expresses something unique in Paul's experience, and does not apply to Christians in general. It is Paul's "Christ mysticism," a way of thinking that is half philosophy and half religious psychology, and quite peculiar to Paul's personality. He felt himself to be "a man in Christ," but that is not expected of an ordinary Christian like you and me.

We can dispose of the whole business in that way. Having got it labeled as "Paul's Christ mysticism," we can put it in its proper place in our intellectual filing system, and it need not bother us any more. Are you satisfied to let it go at that? I am not. I might do it if such ideas were confined to Paul's letters, but they are not. The whole New Testament is full of them.

To save time, let me first state it in general words, as a thesis. From first to last, the whole New Testament's picture of our Christian existence is the picture of a corporate existence, not an existence as independent individuals. It is the picture of an existence in which no person can be a Christian in himself alone. No man can be a Christian except in vital union with Christ, and no man can be in union with Christ without being in vital union with all other persons who are in union with Christ.

We have no time together in which to reread the whole New Testament in support of this thesis. Yet if it is true, we shall have to restudy the whole New Testament in its light before we can interpret it or preach properly on its most important texts. Until we do, we shall go on trying to put its message in terms of an individualistic philosophy that cannot convey its message, the gospel.

We cannot reread the New Testament today. But we can begin to look more closely at two or three other images it makes use of to describe our life in relation first to Christ himself, and then to one another.

There is the image of the vine and branches. It does not belong to Paul's Christ mysticism, but to the words of Jesus himself as reported in the fifteenth chapter of the Gospel of John. "I am the vine, you are the branches. He who abides in me, and I in him, he it is that bears much fruit, for apart from me you can do nothing. If a man does not abide in me, he is cast forth as a branch and withers; and the branches are gathered, thrown into the fire and burned."

That's a pretty basic condition for existence as a Christian, is it not? Here it is not simply a question of fruit. It is a question of life as well as fruit. The life is the vine's life. It is never the branch's life, never exists in the branch apart from the vine. The life is Christ's life, never mine. I live only because Christ's life is in me, and only so long as I am joined to him. The Christian lives only by sharing Christ's life along with the other branches, and he shares that life only so long as he is organically united with Christ. When detached, he withers, because he has no life of his own. This "apart from me you can do nothing" is quite explicit. "Apart from me"—not "apart from the vine the branch can do nothing," but "apart from me, you can do nothing."

How are we going to preach a text like that? Shall we explain that the Lord was exaggerating for effect, that his figure was overdrawn and perhaps misleading, suggesting more than he intended? Shall we imply that the great teacher's choice of an illustration was not a perfectly happy one at this point? And shall we then proceed to reduce the mystery of life in Christ to something obvious? Shall we explain that when Jesus said, "abide in me," he meant in his truth, in his teachings, or in his way, the way of ethical and religious rectitude? This is what has been preached from the text a thousand times.

But it is not so simple and reasonable as that. We cannot explain the New Testament by reduction and simplification at this point, without running into its sharp opposing words at a dozen other places where they cannot be simplified. This Jesus, who here calls himself the vine, did not say, "I teach you the truth in which you are to live." He said, "I *am* the truth." He did not say, "I show you the way." He said, "I *am* the way." He did not say, "Do as I tell you, and you will have life." He said, "I *am* the life."

How shall we explain that in a few words to our intelligent high school student? And what if the simple and reasonable explanation is always a false explanation? What if every person's existence is a mystery of Christ, a mystical union with Christ, even yours and mine, so that none of us can live outside of this mystery? What then? Are we so audacious as to promise people life eternal on terms we think more reasonable than those God provides by his deed in Christ? And dare we offer the cheap substitute in Christ's name? How do we preach this text, or do we?

This as regards the union of every individual believer with his Lord. The New Testament is far more profuse in its images of the corporate existence of all believers together in the Lord. Some of them we, in our inveterate individualism, habitually overlook. Others we have, in my opinion, misinterpreted. But there are so many of them, and they are so striking, that I need only to recall them to your attention, I am sure.

There is the house which is not a temple. Let us take it first because it too is not in Paul. It is in First Peter (2:4, 5). That house begins with a stone like no stone ever seen, for it has life in it, it is a "living stone." It rises as many dead stones become living stones by being joined to him. It ends as a house like no other house, a spiritual house that is also a royal priesthood, a chosen race, a holy nation. What has become of the individual stones here? The priesthood pertains to the structure, not to the individual stones separately. There are not as many priesthoods as there are stones. There is only one priesthood, and we do not have to guess whom that belongs to.

Paul also describes our joint existence in Christ under the figure of a household, a building, a temple. Always the point is that Christians together comprise one household, one building, one temple. Translations do not always make this clear. Indeed, the dominant individualism of Western language as well as thought has made it difficult to translate these passages into modern English, and has resulted in frequent ambiguity and occasional mistranslation. One trouble is that north of the Mason-Dixon line American English has no second person plural, no way to say "you all." To many people it is by no means clear why an individual person must sometimes be spoken to as part of a "you all." Yet without a sense of "you-all-ness" it is impossible to understand what Paul is saying.

For example, in the third chapter of his first letter, Paul says to the Christians at Corinth, "Do you not know that you are God's temple and that God's Spirit dwells in you? . . . God's temple is holy, and that temple you are." This is the Revised Standard Version, and it is a correct rendering of the Greek, except that the "you are" is ambiguous. It is plural, *este,* "you all are." And "God's temple" is singular, *naos theou,* not many temples but one temple: "You all together are God's one temple."

The English of King James' time could and did not make this distinction, "ye are" not "thou art" God's temple. Moffatt, Goodspeed, and the New English Bible are necessarily ambiguous, as the Revised Standard is. Phillips misinterprets it, making the temple plural and saying something the Greek does not say, "Don't you realize that you yourselves are temples of God . . . . God's temples are holy." But this is the voice of Western individualism, not the voice of the New Testament. The picture here is not a lot of little temples all over the place. The New Testament knows only one temple. It says to Christians, "You all together as one in Christ are something no one of you could be in his apartness. You are God's temple, and that temple is holy; God's Spirit dwells in it."

Why make so much of this point and this one short text? Because even so short a text makes clear a basic New Testament concept of Christian existence as a corporate existence together in Christ, not a private affair between God and the solitary individual in his separation and estrangement from other persons. It is a thought very hard for us to take in, but we cannot understand or rightly interpret the New Testament without it.

The figure of a living body is of course the one most frequently used in the New Testament to describe our life together in Christ, and the most explicit one, it seems to me. Surely I need not belabor its interpretation. I only ask you to remember that it and all the others say the same thing, and say it concerning every one of us. They do not point to our duties and possibilities as individuals apart from one another. Nor do they merely point to a doctrine of the church as the body of Christ. They are talking about something more fundamental than that, about the nature of our very existence, and they assert with one voice that we exist together as one and not as many apart, that we live because the life of God in his Son is in us too, by the mystery of our union with him—a union created by his act of uniting himself with us. They assert that we have this life, not each for himself, but all together in a corporate body in which he lives, and that apart from this body we do not live but die.

Now, this is community. This is community as God intends it and creates it, if the biblical word about it is his word. This is the community that has not been created by us, and will not be created by us, by our feelings and attitudes and behavior. We may deny it, reject it, shame it, spurn it, disgrace it, profane it. But we shall not create it. Each of us will find himself and inherit the blessing it has for him, in that moment when he recognizes with joyful thanksgiving that God's community lies all around him, and that Christ put him there.

Now it may well be that this is not what we have in mind when we talk about community. It may be that we are thinking about something much less than this, something less mysterious, more reasonable, and more attainable. So we think, perhaps. But on the contrary, it may be that this is the only kind of community that is attainable, that we cannot possibly have a genuine community on any lesser terms than these. It may be that the choice is between God's kind of community and no community at all.

How shall we preach this mystery of existence? Just here, it seems to me, we are in grave danger of misinterpreting the Bible. Let me call attention to the astounding, almost incredible manner of biblical speech about this community, this oneness of us all and oneness with Christ. The New Testament makes two statements about it and that must stagger our imaginations and tax our belief. The first is that this corporate unity includes and transcends all human differences whatsoever, no matter how fundamental those differences may seem.

The second is that his corporate unity actually exists now on this earth, in spite of all evidence to the contrary.

Let us take the last first. In the language of the New Testament this community exists. The word does not say that we ought to be a community of this kind. It declares that we are that community. The word does not call us to become a community. It does not set this corporate existence before us as an ideal, as a goal to be striven for and reached, so far as we are able here and now, but really only in heaven, perhaps. That is the way we talk about it, and I fear that is about the only way we preach—in the imperative mode: "We ought to be as one"; or in the conditional mode: "It would be wonderful, if we were as one."

But that is not the way the Bible talks about it. The word of God speaks in the indicative mode. It speaks of this corporate existence not as the ideal but as the basic reality, not as the goal but the starting point. It calls us to begin by recognizing that we exist as one.

We shall have to read our texts very carefully if we are to get this straight and keep it straight, because it does stagger our imagination and tax our belief. For example, I do not know how it is in your seminary, but I know how it is in mine and some others. Most of the attention is centered on the contrary evidence, resulting in more or less constant complaint. It runs as follows: "Here in this favorable situation we ought to have a real Christian community, a *koinonia*, a genuine fellowship of love and mutual helpfulness, but we have no such thing. Why don't we have *koinonia*? Whose fault is it?"

I think the seminary campus is a picture in miniature of our world and our world's disastrous mistake. It is of course a flat contradiction of what God says to us. God says to a community of believers like yours or mine, "You are not an aggregation of self-contained and solitary individuals; you are one body of life, Christ's body." We say, "Maybe we ought to be that, but we certainly are not." Likewise, God says to all the people of all races on earth, "You are one creation, one blood." But we answer, "That may be a beautiful ideal, but it is quite impractical; we are hopelessly divided."

The trouble, you see, is that the reality God's word proclaims as a fact overtaxes our belief. You may yourself be asking, "How on earth can we start with such community as a given fact in spite of the evidence? We might suppose that it was easier for a first century Christian like Paul to think this way than it is for us. Is that so? The most explicit and detailed description of life in the body of Christ is in First Corinthians. And to whom is Paul talking there? To a community that exemplified the unity he was describing? Quite the contrary, as you well know. This was a very community whose divisions and bickerings and partisan strife we know the most about. Yet to them Paul does not say "You ought to be one body in Christ and every one members one of another." He says, "Now you are the body of Christ and individually members of it." Dare we preach this as Paul preached it?

The New Testament's second assertion about our community in Christ is that it includes and reconciles and transcends all human differences, however basic those differences may be. The word does not ignore the existence of differences of their basic character. It looks at them realistically. There they are, big differences and little differences. There are big differences that set the divisions of mankind over against each other sharply. The Jew is not a Greek, the slave is not a free man, the male is not a female. The significance of the assertion lies exactly in that the differences are real.

It is good news that, nevertheless, there is a unity of existence, divine existence and human existence, in the divine and human Son of God, by whom all things were made, whose power upholds the universe. There is a unity of existence, divine and human, that is greater than the quite fundamental differences between slave and free man, Jew and Gentile, and even male and female. The unity shows itself precisely in that it includes the people of both sides of the wall. It reconciles them so that the wall is no longer a barrier. It needs and uses all differences in the structure and functioning of the one body of life. The unity exists in spite of the differences, it is true. But perhaps it is more accurate to say that it exists through the differences and because of them.

The divine-human body of life becomes a unity by incorporating and using all differences for the upbuilding of the whole. And the measure of that unity is the measure of all mankind as created by God and under his hand. Jew or Gentile is not the measure of mankind. Male or female is not the measure. A race or a nation or an ecclesiastical community is not the measure of mankind under God. The whole is vastly greater than the sum of all its parts. Without the whole, the part has either no meaning or a false meaning.

It is the same with respect to the little differences among people very much alike, in the same home, neighborhood, or tribe. The individual is not the measure of his group. Together we are something no one of us is or can be apart. Indeed, only within the community and through the shared gifts of the community, can one become a real person, a self in the true sense. Apart from the community, you and I would not possess its corporate experience and accumulated knowledge, its clothes, tools, language and all the thought-stuff that goes with language. Only in community can we have such things. Apart from the community, we are not even human. Everything that marks us as definitely human is a corporate possession which we can receive only in community and use only in community.

I must stop here, though we have caught only a faint glimpse of the radical reappraisal of ourselves and our world which this truth demands. Least I be misunderstood and tagged as a collectivist of some kind, let me call attention to one thing more. An unrealistic and distorted individualism has not made us strong enough to resist the subtle encroachment of new collective tyrannies, of which communism is one demonic form, but not the only one. We face the danger that while rejoicing to feel saved as individuals, we may be judged and destroyed in the mass. And in every mass failure, it is the individual that suffers first and last.

The gospel of the unity of life does not destroy or submerge the individual. It makes him possible. It and it only promises him his final emancipation from all tyrannies and his inheritance of eternal life. So I must leave you with a question not to be answered with words, but surely to be answered by all of us in our work from now on. How shall we preach the gospel of community? I shall not try to provide you with the answer to that question. If I did try, you ought to set me down as a fake. ℞

The Moment of Recognition

Everything I have been saying about preaching up to now implies that the proclamation of the gospel, the word of God, is a special and in fact a unique function. It calls for a special kind of speaking that is appropriate to its nature. Preaching is not a monologue by the man in the pulpit. The speaking of the divine word, the personal and contemporary word, is a dialogue between the Lord and anyone who will hear him. In this communication the preacher must remain primarily a hearer, even in the act of speaking the word. The preaching and hearing of the word is an interaction between the Lord and the persons in the pews, which the man in the pulpit must serve while being himself one of those who are acted upon.

Of course you have been asking how this is to be done, and you were quite right to be asking. You would be no use to the Lord if you were not asking. You would have every right to be impatient with a lot of tall talk about preaching that did not come to grips with the question of how it is to be done. I agree with you. We would stop short of our purpose here, if we did not get closer than we have yet done to the actual process by which a sermon comes into being.

Today we must consider the *how*. Of course we must realize that if preaching is what we have said it is, there can be no patented formula for it, and we must not expect one. It is part of any sound homiletical method to understand that the act of God in his word is not brought about by self-conscious effort, technical craft, or calculated skill. The work deserves the highest possible craft and skill, and to give less is to insult the Lord. But when you ask, "How can I do it?" in a very deep sense the answer has to be that you can't. But we must preach, and we must ask how.

How, then, does a real sermon, the kind we hope to preach, come into being? Let me put it as a proposition. Just because preaching is what it is, a genuine sermon is a thing given to the preacher, in the first place, a thing that comes to the preacher. And it comes characteristically in a moment that can best be described as a moment of recognition. A genuine sermon is more like something done to the preacher than like something he does, and it begins in a moment of hearing the word as if he had never heard it before, in a moment of vision, of seeing freshly, as if his eyes had suddenly been opened for the first time.

Now, if this is true, then the swift moment of receiving what is given, the act of hearing, vision, recognition, is not marginal or incidental in sermon preparation. It is the very essence of preaching, and it is the very first item of the *how* of preaching. It is the first prerequisite to sound work on any given text or sermon. The most fatal technical error you could make is to forget it or go to work on your sermon as if it were not so. It is this moment of recognition that I ask you to consider today.

I want to talk about this moment of recognition. I want you to hear descriptions of this moment by workers in different fields who have experienced it, so as to get a better picture of what it is and how it happens. I want to try to show why it requires exactly that unique operation of a man's powers that we should expect, if preaching is what we say it is.

We should not be surprised that the powers it requires are the human powers of mind and spirit that we all share, since we have no magical or supernatural powers to take their place. On the other hand, we should not be surprised that this process requires a higher activity of the mind, an act of the spirit that is more intense and swift and spontaneous than usual, like the so-called "creative" experience in which all art and science, all fresh and original works of the mind are born. Many reliable witnesses report that fresh discoveries take place in an unexplainable way, and in a moment that is commonly called a moment of creation, but which is more accurately described as a moment of recognition.

I am not forgetting the difference between the impersonal truth of science and the human truth of art, on the one hand, and the divinely personal word that must find voice in the preacher. I am saying that if the revelation of truth in science and art requires a special operation of the mind and spirit, much more does the revelation of the word of God require a special operation of the mind and spirit of the preacher. It is that operation and the moment in which it occurs, that we are concerned with today. Let us hear some evidence as to what it is.

A great many persons have spoken and written about this process. If you would like to study it for yourself, let me recommend the book from which I am drawing freely in this lecture. Its title is *The Creative Process*. It is a symposium edited by Brewster Ghiselin, published by the University of California Press in 1952, and as a Mentor paperback in 1955.

The poets and other literary men are, of course, the most articulate about this experience. But just to correct any mistaken notion that it belongs especially to them, I will start with a quite different example.

Henri Poincare is a great French mathematician who has made original contributions in the field. He describes a mathematical discovery that came to him suddenly. Please note that his is the kind of experience that does not come to anybody who has not prepared for it. It came to Poincare in the middle of a lifetime of intensive and devoted study, and after fifteen days of work on a certain problem that seemed to get nowhere. This is the way he tells it: "I went to spend a few days at the seaside and thought of something else. One morning, walking on the bluff, the idea came to me, with just the same characteristics of brevity, suddenness and immediate certainty" (*The Creative Process*, p. 37).

"It came to me." That's all he could say about the *how*. We can be certain that it would not have come without the concentrated and intelligent thinking that got him ready for it. It would not have come if he had not done his best to work it out for himself. But he did not work it out, it was given, suddenly it was there, it came, and he recognized it with immediate certainty.

This is the way your very best sermon will come. It will not come without your intense desire and sustained effort to hear, to see. It will not come without the thorough and intelligent and concentrated study that represents your own best attempt. But when it comes, it will come in an act of recognition, and afterwards you can only say, "It came to me."

Is this surprising? Is it the kind of thing that happens only to geniuses? Not at all. We all have these experiences about all sorts of things. In common life we say it: "How did you happen to think of that? And the only answer is, "Oh, it just came to me." And this is what the Old Testament prophet also said, is it not? "The word of the Lord came to me."

But let me stop talking while we listen to some other witnesses. Albert Einstein, with his characteristic reticence, has put it negatively. "He who can no longer pause to wonder and stand rapt in awe is as good as dead; his eyes are closed" (*Saturday Review*, March 4, 1961, p.

23). And this has its own profound implications concerning the possibility of fresh vision.

After Poincare and Einstein, perhaps we can afford to listen next to a literary person. I want to take Gertrude Stein first, because I am indebted to her for the title of this lecture. Whatever we may think of Gertrude Stein's own writings, we have to admit that she has encouraged and helped as many writers and artists as any person in this century. Here she is talking to a young writer about his own work, about writing, any writing, and about how it is done. These are as wise words and as true words as I know about writing, and, in my opinion, we could substitute preaching for writing, and they would be just as true. This is what she says:

> You will write, if you will write without thinking of the results in terms of a result, but think of the writing in terms of *discovery* . . . . It will come to you if it is there and if you will let it come, and if you have anything you will get a *sudden creative recognition*. You won't know how it was, even what it is, but it will be creation if it came out of the pen and out of you and not out of an architectural drawing of the thing you are doing (*The Creative Process*, pp. 159-60. Italics mine).

The temptation to talk about that remarkable statement and to apply it to preaching is almost irresistable. For preaching must be thought of in terms of discovery. The best sermon is a discovery by the preacher. It is not a rerun of a picture he saw a long time ago. It is something he is seeing now for the first time. And even when the moment of recognition comes, he will not yet know for sure what it is that has come, and he will find out only as he lets it come all the way through to the end. But if the preacher has anything, if it is there, it will come if he will let it come.

Here is F. Scott Fitzgerald telling how he wrote *This Side of Eternity*. Somebody asks "How long did it take you to write your book?" And he replies, "To write it—three months; to conceive it—three minutes; to collect the data in it—all my life" (*Saturday Review*, November 5, 1960).

I think this is true, and also hopeful. Three minutes to conceive what it takes three months to write and a lifetime to clothe with flesh and blood! Not bad! It means that if a sublime discovery does not occur every week, a single minute of recongition can furnish what it will take a month to write and perhaps three years to preach properly.

Here is Amy Lowell on how a poem gets born. "A common phrase among poets is, 'It came to me'. So hackneyed has this become that one learns to suppress the expression with care, but really it is the best description I know of the conscious arrival of a poem" (*The Creative Process*, p. 110).

I wonder if you would let me call Mary Wigman to the stand. Mary Wigman is a ballet dancer, and also a remarkably gifted choreographer with many original and highly imaginative dances to her credit. Here she is describing the process by which they are created:

> The fundamental idea of any creation arises in me or, rather, out of me as a completely independent dance theme. This theme, however primitive or obscure at first, already contains its own development and alone dictates its singular and logical sequence . . . . The theme calls for its own development (Ibid., pp. 78-79).

Before I comment on that, I want to put beside it a similar and illuminating remark by Jan Sibelius, the great composer of Finland. When asked if he could tell anything about how he composed those mighty symphonies and haunting tone poems, he said, "I am the slave of my themes and submit to their demands."

The significant work, be it dance or symphony or sermon, begins as a fundamental idea, or theme, that rises in one or out of one. It may be very primitive and obscure at first, but it is the fundamental idea, the theme, and it already contains its own development, and it dictates its proper form, sequence and outcome. And this is what Sibelius means by being a slave of his theme and submitting to its demands.

Now, those of you who read *Design For Preaching* will, I hope, see that this is exactly what I am trying to say and illustrate from beginning to end of that book. I did not steal it from Mary Wigman or Jan Sibelius, for I had not read their words when I wrote. I did know then that all significant works of the human mind are produced in this way and not some other way. But it is encouraging to hear so many diverse workers saying the same thing.

Here is another musician, one of the modern composers, Roger Sessions. He is describing the process by which a few basic musical ideas, notes, rhythms expand into an entire composition. But he might just as well be talking about how a few generative words and phrases expand into a sermon. He says:

> The composer "has an idea" . . . consisting of definite musical notes and rhythms, which will engender for him the momentum with which his musical thought proceeds. . . . The inspiration takes the form, however, not of a sudden flash of music, but a clearly envisaged impulse toward a certain goal for which the composer was obliged to strive. . . . This vision of the whole I should call the conception. For the musician this too takes the form of concrete musical materials—perceived, however, not in detail but in foreshortened form . . . . He is not so much conscious of his ideas as possessed by them (Ibid., p. 47ff).

We have asked how the preacher receives a word that is not his own, how he is possessed and used by it, how in a moment of recognition it comes to him as a germinal but yet unrealized thought, how it keeps on coming, one bit at a time, if he lets it, dictating its own shape, development, movement, and goal. We have asked how it can happen. And these people are trying their best to tell us how it does happen over and over again.

I have kept Robert Frost for the last witness, not only because his description of the process is one of the clearest, but also because I did know it and use it when I wrote *Design For Preaching*. Those words of his on page 163 were not put there to make pleasant reading. They were put there to show how a genuine sermon as well as a genuine poem comes into being. Today I should like to repeat those wise and illuminating words, and add some others from the same essay. And I think Robert Frost will not be offended if I use the word *sermon* where he says *poem* all the way through. Let me bear my personal witness that these words then give as accurate a description as I could possibly give of the way my best sermons have come into being.

Please pay close attention to Frost's words. "The figure a (sermon) makes. It begins in delight and ends in wisdom . . . . It begins in delight. . . . For me the initial delight is in the surprise of remembering something I didn't know I knew . . . . There is a glad recognition of the long lost, and the rest follows."

Let me pause here for a little commentary. If the making of a sermon differs from the making of a poem, the difference is at this point, and the thing that makes the difference is the text. But I am by no means sure there is a difference. There is a glad recognition of something in the text, too. This something that I recognize in the text, when I am ready for it, is something I feel I must always have known, but did not know I knew until now. The recognition is like a sudden remembering, and it comes as a surprise and a delight.

Now let us go on with Frost. "It begins in delight, it inclines to the impulse, it assumes direction with the first line laid down, it runs a course of lucky events . . . . Step by step the wonder of unexpected supply keeps growing." Here Frost is saying that the act of glad recognition, the wonder and surprise of something given, goes right on through the process of shaping a genuine poem. Truer words were never spoken about a genuine sermon.

Frost again: "It runs a course of lucky events, and ends in a clarification of life—not necessarily a great clarification, such as sects and cults are founded on, but in a momentary stay against confusion. It has denoument. It has an outcome that though unforeseen was predestined from the first image of the original mood—and indeed from the very mood.

"A (sermon) may be worked over once it is in being, but may not be worried into being. Its most precious quality will remain its having run itself and carried away the (preacher) with it . . . . It must be a revelation, or a series of revelations, as much for the (preacher) as for the (hearer)." (From Frost's introductory essay in his *Collected Poems*.)

I do not think I need to add anything to those words. I am not sure I can add anything important to them.

In this description of how a sermon comes into being, I have not for a minute forgotten our previous attempts to take the doctrine of the word of God seriously. Quite the contrary. It is the personal word of God, and the possibility that it may be spoken now through the preacher, that make necessary just this way of preaching and not some other.

For preaching is not telling, but being told. It is not a word going out from a man, but a word coming to a man and through him. It is not giving something, but sharing something that is given. It begins not in knowledge, but in vision, a kind of "inward beholding," as Samuel Taylor Coleridge called it. A true sermon is not a fabrication, but a discovery. It is not a creation, but, on man's part a recognition, and on God's part a revelation. Would we like it to be less?

Before I stop, let me say two things about this experience we have been discussing today. The first is that this is decidedly not an easier way of preparing and preaching sermons. It is not a magical trick or a supernatural gadget. It is not even a sermonic method, for any attempt to use it as a short-cut is foredoomed to fail. It is not a life-saver for a lazy man. It is not a substitute for hard, disciplined, prolonged and painstaking work with textual and exegetical helps, commentaries, theological and other books, and everything else that nurtures and instructs the mind and spirit. The sermon will not come without your working hard enough to have made it yourself. But it will come if you let it, and it will be better than the one you could have made.

The other thing I must say is that this experience of recognition is by all odds the most decisive factor in sermon preparation, or in any other original work. In the customary plodding, pedestrian, mediocre practice of sermon fabrication, it does not receive the attention it deserves. It is worth all the costly self-dedication it demands. It is worth more than all the other fussing over incidentals put together. It fits the situation in which we are called to preach a word that must first come to us, too.

And to you, called to preach to the vast body of people in your church, just as they are, let me assure you that God has something new as well as something old to say to them. I don't know what it is, and you don't yet know what it is. But if you can hear that word in the scriptures and preach it fresh as it comes, the Spirit's power will be in it, and it will do its work. 𝕎

Samuel H. Miller

Samuel H. Miller was dean of the Harvard Divinity School when he delivered the 1963 Mullins Lectures. Dr. Miller was the author of such well-known books as *The Great Realities*, *The Life of the Church*, and *The Life of the Soul*.

The theme for his Mullins Lectures was "The Minister's Workmanship." This is the first time these lectures have been published.

The Word of God—and Words

The minister is the servant of the Word. It is the Word which called him, brought him out of the world, plunged him into prayer, disclosed the heights and depths of his soul, stood him face to face with mercy and judgment, put a coal of fire on his tongue, and sent him down his days and nights unable to forget its glory and forever unsatisfied with his own testimony. He is its servant; of that there is no doubt; for he was born of its grace, but his feet will not be fast enough to proclaim its good news, his eyes will seldom catch more than a fleeting glimpse of its epiphanies, and his heart will often be too clumsy or too cluttered to hold the clear water of its eternal life. He will be the servant of the Word, but not because he is worthy of the high calling or adequate for its task; he has been taken into custody.

But the service is not without its danger. There is no place where a man's soul is more in jeopardy. Not because this is not a high and exalted destiny, for there is none higher. But simply because the strain of it creates a temptation few can resist, a temptation to multiply words at the expense of the Word. Because the Word is elusive, and cannot be regulated for public dispensing at ecclesiastically appointed hours, it becomes convenient to fill the void with the noise of sanctified garrulity. Because listening for God's Word implies a superhuman effort, it becomes more comfortable to hear the words men speak about the Word than it does to reach beyond limits for the Word only God can speak. Because the Word, when God speaks it, is so shattering, so radically destructive of our erstwhile comedy of pride and pretension, we prefer to take the job of revelation into our own hands and build the stately mansions of truth according to our own desires. Substitutes flow in from all sides; temptation rises from the very ground; custom and tradition commend the easier way, and ultimately the humble servant of the Word becomes merely the pompous butler. There is no silence left; no sanctity, no reverberation of the earth and sky, no shaking of foundations as when God speaks; there are simply talkative men, garrulous, loose-tongued, lip-flapping speel-masters, glib with God and giddy with gab. None fall so low as those who presume to speak the Word merely by mouthing words. This is a kind of disease, isolated and identified by the witty churchman, Geddes MacGregor, as logorhea. (The term is used by Geddes MacGregor in *From a Christian Ghetto.*)

Little wonder that words have become cheap in our day. They have been produced with a profligacy that confuses and bewilders all of us. Newspapers alone, manufactured daily over and over again, would defy the wildest fantasy if they were stacked up in one place. Add to that the incredible spate of books, the word-filled airways, and one wonders how, with so many words, any sense could be made of it all. It has gotten out of hand, like the sorcerer's apprentice. And with the mass of words, and the speed and turnover, the quality has suffered. Deadpan prose, machine-gun syntax, and sloppy non-thinking pervades a field orginally capable of mystery and magic.

Sermons have fallen under the influence of this undisciplined garrulity. Good words are all used, over and over again, the same way Beecher or Moody or Jowett used them. Listen to a thousand of them, wring out the real juice of the human problem freshly seen, and see if you have enough to fill an old-fashioned thimble. Hang them out to dry, and after a week see if there is anything left except the illustrations, and then check the laundry marks on them and see where they have been. The church in America could stop preaching tomorrow and the effect on human life and morals would be measurable only if you had a very strong magnifying glass to observe it.

I have said that the minister is the servant of the Word, and I have said that he becomes too easily the sluice of mere words. Between the two there is a vast gulf fixed. The Word is a great mystery. One may begin with words, man's speech, the shape of the breath, the image of thought, the bridge of breath between men, the web of meaning, like a constellation of stars hanging in the sky, the heights pointed and the depths heard—one may begin there with sound and sign, with things familiar and others only dreamed of, guessed at, hoped for, believed in; one may begin there with words like the labels of things, the substitute for experiences, the names to use for beck and call—one may begin there and work backward toward the origin of words in the Word, back toward the silence where there are no words because the Word itself is there, needing no speech, no sound, back toward the mystery where words begin to take shape out of the power and clarity and splendor of the Word. One will soon discover that the Word of which he is the servant is a word he cannot speak. It is God's Word, as deep as God himself, and filled with the terror of His mercy, brooded over with the bright wings of a tireless creation. Everything, from the tiniest shell to the heaviest star, echoes to its trills and thunder, yet there is none to speak it outright. The Word belongs to God, not to His world or even to man.

Yet, if the Word does not belong to man, man belongs to it. In a sense, he cannot live without it; it is woven into the warp and woof of his heart and mind, his very flesh and bone. His longings are rooted in it, reach for it, and live by it. His passion demands it, his hope expects it, his faith confirms it. His dreams are built of its largeness, his prayers come to his lips because his heart is haunted by it. The little souvenirs of every ephiphany are treasured because they are the signatures left in its passing. Even idolatry is the evidence of it, an evidence of clutching it too tightly. Man surely belongs to it, for the halo of its hunger marks every deed he does with a distant light and everything he handles with a glimmering wonder of a kingdom not yet born, waiting like dawn for the new sun to rise.

It was Rainer Maria Rilke who spoke so movingly of man's listening for the Word. In his terminology, the Word which pressed man on all sides, the principalities and powers, became the realm of the angels, those great winged beings who stood between God and man, moving swiftly eternally between the ultimate mystery and the intimacy of the spirit. They solicited the openness of man. The terror of this encounter, the magnitude and intensity of human action in such an event is described in the *Duino Elegies*:

> Hear, O my heart, as only
> saints have heard: heard till the grand call
> lifted them off the ground; yet they went impossibly
> on with their kneeling, in undistracted attention:
> so inherently hearers. Not that you could endure
> the voice of God—far from it (*Duino Elegies,* by
> Rainer Maria Rilke, W. W. Norton, 1939, p. 25).

Over against this, one ought to recover the story of Jacob wrestling with the angel of mystery—the heavy darkness, the desperate situation, the utter aloneness of the man, the long agony of struggle, and at last the blessing, a blessing associated with a crippling mark. In the eyes of the world, Jacob would be less admired because he was less capable, but the blessing wrought and received took in his whole nature. Indeed, after he had heard the Word, he was no longer the same man—Jacob had become Israel.

I presume there is in a congregation something of this sort. At least I hope there is, though habit and comfort take a heavy toll of these high and solemn urgencies. Surely if the church is honest about life, and earnest about its faith, then some semblance, or perhaps a remembrance, of this encounter with the Word ought to stir the waters when the congregation meets to turn its heart Godward. Karl Barth reminds us of this:

> On Sunday morning when the bells ring to call the congregation and minister to church, there is in the air an *expectancy* that something great, crucial, and even momentous is to *happen*. How strong this expectancy is in the people who are interested, or even whether there are any people whatever who consciously cherish it, is not our question now. Expectancy is inherent in the whole situation.
>
> Here are *people*, only two or three, perhaps, as sometimes happens in this country, or perhaps even a few hundred, who, impelled by a strange instinct or will, stream toward this building, where they seek—*what?* Satisfaction of an old habit? But whence came this old habit? Entertainment and instruction it is! Edification? So they say, but what is edification? Do they know? Do they really know at all why they are here? In any case here they are—even though they be shrunk in number to one little old woman—and their being here points to the event that is expected or appears to be expected, or at least, if the place be dead and deserted, was once expected here.
>
> It is simply a truism that there is nothing more important, more urgent, more helpful, more redemptive, and more salutary, there is nothing, from the view point of heaven or earth, more relevant to the real situation than the speaking and the hearing of the *Word* of God in the originative and regulative power of its truth, in its all-eradicating and all-reconciling earnestness, in the light that it casts not only upon *time* and time's confusions but also

beyond, toward the brightness of *eternity*, revealing time
and eternity *through* each other and *in* each other —the
Word, the Logos, of the Living God (*The Word of God and
the Word of Man,* by Karl Barth, Harper Torchbooks, 1957,
pp. 104, 105, 123).

It is at this juncture that one must raise the question of words, that
proliferation of speech which tends to obscure or even obliterate the
Word itself. The human heart finds it very hard to stay open, to keep
listening, to be forever hospitable to the vagrancy of the Word. It is
easy to close in and shut the Word up; indeed, it is inevitable to follow
revelation with reflection and confirmation. Significance is the first
step, but description and communication are necessary consequences.
Once the Word is heard, then speech is born.

Now we reach the nub of our embarrassment. True though it be
that the servant of the Word may subvert it by talkativeness, or that
speech cheaply conceived, pretentiously mouthed, and glibly
elaborated may be the Word's worst enemy, nevertheless, just as spirit
without things or God without the creation would be without sign or
substance, so the Word has a direct relation to words; it is incomplete
without them. They, like man, belong to the Word. That which utters
itself in speech, came out of the speechless Word. Words derive their
power and their beauty from the Word which has neither shape nor
form. Words can clutter, confuse, and disregard the Word, but if their
true integrity is maintained, they clarify, contain, and celebrate the
primal mystery of the Word.

In the minister, these two mysteries are joined. He must hear the
Word, and he must speak words. If his speech comes from his hearing,
his words are rooted in the Word. Nowhere will his interior life, the
very breath of his soul, be more instantly manifested than in the nature
of the words he uses. If he has any respect for the Word, if he
remembers its glory well, if he treasures its beauty in his heart, if he
remembers its swift transport of delight and illumination of life, he
will choose his words as a servant chooses his master's clothes, or an
artist his colors, or a housewife her dishes. Into these much used,
battered, broken, bent vessels the golden light must be poured. The
servant will labor to shape them carefully, hammering, molding,
finishing, until at last they fit some portion of the Word.

For words such as a man may use have a mystery not unlike that of
the Word from which they have come. They laugh or cry, leap or

languish, or dance; they stretch with a great reach or they dangle limply, blindly content. They tear people apart and bring them together. They build bridges firm enough to last a lifetime to span vast chasms between races or nations or ages; they dig chasms too deep ever to fill or to forgive. Once they are spoken, life is never the same again and cannot be. There is mystery in any word—watch a child groping for the very first words, learning to "say things," moving by such sacramental action into a world immense with exciting powers. And in the mystery of words there is a magic. Call it what you will: it resembles magic—a primordial power, a transforming, creative, and controlling power by which things are changed, originated, and handled according to the breath we shape for their names.

It is for this reason that the minister is as responsible for the words he uses as for the Word he serves. His service for the Word will be known by his workmanship with words. How far can he cut down the distance between the Word and his words? How can he achieve an intimacy, a clarity, a transparency between them? How well does he shape the words so they will carry some echo of the great Word? Their little mystery should open out into the mystery of the first Word; their magic should catch the sparkling coruscating shine of the great Word's power and glory.

It is interesting to ask what people expect of words. For the most part, I suspect, it is assumed the "words explain things," as when a tag or a folder comes with a new gadget and the directions are given for its assembly or its use. Sometimes I think that is about all some ministers think that words are for—a kind of tag, telling about a certain text or event. A sermon becomes a kind of hortatory direction. But if that is all a man uses words for, then both the mystery and the magic of the divine Word are shortcircuited. In the peculiarly subtle economy of man's total self, words do a great deal more than that, and the minister had better be busy with his duty at such profounder levels.

If we look closely, we can distinguish where the Word and words are joined, so to speak; we can spot the place where words are born of the Word. We must look closely, for the wound quickly closes and after that it is hard to go back through the words in order to find exactly where they were separated from the mystery and magic of the Word. Our eyes must look sharply, our ears must be waiting for the slightest whisper, our hearts must be wide open and on tiptoe. Then where no one expects it, in the midst of a thousand things, the eye will see a slight flicker of beauty burn like a flame at the edge of a leaf, or in the shape of a tree, or in the grain of granite, or in the fingers of a child, or in the eyes of a woman, or in the sound of wind, or the silence of the stars, or the hissing roar of a sea wave—anywhere the flame will leap up and burn away the dross, until glory "shines out like shook foil" and the soul itself takes fire.

> The world is charged with the grandeur of God.
>   It will flame out, like shining from shook foil;
>   It gathers to a greatness, like the ooze of oil
> Crushed. Why do men then now not reck his rod?
> Generations have trod, have trod, have trod;
>   And all is seared with trade; bleared, smeared with toil;
>   And wears man's smudge and shares man's smell; the soil
> Is bare now, nor can foot feel, being shod.
>
> And for all this, nature is never spent;
>   There lives the dearest freshness deep down things;
> And though the last lights off the black West went
>   Oh, morning, at the brown brink eastward, springs—
> Because the Holy Ghost over the bent
>   World broods with warm breast and with ah! bright wings.

("God's Grandeur," *Gerald Manley Hopkins: A Selection of His Poems and Prose*, by W. H. Gardner, The Penguin Poets, Baltimore, Maryland, 1953, p. 27.)

This is where the Word shows itself—in a piece of bread broken in love in the shadow of a cross; in a boy whose heart is torn between the ancient adversaries of Eden while he strives to thrust himself into manhood; in an artist whose very soul has been lashed by the whips of beauty in the world and he learns to translate his pain into the bright colors of his canvas. There are many books in this sacred canon— Conrad's *Lord Jim*, where a man's first disastrous meeting with the Word is followed by such earnestness as only a saint might avow, to recover the soul; or Joyce Carey's *From the Horse's Mouth*, where Guoly Jimson rushes like a drunken, brawling fool from epiphany to epiphany, celebrating the glory of the ceaseless Word; or the poets, like Rainer Maria Rilke, who count on the Word showing itself to the eye which really sees.

Torso of an Archaic Apollo

Never will we know his fabulous head
where the eye's apples slowly ripened. Yet
his torso glows: a candleabrum set
before his gaze which is pushed back and hid,
restrained and shining; Else the curving breast
could not thus blind you, nor through the soft turn
of the loins could this smile easily have passed
into the bright groins where the genitals burned.

Else stood this stone a fragment and defaced,
with lucent body from the shoulders falling,
too short, not gleaming like a lion's fell;
nor would this star have shaken the shackles off,
bursting with light, until there is no place
that does not see you. You must change your life.
(*Rilke: Selected Poems*, University of California Press,
1956, p. 93.)

The attrition of soul, the slow accumulation of tough barnacles, the growth of custom taken-for-grantedness leaves us heavily encased, unable to perceive the subtle signs of the Word in being revealed. Buber speaks clearly of this:

> Each of us is encased in an armour whose task is to ward off signs. Signs happen to us without respite, living means being addressed, we would need only to present ourselves and to perceive. But the risk is too dangerous for us, the soundless thunderings seem to threaten us with annihilation, and from generation to generation we perfect the defence apparatus. All our knowledge assures us, 'Be calm, everything happens as it must happen, but nothing is directed at you, you are not meant; it is just "the world," you can experience it as you like, but whatever you make of it in yourself proceeds from you alone, nothing is required of you, you are not addressed, all is quiet.

> Each of us is encased in an armour which we soon, out of familiarity, no longer notice. There are only moments which penetrate it and stir the soul to sensibility. And when such a moment has imposed itself on us and we then take notice and ask ourselves, 'Has anything particular taken

place? Was it not of the kind I meet every day?' then we may reply to ourselves, 'nothing particular, indeed, it is like this every day, only we are not there every day'." (*Between Man and Man,* Martin Buber, London, 1947, pp. 10-11.)

This is where the right word must be found. And the workman will know when he finds the right word. Any old word will not do. As Mark Twain put it so pungently, "The difference between the right word and the almost right word is the difference between lightning and the lightning bug." For most of his agonized life, Beethoven strove to perfect a phrase of music which haunted him incessantly. In eighteen different places in his compositions he labored with it, shaped it, did everything he could to bring it to its final form. But it was not until he wrote the Ninth Symphony that he finally broke through all the halfway successes, through the "almost right word" which would have satisfied anyone else, and in a moment of time reached the splendor which had tormented him for years.

One of Wallace Stephens' poems has a beautiful picture of man in it. He is a guitarist, a metaphysician of sorts, plucking his strings, and holding his head down to listen, a man striking the strings up through the singing tones, until he has the right note. All our lives we are trying to do that—to match the glory we have heard or dimly guessed with the right note. To strike our strings, our human instrument of mind and heart, flesh and blood, until we can say the word that witnesses to the music of God's word.

The truth of it is that things are not complete until they are named, and named rightly. The realist who boxes up reality in *res* truncates the world, beheads it, leaves it without spirit. Things stand halfway between the Word by which they were created and the words by which they are fulfilled. Nothing is describable in terms of itself. My love begins to reveal its inner glory only when I add the words of metaphor—my love is like the red, red rose. Or again, a man is troubled and bewildered by a torrent of new experiences, until in dialogue someone describes and articulates what he has been through, and he cries, Yes, Yes, That's it! That's it exactly! His eyes are lighted and he knows, not only the feel of the experience but the shape of it. The words are like handles by which he gets hold of it all and begins to possess it, rather than being possessed by it. He is free again in transcending what overwhelmed him, and it was the word which did it.

One has the sense of Jesus' seeking the right word in Mark 4:30. He asks the searching question, "Whereunto shall we liken the kingdom? Or with what comparison shall we compare it?" And then goes on in a series of efforts to find a word or a picture that will be identifiable in the experience of the listener. His sure sense of "touch," the precision of his pictures, all point to a remarkable clarity and perceptiveness of mind.

I know it is not an easy thing, this working with words. As Eliot puts it in *The Four Quartets*:

words strain,
Crack and sometimes break, under the burden
Under the tension, slip, slide, perish,
Decay with imprecision, will not stay in place,
Will not stay still. Shrieking voices
Scolding, mocking, or merely chattering
Always assail them.

Or later, when he speaks of twenty years, largely wasted

Trying to use words, and every attempt
Is a wholly new start, and a different kind of failure
Because one has only learnt to get the better of words
For the thing one no longer has to say, or the way in which
One is no longer disposed to say it. And so each venture
Is a new beginning, a raid on the inarticulate
With shabby equipment always deteriorating
In the general mess of imprecision of feeling,
Undisciplined squads of emotion.

Here is an author's confession, but any minister who still has a live soul wrestling with the imponderables of man's tangled dust and destiny, knows what it means to put pressure on the inarticulate, to muster up the squads of emotion, to get some clarity and order out of the mess of human circumstances. It is never easy to name things, or to name them so well, people will say Yes, yes, that's it, or, My God, that's me! But if the minister fails here, no amount of talk will throw light upon the Word.

This struggle becomes plainer, and the function of words clearer, when I perceive that the search for the right word is always an attempt to articulate the nature of the event which until now has not been described. It is part of the new creation, it is the happening of the world, it is the event which has just occurred. Homer or Dante, Moses or Socrates, Aquinas or Luther may assist us somewhat, but whatever they did for themselves, they cannot do for us. We stand in Adam's shoes and must name the circumstance which falls to our lot. We must shake the meaning loose, breathe it into the peculiar shape of our breath, anchor it for all time in the singing whisper of consonant and vowel.

Look at any congregation! They have suffered a thousand experiences, endured as many ecstacies and humiliations, shocked by sudden sight of themselves, disguised in ways they can no longer see themselves, with tremendous storehouses—attics and cellars bulging—with experiences they have never unwrapped, never identified, never named. They merely experienced them, got them out of sight quickly, and moved on to others as quickly dropped into limbo. This is the wasting of sorrows, of mortal time, of human substance, of priceless grains of eternal wheat. The minister's duty is to life these forgotten worlds into view, to take the castoff events and name them, to let the light of imagination shine on old circumstances till the glory is revealed and the truth stands out. Most people who say they have never had a religious experience have had hundreds of them but did not know how to identify them. And the burden of their ignorance often lies back on the stupid dullness of the minister, who never attempted to bring human experience up to the light of day in such well chosen and disciplined words that men could see the reflection of God's work in their own lives.

This is the text which stands today in need of the profoundest exegesis. The key to the scripture is not to be found in Hebrew or in Greek, in historical criticism or Formgeschichte, however helpful such devices may be. The key to the Word which lightens every event is to be found in man, that is, in Jesus, who is Christ, the being who unites the logos and the logoi, the heavens and the earth, the divine and the human. Until we learn by discipline and insight to get the right word for what happens in man, in the human being, we shall be multiplying words, often very sacred words, to no end. The servant of the Word must fashion words precise and pungent, adequate and awesome, to elicit the full reality of man, in short, to open the way for his fulfillment in the new being, for his life in the kingdom. ℞

The Vision of Reality—and Art

To have said at the beginning of the first lecture that "the minister is the servant of the Word" was so supremely safe that it is doubtful if anyone saw the danger in it. But I dare say that if I declare at the beginning of this lecture that the minister is an artist, it would explode like a bombshell, and in less courteous surroundings the audience would immediately withdraw in disgust. What business is there between faith and art? To call the minister an artist intimates that he is a dilettante, a fop, a dabbler in making pictures, perhaps even a bit loose in morals.

Let me ask you to suspend judgment long enough for me to say what I mean by art, and then to outline briefly certain ways in which art and religion have always had something in common, which, if lost, impoverishes both of them.

At the primordial origins of the great religions there is a vision of reality. Usually called a revelation, it determines the basic character of the faith throughout its history. It is a vision of such profound impact that neither catastrophes nor migrations nor changes of civilization do more than slightly alter its shape or affect the language of its remembrance. From such a vision, there is derived a quality of life and behavior, a system of morals, a philosophical stance, and a common focus of belief. Society, culture, destiny all take their color and style from the vision.

With Israel, it was no doubt the Exodus. With Buddhism, the Enlightenment under the Bo tree. With Christianity, it was Christ on the cross. Through these events, the people broke through the limits of repetitive history and touched a level of experience which made sense of life in an extraordinary way. Everything complex or contradictory, everything good and evil, everything sublime and common, literally everything was seen in the light of such an event, and was reconciled. This was reality in its broadest, deepest, highest dimensions, in its most terrible tension and vast extremes, in its shocking rudeness and its dull routine—yet it was reality uncommonly seen, reality perceived in a vision. For a moment, the eye had seen what the pedestrian reason could not reach in long years of plodding steps of logic. And if the minister has no vision of reality, if he has not been initiated into anything deeper than the ordinary sequence of happenstance, if he has not blundered or broken through the limits of this all too present world into the realm of reality, where the foundations cannot be shaken and things are everlasting, then he is not merely poor, he is pathetic, a clown with a make-believe sceptre.

The question I want to raise at the outset of this lecture is why we train men to use words so as to be precise and powerful in their testimony in regard to the Word, and completely ignore their training in such images as would enable them to transmit their vision of reality. Ministers ransack literature and do everything they can to increase their vocabulary; why not ransack art and do everything we can to develop our perceptiveness? Why does there seem to be such a vast gulf fixed between the man who listens and the man who looks, between the speaker and the seer? Did God not make the eye even as he made the tongue?

To be sure, we do not have to look very far in our history to come upon some of the factors which have caused us to devalue the work of the eye in the kingdom of truth. In the medieval world everything that truth had to say was put into eyework. The Bible was translated into stone and glass; worship was translated into ceremony, vestment, ritual; meaning was translated into color; significance was elaborated in symbols and signs. Language was poor in comparison to vision; the solemn language of high things was the aristocratic Latin; the vernacular was vulgar indeed. With widespread ignorance, eyework was simpler, more direct, and less reflective. But then, like every good thing, it was pushed to extremes. It became specious, hollow, contrived, a silly game, a play with fashion. The most solemn sanctities were not safe from its foppery and cheap extravagance. Take, for instance, Alain de Roche's symbolic speculations:

> His symbolic speculations are very highly elaborated and somewhat fictitious. In order to obtain a system in which the numbers fifteen and ten enter, representing the cycles of 150 Aves and of 15 Paters, which he prescribed to his Brotherhood of the Rosary, he adds the eleven celestial spheres and the four elements and then multiplies by the ten categories (substance, quality, etc.). As the product he obtained 150 natural habits. In the same way the multiplication of the ten commandments by fifteen virtues gives 150 moral habits. To arrive at the figure of fifteen

virtues, he counts, besides the three theological virtues and the four cardinal virtues, seven capital virtues, which makes fourteen; there remain two other virtues: religion and penitence; that makes sixteen, which is one too many; but as temperance of the cardinal series is identical with abstinence of the capital series, we finally obtain the number fifteen. Each of these fifteen virtues is a queen having her nuptial bed in one of the divisions of the Pater Noster. Each of the words of the Ave signifies one of the fifteen perfections of the Virgin, and at the same time a precious stone, and is able to drive away a sin, or the animal which represents that sin. They represent other things as well: the branches of a tree which carries all the blessed ones; the steps of a staircase. To quote but two examples: the word *Ave* signifies the innocence of the Virgin and the diamond; it drives away pride, or the lion, which represents pride. The word *Maria* denotes her wisdom and the carbuncle; it drives away envy, symbolized by a black dog. Sometimes Alain gets a little entangled in his very complicated system of symbolisms. Symbolism was, in fact, played out. (*The Waning of the Middle Ages,* by J. Huizinga, Garden City, New York, 1954, p. 208.)

In such a jungle of undisciplined fancies there is neither sense nor seriousness. It all ends up in sheer monkey play, and life takes on the paper-thin mockery of a *tableau vivant.* Disgust on a wide scale set in against this disregard for plain reality. A vast movement of iconoclasm permeated every level of society and culture, slowly purging it of symbol-sickness. With a rising tide of rationalism, every sort of imaginative activity became suspect. The sobriety of science, the stripping of rhetoric from prose, the pragmatic, moralistic, made short shrift of all eyework, put the artist under a cloud, and struck out wildly, violently, at anything that seemed to smack of idol worship.

Religion in its own way turned its back on eyework. Symbolism was reduced to a minimum, eliminating every vestige of art from the sanctuary. The centering of worship in the Bible, in sermons, in devotional reading, in catechetical instruction turned the Church into a listening shell—an auditorium. The tongue came into undisputed sway and raged with fury and inexhaustible garrulity. It seemed so much more sophisticated, so much more rational, than the eyework of the medieval faith. The work of the eye became negligible, the artist an outcast, the minister a man glib with his tongue and a Philistine in the arts.

Having come so far, let me jump into the very middle of this question by declaring that great art has a religious function, and without it the minister is impoverished for lack of means to communicate the profound vision of reality which lies at the heart of faith. And not only is the minister impoverished, but the congregation with no soil deeper than that of hearing, of hearing abstractions, sacred syntax and holy grammer, should find itself only with small change, afraid to embark on large ventures of sight and symbol, fearful of the depth and the power that crowds into and out of God's own created things, ready to leap into light when the eyes see and the heart feels. A congregation without great art tends to be blind. As George Bernard Shaw put it: "You use a glass mirror to see your face; you use works of art to see your soul."

Let us begin with the central vision of reality in the Christian faith, namely, the cross of Jesus. If the minister thinks this is a candid picture, a photographic copy of what happened on Golgotha, a realistic substitute for a single event, he has missed the theological meaning entirely. The cross of Jesus is a symbol of an event, in which there is an intense compression of meanings which interpret the true nature of reality. It tells about Jesus crucified, to be sure, but it is an open-ended event through which one can see the total scope of history as it is compacted in this event, and it is open-ended in that one's own experience is totally engaged and clarified by it. It is not an event, quite unlike all other events in history, but actually the point at which all other events in history reveal their essential meaning. It is the concrete symbol of the hidden significance of all historical existence. It is the picture of reality, the picture of everything once the veil of obscurity is removed.

Now this is art in its profoundest character. No art worthy of the name is ever an imitation of appearances. Neither art nor religion is concerned with appearances, or with the surface of life, or with superficial likenesses. Listen to Franz Marc: "Art always has been and is in its very essence the boldest departure from nature and 'naturalness.' It is the bridge into the spirit world." Or turn to the sculptor, Henry Moore: "Because a work does not aim at reproducing natural appearances, it is not therefore an escape from life but may be a penetration into reality." Or listen to Paul Klee: "Art passes beyond the object . . . . One learns to look behind the facade to grasp the root of things . . . to dig down, to uncover . . . ." Or, again, let us pay attention to Max Beckmann, the Expressionist: "In my opinion, all important things in art since Ur of the Chaldees, since Tel Halaf and Crete, have always originated from the deepest feeling about the mystery of Being." Or let Ernst Barlach testify: "It is my belief that that which cannot be expressed in words can, through form, be comprehended in someone else's soul." In short, art itself, like religion, is searching for a reality which must be found beyond or in back of appearances, underneath the ordinary surface of life. They both search for a reality which must be elicited, or, as the Christian says, must be revealed. And, further, when it is revealed it is revealed in the flesh, that is, in concrete form, in all the difficult straits and constraints of space and time. The forms of art constitute a living testimony of the doctrine of the incarnation.

This is why the literalist in art as well as in religion is always a liar. The reality cannot be captured in any one form once and for all. The living Word, the true reality, is not static. It moves, enters relationships, creates and transforms, forever surprising man with its inexhaustible energy and beauty.

Reality, for both religion and art, spelled with a capital R to distinguish it from the superficial appearances of life with which it is often confused, is more than something out there, something to be identified as an object. All great art is a subtle and powerful interpenetration of the man and the world. Wherever man's agony of insight and imagination elicits the hidden mystery of Being in anything, whether it be miner's shoes, a kitchen chair, a Madonna, a clown, a cypress tree, a dancing girl, or a crucifixion—whenever the mystery of Being is elicited and wedded indissolubly, sacredly, with the spirit of man, there Reality is revealed in all its everlasting vivacity, its overflowing exuberance, its quiet and ineradicable terror just beyond the edge of the visible. Giotto and Rembrandt and Van Gogh and Picasso will be as different as Abraham and Hosea and Jesus and Paul—but their uniqueness of revelation is the evidence of their religious vision. They have put their souls into the world, at great cost and danger, and what they found was greater than the world itself—a Reality in which man and his world were reconciled.

If you have not seen in Van Gogh's "Potato Eaters," or in Rouault's "Clowns," or in Picasso's "Guernica," then I do not know how you read what you see in the cross of Jesus. If we talk of atonement, it must be to bring man together, intimately and thoroughly, with his world. The theological term "reconciliation," if it means anything at all, means sharing in the reality where all things work together for good, where all the seeming contradictions of life are seen in the light of a deeper unity, where the infinite and frightening gap between the awesome nature of the eternal and the pathetic fate of created things, between the holiness of God and the sinfulness of man, between the glory and the shame, is suddenly closed, brought together, so that they no longer deny each other, but reflect and justify each other. Then the artist or the minister are also reconciled, for then they see alike, that the Word is forever made flesh in the ceaseless creation of the Eternal Father, and that everywhere in the breaking of the bread we can see and eat, there is a breaking of the bread of heaven which cannot be handled or seen. The apples and peaches Cezanne paints are windows into eternity; the little children Picasso paints with such consummate sensitivity are of the kingdom of heaven; the wheatfields and cypresses and blackbirds of Van Gogh are like the writings of Genesis, a glimpse of God's creative energy at work; the lithographs of Rouault, portraying the agonies of the war, are portraits of the crucified; in short, artists are men who have seen the Glory, the light of heaven, the greatness of eternity, and then by their skill they have turned and twisted the little common things of earth in such a way that you can see past them into a Reality, into a Mystery called Beauty, into a presence which stays forever.

The genius of an artist is that he can see so much in a loaf of bread and a glass of wine on a table, or in a clown grotesquely painted, looking longingly into the distance, or in the wrinkled face of an old woman; or in old houses cluttered on a hillside; or in a kitchen chair marked and worn; or in a woman looking at her firstborn child. The genius of a minister—is it any different? Is he not to see grace in common things, unexpected mercy in routine, the kingdom of heaven within the heart of ordinary man, the beauty of the Lord in the habitations of men, the hallelujah of the heart in plain homespun lives, the sight of angels in sordid places? What is the minister but one gifted and trained to see in life what others may miss? Is it not his plain duty to see God, not in heaven where all may get to see Him easily enough, but here below, where we see through a glass darkly? Our task is not alone to see the Glory behind things, but to use things so the Glory can be seen. The bread and wine of the Lord's Supper are sacred when as things they are handled in such a way as to disclose God's presence in the world. The cross is sacred when it is seen, not as a souvenir of an ancient sacrifice, but the focus of that mystery which transforms the suffering of this world into hope and salvation.

What do you "see" in the bread and wine? How much of life and death crowd into them? How deep into sin and darkness and shame do you see, and how high into mercy and compassion and faith? How much of this world's anguish and its black hate and its spite, how much of man's incredible trust and bright willingness to suffer and his invincible hope—do you see far back to men who were more like apes, hairy hunters, sitting about their meal, dimly feeling the stirring of a bond between them? Do you see the wild grain, the tilled soil, the dark of the roots, the wet of the rain, the blow of the wind, the threat of the storm, the feel of the grain in the hand, the white flour on the stone, the magic of fire, the making of bread, the gift of eternal benedictions, derived from countless agonies, the mark of God's sustaining grace? Do you see the fumbling mistakes, the burnt hands, the laughter of ridicule, the harsh pain of hostility, the dull ache of fear, the cold thrust of sudden death, the fears and fury, the joy and peace, the thinking and dreaming, the labor and loneliness? "Art is that medium thanks to which the ineffable does not have to remain imprisoned in the secret places of each individual's life. Poetry and art are based on images; and images possess the power of penetrating into the individual soul and extracting from it and communicating to others its secret treasures" (*Ideas and Images in World Art*, by Rene Huyghe, Harry N. Abrams, New York).

I rather like Louis de Rougemont's word about art, where he speaks of it as "a calculated trap for meditation." It does not take too much imagination to transfer this brief phrase to the realm of religion. Isn't worship a calculated trap for meditation, by which we hope to bring men and women, ourselves included, into the deeper realities of the kingdom of God? Isn't prayer a calculated trap for meditation, a way by which we open our hearts and minds methodically and deliberately to the searching judgment of God in the hope of ordering our wills more closely with His? Isn't Bible reading a calculated trap for meditation, recalling the testimonies of saints and prophets in their several ordeals whereby they won through to a more powerful faith, in the hope that we can open up in ourselves the same resources of courage and perseverance?

Whether it is the artist or the minister, in this situation, we must make it unmistakably plain to both of them that we do not want to be entertained; we want to be redeemed. Most of our trouble both in art and in religion is that we have confused these categories. Entertainment exists on the surface; it is playful; it has no serious intention or depth. It does not presume to lead us into reality; indeed, it tends to offer us escape, to treat reality lightly and fantastically. It runs along the ground, scarce touching it and is not halted by any of the darknesses or shames of life. Generally speaking, Hollywood is entertainment. Indeed, nothing is more characteristic of the situation of art in America than the phrase "the entertainment industry." Everything is fashioned to fit the vast demand for irresponsible play. The ghastly consequence becomes evident when Cecil de Mille can take a biblical revelation of the Law, and make it into a blasphemous entertainment of such superficial excitement that multitudes of Christians, and not a few parsons, are deceived into thinking they are seeing a religious picture. It is not the amorous intrigues which vulgarize the picture but the utter unawareness of the nature of religious revelation. This is not a calculated trap by which men are led deeper into a vision of reality; reality is completely destroyed in the search for excitement and entertainment with which to titilate the jaded nerves of lost souls. Like Lloyd Douglas' novels, all the claptrap and paraphernalia of religious signs and miracles are present, but religion itself is absent. This is sheer entertainment, not redemption.

What I mean by redemption is simply that great art certifies itself not by mere pleasure as entertainment does, but by changing the life of the person who sees it. This is indicated in Rilke's poem on "A Torso of Apollo," in the last line where, after describing the power of the stone it is as if the torso itself spoke, saying, "You must change." This is the effect always of true art. One does not see Rembrandt or Giotto or the "Winged Victory of Samothrace," or Giacometti's "Walking Man," or Dante's "Divine Comedy" and remain the same. The dimensions of life are altered, the soul has seen, and there is no way to go back. This has been the power of Ingmar Bergmann's movies like "The Seventh Seal" and "The Virgin Spring." They altered the fundamental sensibility of the audience, both in terror and in pity. They were cruel, but creatively cruel.

One must raise here a problem which is deeply associated both with the idea of art as entertainment and with what H. G. Wells once called "the fatalistic optimism" of the American culture. We do not take kindly to any kind of unpleasantness in art. We prefer it to be pretty, to raise no questions, and to probe into no darkness. But if art at its best is redemptive, then obviously we have denied it. I suspect the great masterpieces, whether they have been in the literary or the plastic arts, have never given pleasure. They are too complex, too profound, to be mere entertainment pieces. They demand too much of the reader or the observer; they elicit his own buried reality from the dormant depths and they probe by reflection the distant roots of his own pain and ecstacy. Art to redeem, to transform, to illuminate the mysteries of this mortal venture, must not stop at discomfort, or anguish, or blind resistance.

What this means to a minister can be seen quite quickly. The distinction between entertainment and seriousness is kept no more carefully in the church than it is in art. All I need to do is to ask the simple question: How much religious activity today is more than a passing entertainment for people already calcified in their complacent respectability? How much of it is dynamic enough to effect a real change in the sensibility of the people who play at it in their Sunday clothes? The entertainment principle has permeated the church as thoroughly as it has permeated Hollywood; in Hollywood it tends to be vulgar and exciting, while in church it tends to be respectable and boring. But there is no dimension of redemption in one or the other. Life is not deepened; motives are not changed; what has been is corroborated and confirmed and will continue to be.

It is precisely here that one must enter an apology for what may be called unpleasant art. People who like Sallman's Arrow Collar ad of Christ or the saccharine illustrations of Sunday School lessons usually dislike the agonies of Picasso or the difficult art of the non-representational artists alike. Their objection is that these things are not beautiful and they do not want to look at such things constantly. Strangely enough, these same people do not suggest that we remove Ecclesiastes from the canon of the Old Testament because of its despair, or the terrible pictures in Jeremiah, or Isaiah, or the twenty-third chapter of Matthew, or the fall of the city in Revelation. The modern artist, as I suspect the modern minister, if he really has a call to serve God, is forced to make some kind of discriminating judgment about life. If he has a vision of reality, it means he is face to face with saying what he thinks the condition of the world is in respect to reality. If all he wants to do is to entertain men who are lost, and thus try to make them forget they are lost, if he is intent only on putting poultices on cancers and giving crazy men tranquilizers, then he has a right to object to modern art. But if the artist or the minister has caught a vision of reality, or real reality if you will, and must compare it with the unrealities, corruptions, and perversions represented by our age, then the matter must be faced.

The modern artist, first of all, is more concerned with reality in its profound sense than with beauty in its superficial sense. He is trying to recover the realities which govern the life of modern man. If all hell breaks loose, if old men and animals and little children are blown to a bloody mess by absorption bombing, Picasso breaks all the bounds of prettiness, all the laws of classic decorum, and stretches every dimension of the human figure to paint "Guernica." If modern man no longer has the ability to see himself whole, if he has no power by which to integrate the diversified and contradictory aspects of his experience, if he has fallen to pieces as poets, psychologists, and novelists suggest, then Picasso has shown him this way, in fragments, piecemeal, tortured, and distorted. If the world itself has lost its order, and has become demonic, if in its violence and loss of proportion it has disregarded the human and elevated the technical, if it has all the signs of an end of an era and the chaos of a beginning about it, then something of this will be seen and seen directly in the work of Kline, deKooning, Leger, and Kandinsky. They witness to that which has been lost. If the minister is to fulfill his role as prophet, he should not retreat from the necessity of rightly dividing between the reality of God's kingdom and the unrealities of this world. He, too, should be a witness, capable of articulating the cruelty and chaos of our time and pointing out by such unpleasantness the nature of a better world under God. If the minister operating under the fatalistic optimism of our present desire to be affable at all costs, refuses to discharge his duty, the artist, novelist, and poet are obviously willing to take this burden on themselves, although it is at great cost, often by being anathematized by the very people who ought to be engaged in it themselves.

Before I finish, I want to make sure that you do not think I am talking only about masterpieces. I am talking about masterpieces only to make plain what I mean by eyework in achieving a vision of reality. Masterpieces become masterpieces simply because they do in an extraordinary fashion what we are always trying to do in ordinary circumstances. All our work, whether it is art or religion, is trying to see the sign of glory in the commonplace. The intense power of such eyework manifests itself in the unforgettable images of the parables, such as the Prodigal Son, or the Sower. Or we can see it closer home, in the white whale of Melville, or the plague of Camus, or the castle of Kafka, or the dustheap in Dickens' *Bleak House*, or the wild duck in Ibsen. These images are crammed, packed full and running over, with meaning compounded and multiplied. There is an eternity on the other side of each of them.

To tap the great resources of art, to be able to see as well as to hear, to train the sight to penetrate beyond the surface, to liberate it from mere surface seeing until it becomes creative, revealing, redemptive, is our large task. The discipline to become perceptive, to sharpen our skill and to move it with imagination, is to be aware that God has more than one way to speak.

Let me close with words from Louis de Rougemont: "Art is the exercise of the whole being of man, not to compete with God, but to coincide better with the order of Creation, to love it better, and to reestablish ourselves in it. Thus art would appear to be like an invocation (more often than not unconscious) to the lost harmony, like a prayer (more often than not confused), corresponding to the second petition of the Lord's Prayer—"Thy kingdom come." ⟋

The Care of Souls—and Faith

When Jesus in his last importunate interview with Peter asked him to care for his sheep if he loved him, he was laying down a primary injunction on which our work as ministers is founded. Our basic service, if we love the Lord, is the care of souls. Others may care for their bodies, some may care for their minds, and still others for their wealth, but our duty is to care for their souls. And this is not to infer that we have no concern for their health, or their education, or their security. It is simply that we are so deeply concerned with their total well-being that all these things are included, and with these things something more, namely, their relationship to God.

I wish at the outset that I knew how to salvage this word "soul" from its spurious connotations and disguises. It has been spiritualized to such an extreme that nothing human remains in it. It has been Platonized until it floats far above our common life, quite disembodied. It has been purified until its impeccable, untouchable perfection reminds one more of a whited sepulchre or a blatant pretension than of holiness. I say I wish I could salvage the word, by humanizing it, by recovering its participation in the flesh and blood realities of our life, by disclosing its rich involvement with historical existence. Perhaps the best way would be to drop the word "soul," and then to say it is the care of human beings which is our primary duty. Yet if we do that, then we must think of human beings in their largest and profoundest magnitude. They are not merely animals, or even thinking animals, or socialized animals, or tool-making, bomb-making, fun-making animals. They have dimensions which can only be described as implying some kind of heaven or hell, some kind of eternity, permanence, destiny. They are souls—in the subtlest, most imaginative, and truly classically religious sense of being related to God. They transcend nature; they stand outside themselves and judge themselves; they have a hunger, a metaphysical hunger, that desires more than the world supplies; they grapple with reality, both their own and their environment, and transform them; they make impossible demands on themselves, and endure incredible suffering for causes that seem hopeless; they see visions, and dream dreams, they go without food and dress in rags to serve some invisible beauty

248 / *Preaching with Purpose and Power*

they strive to enshrine in verse or stone or stage; they kneel and lay their heads on the executioner's block with a prayer for their accuser; they sing their "Te Deums" with invincible joy and turn to kiss the sores of lepers; they follow the path of the stars with their crafty sight and uncover the primordial structures of God's wisdom; they share in the power of creation and watch with unspeakable wonder the miraculous child they beget; they build cities and bomb them; they wage wars and assist their enemies to rebuild; they unleash the dread of universal death and play with the gruesome destiny of a misshaped humanity, and yet in every catastrophe they leap across every prejudice, every barrier, to bind up the broken and to assuage the sorrowing. These people, these human beings, these souls in all their muddled magnificence, in all their dubious destiny, are to be our care.

Certainly one must begin by saying that nothing human is foreign to the soul. It shares in every level of our human condition. It is affected by every aspect of our human life. The reality of it is woven into the warp and woof of our very existence. It is no aloof autocrat observing the parade of lesser lights, the serfs and soldiers of our mundane bodies, concerns, and desires, from some high balcony of supercilious sanctity. The soul is colored through and through by everything we are and by everything we do. It has deep and radical relationships and responsibilities throughout every level of our life, both in ourselves and in the world.

But having said this, we must say more. When we say "soul," we put an accent on the very nature of being human, which enhances the meaning of man and suggests a dignity in his being which must be taken into account. There is a significance in being human; there is a certain weight or gravity in man; there is a strange excess, a tangential thrust, the promise of a certain trajectory in the sum total of his deeds, which adds a most explicit mystery, a strange and eerie radiance, not unlike an ancient halo, about his humblest deeds and stumbling questions. The man has a ghost, so to speak, a ghost that haunts him, helps him, torments him, hides him, harasses him, lures him, gives him no peace and yet delights him, tips his tongue into speech and his hands into skillful labor, makes his eyes dance and his heart leap for joy, blinds him in sorrow and shames him in sin, whispers of God in the great fecund silences, and shouts like a mad man in the river of his blood. Yes, man has a ghost; or perhaps we had better be patient and not so infernally snobbish with words—perhaps we had better say,

Man at best, or man at bottom, or man when he consents to be himself, *is a soul.*

In short, he is a creature with extraordinary powers of penetration. His skin does not contain him; he extends in all directions. He thrusts his hands among the stars; he descends the dwindling stairs among the invisibles and counts the atoms and mesons; he turns his back on time and runs down every street of history into the ancient epochs of long forgotten times. There is no horizon too tight to shut him in, no direction he will not take, no darkness he will not invade, no dream he will not try out, no new thing he will not taste, no far world he will not seek to reach. He is *homo viator*, traveller, pilgrim, the inveterate penetrator of all distances. He measures every dimension of the cosmos. Like the sun, his rays reach out in every direction and are tireless in their journeys.

And even as he is penetrator, so is he the most permeable of all creatures. His hospitality is enormous; he welcomes all manner of things, far off and near, commonplace and sublime, past and future, facts and fancies, into the capacious experience of his mind and heart. The past is rooted in his memories; the future in his hopes and fears; other ages, other people, other faiths, in his imagination; Socrates may be close enough to be his brother, Moses to be his father, and Dante to be his counsellor.

Never underestimate the mystery of a man! Just a plain, everyday, *nobody!* Be careful, he may seem drab, his face neutral, his clothes a bit shabby, his hair gone, his eyes dull, his voice unsure of itself, somewhat confused, his direction lost, wary of questions—then take off the mask, if God will allow it, strip away the old husk, get down to the bright colors hidden and worn, and see, if you can, what his soul is like. Look at all the levels of it—infant, child, boy, man. Look closely at the bright shapes of ecstasy and the dark shadows of tragedy; take time to unravel the days of drama when heaven and hell fought over this man; look at the glint of golden love which runs through the story; stop awhile and learn what these strange marks mean of miracles never to be forgotten and mysteries still to be unfolded. There is more wealth of human mystery and miracle in any six people taken at random from our congregations than we as ministers can care for and illumine in a whole lifetime of service. Read *The Diary of a Country Priest*, by Georges Bernanos, and keep in mind the fact that this parish was "eaten up with boredom," miserable little houses huddled together in the mud, gritty, dull, a parish like most parishes. Remember that the priest is not very bright, not an intellectual, not at all popular—just a country priest. Then read on, read into the slowly appearing landscape which appears in the souls of the people, and in the soul of the priest himself, read into the bright and awful glare of evil and the dark tide of death, read into the tremendous excitement and brilliant color of souls seen from within. Even the nobody has a soul, sometimes surprisingly vast and deep and full of sights not seen from the outside.

The first thing we must learn if we are to care for human souls is that they are in the hand of God. This is difficult to learn. So often they seem to be anywhere but in the hand of God, but in truth we must not be deceived by appearances. What I mean by being in the hand of God is that they are free. This is their right as a soul. They have a right to stand in their own relationship to God. They have a right to be free from our meddling. Nothing is so amazing as to see God do something for a man, and immediately a minister rushes in and undoes it. God puts a burden on a man, and as soon as the minister hears about it, he rushes pell mell and drags it off the man with all kinds of cheery advice. God sends a gray sorrow to a man to wear for reasons we may not know, but you can be sure there will be a minister who will quickly rush to his rescue, drag the drab garment from him, and find a bright, red, gaudy thing of optimism and smiles to wear for his own good. The amount of downright subversion, of delivering souls from God's good but often stern grace, of getting in the road of God's almighty hand, of fussing, fuming, and helping until everything God might have done for a human soul has been undone by busybody flubdubs anxious only to make a body comfortable when God might have been trying to make a soul glorious, is beyond belief. We simply have no contract to interfere with God's work if we care for his sheep.

It takes a long time for some of us to learn that there is a vast difference between helping a soul and making it easier for him. It takes a great deal of self-discipline to learn how to stand by, to keep one's mouth shut, to avoid getting between a man and God when God is trying to do something with him. It takes insight and modesty to know that compassion often means letting a man bear his burden, carry his sorrow, wrestle with his shame, and win his own victory.

Nothing has so degraded the repute of love as a Christian virtue as the blind and silly actions which are set in motion by people who only want to prove to the world how good they are. A not inconsiderable amount of the good works is perpetrated for self-satisfaction of the doer, and has no relevance for the conditions of need or their lack in their unsuspecting victims. Even such a sacred word—at least sacred to some—as *agape*, the tendency is to think there is some kind of absolute goodness about it. One does not ask about the other person, what his needs are, where he lives, and how he reacts—one merely pushes the button, gives him a swift treatment of *agape* or love, a single onceover of guaranteed help-you-whether-you-want-it-or-not, and he is bound to be better. What nonsense! Indeed, what a sin against the Holy Spirit! There are too many dangerous people in the world, both in the ministry and out of it, full of excess love, spraying it indiscriminately into everybody's face, without asking whether you like its smell or not.

Love, as I perceive it in the actions of Jesus, is restrained and modest; it is accompanied always by a dignity of measure, and a singularly perceptive insight as to the appropriate means taken to answer a particular need in a specific person. It is realistic, not romantic; it is religious, but not sentimental; and, above all, it never encroaches on the integrity of the individual, it never offends the freedom of the soul. The man remains more than ever himself and is not absorbed, swallowed up, slavered over with the foamy froth of a gratuitous love potion. Love is not specious praise, squandered promiscuously. It is not professional flattery unctuously dispensed for the occasion. Love in Jesus always begins with a real relationship; it is not a sloppy extravagance (between a super-soul and a sub-soul). There is as much hubris in many forms of love as there is in evil. Love is no more free of corruption than anything else in this world.

Love, to be Christian, must know its own limit in the face of God's prevenient care. If we are to care for human souls as the basic duty of our ministry, we must be purged of any thought that love is the tool of our omnipotent desires and subtly disguised arrogance. In short, the care of human souls rests under the constant judgment of God's mercy and mystery. We are only fitted for such a task to the degree that we have faith in God's ceaseless action both in men and for men. What a travesty if we assume they have no other hope save what we can do!

One must be cautious here. In any effort to reassert the singularity of the soul and its non-negotiable responsibility to stand before God, I do not want to obscure completely the reality of our sustaining mutuality. "No man is an island unto himself." Quietly and pervasively we are sustained by each other. But blind mutuality, a kind of unconscious, indiscriminate Rotarianism is one thing: it is quite another thing to be sustained by a wise and penetrating compassion. W. H. Auden puts it clearly when in *The Age of Anxiety* he says:

the ego is a dream
Till a neighbor's need by name create it.

Let us turn then to ask how we can nurture a soul, skillfully assist it as it goes from glory to glory and strength to strength. We began by referring to his freedom as a right to be himself, to stand in his own right before God. But freedom is not only a right, it is also his profoundest burden. It is fraught with great risk and much anxiety. Freedom exists at the edge of his existence, at the very edge where the darkness hides all kinds of possibility, where his foot can feel nothing yet where he must take a step if he is to break out of necessity into freedom. His freedom becomes real when he labors to be born, not once but a thousand times, in a thousand ways. Man is a creature of manifold possibilities, and he can scarcely be said to be himself unless he fulfills them. Birth is not so quickly ended with the first breath of air drawn in, but always after there is a continual travail by which he gives birth to himself in larger and larger measure. If he is a "great" soul, this does not end with any of the ordinary and inevitable necessities of his physical self, with the adolescence or maturity, but in a thousand ways and in a veritable multitude of experiences he grows out of himself and into himself, fulfilling the image of God which marks him as a creature apart from any other creature, somewhat joined with God in an infinite destiny.

Nor is it always possible to tell which way a soul is going. Sometimes it may seem to be going up when really it is going down, and often it may be going down when everyone takes for granted it is going up. For the growth of the soul is not so obvious as the growth of the body, and its progress is much more secret than the progress of the brain. It must have seemed to most people that the road Jesus traveled from Galilee to Golgotha dropped with sickening rapidity as popularity declined and persecution increased until at last the cause seemed lost as its prophet was crucified ignominiously between thieves. That downward path from popularity and respect to condemnation and disgrace ended nearer God, however, than any seemingly upward path anyone has ever climbed. He grew. The growth of the soul is a mystery, a mystery in the hands of God, easily misread by men intent on things God does not value.

This may be the hard thing for most of us to learn—that the progress of the soul does not coincide with climbing up in the world. The spirit has its own path, vague as it may seem, and, once discovered, it will not be mistaken for any other. In it, "God moves in a mysterious way His wonders to perform."

Souls cannot be treated in bundles. They are different, each one patterned by the mystery of forgotten circumstances, turned and twisted by the very grain in the self, knotted by the idiosyncracies of accident and perversity. Each soul is a world, a vast and complicated world, with a landscape as varied as the earth, with mountains, prairies, rivers, with arctic wastes and tropic jungles, with islands, seas, and sandy deserts, with bogs and alpine crags,—the life of the soul has its own inscape, and one's explorations are often attended by dangers and terrors as well as pleasures and delights. The man who does not sense the difference between Prince Hal and Hamlet, or between Ahab and Starbuck, or between Lord Jim and Krueger, would make not only a bad novelist but would be equally a very bad minister. One soul has no ear for music, another cannot understand the pursuit of truth, and still another pours himself completely into serving a colony of lepers. One will center his life in beauty until it radiates into every action; another will seemingly have no center, but always and everywhere be ready to leap to another man's need; still another will hide himself away and labor secretly, yet the consequence may be good for all men.

What a minister must have is perceptiveness, or insight, or imaginativeness. He must learn to look; he must train himself to see not only what is visible but what is hidden; when he cannot see, he must learn to feel, by intuition and by the subtle signs which would normally pass notice. He must not frighten, blunder in with disregard; he must stand at the door and knock, and know how to wait. He must know there are times when not to ask questions, times when silence is his best speech, times when listening keenly and with the profoundest humbleness in his sacred service. He must hold himself open, letting the world and the gestures of the soul he is trying to help run in and out all the corridors of his awareness, up and down the stairs, to discover what they mean, to stop here or rest there or pick up something, until they make their mission known. They may try to disguise themselves, to pose in gentleness when they are wild, or make believe they are friendly when they are murderous, or laugh casually when they are inwardly desperate. You will have to probe the disguises, follow them till they are tired of masquerading; watch for the moment when they try to give themselves away, or give you a chance to discover them. You must not think it is easy or pleasant, or an idle entertainment to follow a soul, to reach the trysting place far from public sight, to have courage and modesty and true love enough finally to assist in the act of revelation, of self-recognition.

One may understand the numinous terror of such an experience from *The Diary of a Country Priest* in Bernanos' novel, where the long interview with Madame la Comtesse is filled with the priest's extraordinary penetration into the heart of a woman who had turned against God and how finally in a veritable wrestling of soul with soul, he had brought her peace. She writes him, "Monsieur le Curé . . . I wonder what you've done to me. How did you manage it . . . . All's well. I didn't think one could ever possibly be resigned. And this really isn't resignation. There is no resignation in me, and there I wasn't wrong in my presentment. I'm not resigned, I'm happy." That night the Madame la Comtesse died . . . . You must read the whole chapter to know the terrific struggle, the "fight for eternal life from which she had emerged exhausted, victorious . . . ." As the priest concludes, as he thinks of his own tormented heart, "Oh, miracle,—thus to be able to give what we ourselves do not possess, sweet miracle of our empty hands. Hope which was shrivelling in my heart flowered again in hers."

One of the heresies which besets the ministry is that the care of the human soul is assumed to be a simple matter. Out of good intentions, plus a pastoral call now and then, particularly when there is sorrow in the family or a scandal, taken along with some cheerful encouragement to attend church, the method becomes a kind of ecclesiastical technique, not so much for a wise diagnosis of the spiritual condition as a gambit by which the real situation can be avoided in as pleasantly a respectable and religious a manner as possible. If real illnesses were treated by a physician the way most ministers treat the soul suffering from some sickness or shame, they would ignore the symptoms, disregard the fever and pain, and prescribe a hearty meal for the patient, to be followed by dancing a tarantella in order to restore the sense of health.

We have been slow coming to the final point, and, I think, justifiably. No other skill is as deeply and profoundly obscured by mystery as our care of another man's relationship to God. This is what we mean by his soul. And this is exactly the most presumptuous purpose of our ministry. By what right or with what kind of skill do we dabble in such a mystery? Is there any wisdom we possess, or by training achieve, which would enable us to walk inoffensively into that most sacred of all freedoms where each man faces God alone? Yet having said all these things, I must also say that from every page of the gospels there appears the incontrovertible evidence that the work of Jesus was precisely the care of men's souls. He was immensely careful not to encroach upon their soul's freedom; he neither wheedled nor threatened, pampered or ridiculed; he spoke with a terrible simplicity, a transparent honesty, a fierce restraint. He found people caught and tangled in fears and futile efforts to hide them; they were inwardly perplexed and outwardly boisterous; they were hemmed in, frustrated. tormented by a darkness they could not throw off; they were shackled, they limped, they were blinded, they went round in futile circles, they whimpered and raged, tantalized by a legion of devils—and then he came, with a swift word both of clear insight, and the darkness lifted, joy came in with a surprising peace, and with it all a surging burst of power that seemed to come from God, and it set the soul on its feet and thrust it into the world singing and shouting its praise of God's everlasting mercy.

How did Jesus do it? That is too high a mountain for my poor feet to climb, but I can see some things plainly. Jesus held a mirror up to men in which they saw their own souls. Look at the parables: Were there ever such perfectly polished instruments of reflection? Jesus did not ransack a man's privacy; he did not violate his soul; he did not turn it inside out for the sake of overwhelming the man. He dealt indirectly with the soul, as one must always. He did not speak except in parables; and each parable ended with a question: What think ye? The hearer was to carry the message into his own house and down the stairs to the secret keep where alone he faced himself and his God.

Notice the extraordinary restraint which characterizes the wisdom of that saintly scholar, Friedrich von Hügel, in a letter to his niece, Gwendolyn Greene, whom he was training in the spirit:

> I wonder if you have seen how much you will be called on to
> help people—to help souls. The golden rule is, to help
> those we love to escape from us; and never try to begin to

help people, or influence them, till they ask, but wait for them. Souls are never dittos. The souls thus to be helped are mostly at quite different stages from our own, or they have quite a different *attrait*. One should wait silent for those who do not open out to us, who are not intended, perhaps, ever to be helped by us—except by our prayers (the best of all helps).

What this does is to commend to us a new gentleness, both in our preaching and in our pastoral work. It is a characteristic Protestant failing to go at our work "hammer and tongs," to lay about us with fearful strokes, and to give every impression that if we are not invited into the soul we will break in anyway. Some of the saddest memories I have of the church are of ministers bellowing, braying madly, roaring like madmen in the ear of God, or setting upon a congregation as if the very hounds of hell were about to tear them apart. Most of the tradition of exhortation is violence substituted for the lack of imagination; sound and fury to take the place of insight; militant attack instead of merciful understanding. The letters of Fenelon, the acts of St. Francis, the superb good sense of Teresa of Avila, the lightning-like flashes of Luther, the patiently stern but compassionate self-diagnosis of Augustine—all these evince a gentleness in the care of the soul not because of a sloppy sentimentalism but because, like good physicians, they were intent on clearly understanding the causes of illness in order to effect a real cure, and not a false euphoria. Their sight was deep and far behind the thick walls of the flesh, they kept their eyes intent on the living soul as it struggled with each day's circumstance to find out God's will and to stand in His presence if they might, humbly and hopefully to sing the hallelujah of their surprise and joy amid the darkness and pain of mortal strife. ✎

The Insight of Saints—and Morals

The lectures so far may be seen as descriptive of our professional function as ministers, first in the care of words, for the sake of the Word; second, in the care of art, for the sake of reality; third, in the care of souls, for the sake of faith. This last lecture is the care of saintly ideals, for the sake of morals. Or, to put it obliquely, without saints morality becomes unbearable. And if you ask what that has to do with ministers, I should say without equivocation, it means that ministers are called to be saints.

A rather uncomfortable calling from any point of view, but especially uncomfortable and even distasteful from the American or Protestant point of view. We dislike saints, and we are not disposed either to hide our dislike or to dignify it by careful rationalisation. We dislike saints—naturally; and we dislike them—by inheritance and tradition as well. The ancient saints were anti-social; the medieval saints were queer; the puritan saints were unlovely. All together, they represent everything we dislike, and so we repudiate them in one large gesture of disdain and repudiation.

Indeed, the Protestant movement as a whole manifests a rather general and deep-seated aversion to saints. We have missionaries, heroes, executive secretaries, even martyrs, but not saints. The forces of democracy, operating over a long time, have produced a levelling down in the ranks of the church, so that we not only boast of church democracy but every vestige of hierarchical order has been devalued in such a way as to cancel out its substance. Saints went out with the aristocrats; they represented a royal class in the realm of religion. Today everybody is alike, or at least we like to believe they are. A general assumption of mediocrity is more comfortable than the implicit criticism of our condition by the presence of one whose goodness is so plainly superior to ours.

But I believe in the saint. I believe he has a place in the world. Without him, religion loses its most intense and redemptive witness. The church that does not produce saints reveals that it is in the business for no other purpose than keeping the *status quo* intact and inflating its own self-indulgent prestige. The disappearance of the saints in religion would be parallelled in science if we had been able to

258 / Preaching with Purpose and Power

eliminate the Curies, the Einsteins, Openheimers, Bohrs, Schrodingers, Enders, and had rested content with third-rate technicians repeating the classical experiments for things already proved.

Fundamentally, the main insight of the saint is that there is a level of morality far above the general respectability of the world. What passes ordinarily for "moral conduct," what makes men appear worthy and decent, what moves them and satisfies them in the eye of the public, is only the first level of human behavior, a kind of kindergarten, a place to learn the ABC's. Far above that, there are realities, structures of meaning, higher motives and more permanent satisfactions, to be reached only by the discipline of saintly practice and insight.

I have a suspicion that the saintless Christianity of our day is little more than a kind of worldly respectability, confirmed, sanctified, glorified by a service of worship in which the insights of the saints have long since disappeared. The morals are worldly morals, good as far as they go, but without much penetration either into the sublimity of grace or into the dangers of damnation. As Eliot put it, so long ago; "decent goodless people," meeting the requirements of public morality but quite without any imagination as to the higher reaches of beatitude or any idea of what spiritual aridity or the might of the soul means. They measure up quite well to what the world means by being good, but when they face the higher calculus of the Beatitudes, they are simply lost.

The first thing we must recover, if we are to understand the saints, or, for that matter ourselves, is the marked difference between contemporary morality and the insight of the saints. What we must do is to get a "firm fix," as the surveyors say, on what morality means at the present time, and then we can see what the insight of the saints means in reference to it.

For three hundred years or more, we have been developing a new set of mores, derived mainly from two historical forces, the first, individualism from the Renaissance and the second, mass production or prosperity from the industrial revolution. When these two forces are mixed dynamically in the imagination of man, they produce a way of life qualitatively different from the medieval world. Indeed, so marked is the difference that Lewis Mumford, describing the change, says that in three hundred years the cardinal vices of the Middle Ages became the cardinal virtues of the modern world.

What are the mores which have resulted from such a development? One can begin to isolate them by a careful examination of what it is that motivates modern man and satisfies him. What is the spring of action and the reward which he prizes highly? One is immediately confronted by such lively realities as ambition, success, prestige, of getting ahead in the world, of attracting attention, of having your name seen in the papers, of being popular; in short, the aggrandisement of the individual. And this in turn is measured, largely by quantitative terms—the size of his house, the extent of his wealth, the number of votes or the place on the TV, or the noise he makes in the papers. Two things characterize this new set of mores—first, an overall aggressiveness, constantly accelerating the speed and scope of ambition (for ambition today tends to be action hypostasized by neurotic compulsion till it becomes self-destructive), and a judgment principle which measures everything in quantitative terms.

If you have difficulty isolating these factors and seeing them operate in unqualified terms in all their raw nakedness, just observe the way churches report their annual progress or justify their existence. Ask most ministers what *kind* of church they have and they miss the question altogether; they will immediately tell you how big it is, how much money it spends, how large a congregation attends, how vast the parking lot, and how many ministers are on the staff.

Behind this quantitative success, morality is a pervasive dependence on "appearance rather than being." Conspicuous consumption, the chromeplated motor car as a status symbol, the feverish moving from one neighborhood to another in order to be in the right set, the assumption that a good reputation is equivalent to righteousness, the shocking ignorance and emptiness behind much ecclesiastical conformity—all point to a social morality which keeps up the appearance at the expense of reality. "Save the surface and you save all" may apply to paint, but not to people.

Let me press the matter by turning specifically to the Beatitudes. We take for granted that we are all Christians, and that we are seriously devoted to Christian morality as Jesus enunciated it. Surely at the very basis of the faith was the Sermon on the Mount. Few of us would repudiate it, at least in an outright fashion. But have you looked at what it says, carefully, thoughtfully? It begins: "Blessed are the poor." Let's stop there for a minute. Do we believe that? Can we swallow that? Do we believe in poverty? Have we taken time to look the situation over and make up our minds what it is that makes it blessed to be poor? In all honesty, isn't it true that we really believe in prosperity, in the American way of life, in the "Revolution of rising expectations," in the faith that it is better for everybody to have more and more; we certainly are not motivated to become poorer and poorer! As Santayana once pointed out, the ideal of poverty is simply not understood in America.

Now, of course, some of you will suggest we should turn from Luke to Matthew, where the Beatitude seems to be moderated: "Blessed are the poor in spirit." But is it moderated? Do we believe that the poor in spirit are blessed? Rather, isn't it true that if a man is worth his salt he will have some ambition, some get up and go; he will fight his way ahead and make a place for himself. We say he has a "lot of spirit"— not poor in spirit.

Run down the whole line and see if any of it fits into our moral standards. The meek—we smile at that! We do not really know what it means unless it is something like Mr. Milquetoast, or meek as a doormat. Or they that mourn—how does that fit into our "fatalistically optimistic" way of life? How does that match the eternal grin, the frozen, evangelical smile, the sweet cosmetic joy with which we keep up false appearances in order to inculcate a semblance of inner joy? Or the pure of heart, or the peacemaker, or the persecuted: How are these really blessed? How do they fit into the virtues of our aggressive, good-natured, happy-go-lucky, wildly clambering getting-ahead-at-any-price kind of morals? The two do not mix very well, if at all. Indeed, you can put up an easy yardstick with a simple sentence: Most people, inside and outside the church, would rather be insured than saved.

What has happened can be stated in several ways. A new evaluation has grown up inside the old one, and most people do not know that the old one is dead and the new one, in this case, the technological civilization of industry, is calling the time and setting the standard of morality with its own virtues appropriate to mass production and consumption. Or you could say that people themselves simply do not live any longer where the biblical morals have any meaning or relevance, and so they may revere them when they are read in service, but they do not feel them because they are no longer operative; they do not affect us, or motivate us, or excite us, or lure us, or satisfy us. We are travelling in a different orbit. Or, again, one might say that this is the way it has always been—most people living according to worldly standards, keeping their reputations clean and, for the most part, being good neighbors, but unlike previous ages, we do not have eccentrics who insist on a higher standard and so we rest content with the lower; indeed, because there is no testimony to anything higher, we take the world's morality into the church and sanctify it, label it Christian, and measure the realm of God by the standards of the world. At any rate, a classless society tends to excommunicate the saint as a suspicious, if not a subversive, character, and then we are no longer disturbed by the tension between God's rule and worldly rule.

Let us not quibble. The saint is a revolutionary both for the world and also for the church. The rules he lives by are not the world's rules, his goodness stems from a different quarter, and his judgment lies athwart the easy ways the world justifies itself. The saint is a radical, not in the sense of choosing the extreme left in preference to the extreme right, but in the sense that he eschews both and reaches into a depth which neither of them has ever seen, or seeing would believe. The saint is a true religious, because he has no interest at all in appearance, but only in being; he is willing to appear like a fool, if he can work his way into reality, slough off all manner of pompous deceits and find the substance of his soul. He smiles at the masquerade, the silly poses, the masks and subterfuges of impeccable ecclesiasticism. He is intent on a mystery that often manifests itself to the poor, the meek, the pure in heart, the failure. He chooses the poem and repudiates publicity; he prefers a cup of cold water to a church council; he remains unstirred by headlines but boldly flings his whole energy into an unknown private event. His scale of values is the very reversal of the world's.

He represents, it seems to me, the breakthroughs which liberate a man from the tyranny of the world's law. His function is movingly described by Albert Camus where he "wants man to act so as not to add to the unbearable misery of the world, but only to designate within the obscure walls against which we go agroping, the places, still invisible, where gates may open." He searches for the gates, often in directions unsuspected by worldly goodness; he stands where they open into freedom, and testifies by his acts of their higher validity; indeed, he becomes himself the gate, the place where life breaks into new possibilities, more profoundly human, more substantially real.

This brings me to a sentence which I used in the opening paragraph of the lecture. The saint, I said, makes morality bearable. What I meant by that, and what becomes increasingly plain, is that the boredom and burden of the world's morality can only be carried if man finds a way to transcend it. Paul recognized that the law had become an unbearable burden in his own time; it darkened the life of man with its strictures and rigor; it smothered every vestige of spontaneity, straitjacketed the vital, and frowned on freedom. It became a prison, shutting in, barring out, restricting, restraining, until man felt himself, at his most human and essential level, stalemated. Morality, in order to maintain its affirmative character, must be counterbalanced by means to affirm man's freedom and the will to creation. Without the insight of the saint, it calcifies and encases life in a rigidity which is death to his soul. This is what happened to the scribe and the Pharisee, and many centuries later to the Puritan. Morality, in short, needs to be redeemed; taken alone it is almost as deadly as evil.

The insight of the saint then, breaks through the legalism, reasserts the freedom of the soul, restores the springs of spontaneity, confirms the vital, and opens the gates wherever they can be found into the realm of God's continuing creation. He strives to be poor, in order to achieve simplicity while everybody else is buried under high-priced rubbish in order to be prosperous and unsatisfied. He becomes meek, stripping himself of pretenses in order to accomplish an inner disciplined strength which does not need to dominate others or to coerce them violently in order to be something himself. He finds other virtues than aggressive or rebellious ones by which human excellence can be achieved. He does not require a majority vote to assure him of truth or a global victory to make him content with such truth as he knows.

There are three dominant motifs to the insights of the saints which seem pertinent to our own day as we try to grope for the gates in the obscure walls of life where we may find a new hope for our time. The first motif is Christian in nature. It sees morality not in terms of power, possessions, success, or appearances of any kind, for these are all dubious bargains with the world as such, and usually in the end reveal their superficiality. The insight of the saint fastens on the question of life and death, on how man can live his life in the sure knowledge of his death, how he can transcend the tragic nature of existence. Certainly not by collecting newspaper clippings, or by buying more than he can use, or by accumulating money. For the saint, the crucifixion and resurrection was an epitome of the mystery by which dying, we live, and living, we die. Under the sign of that mystery all our love, all our living, all our labor and laughter, must find a way to be reconciled. The motif of the saints, in other words, is life itself, not its accessories; life in all its profoundest realism and contradiction, with its human value standing higher than all others. "There is no wealth," said Ruskin, "but life itself." It reaches into a much more complex mystery where black and white are not so discernible and yet where the difference between life and death, reality and unreality, being and appearance are much more sharply divided than at the worldly level.

Perhaps nothing expresses this first motif more plainly *vis-a-vis* the world's morality than in the matter of forgiveness. This simply does not make sense in the moral structure of the law, and it is not strange that the Pharisees were frightened by Jesus' seemingly promiscuous forgiveness. Forgiveness is a surd, a new dimension, a subversive factor in any strict morality. It relaxes the structure, introduces an unmanageable freedom, and throws the system into chaos. Yet life itself, the dying and living, does make room for forgiveness; indeed, forgiveness at the moral level represents the resurrection. It is a new beginning, a fresh spurt in creation, a new center from which life can be reorganized.

The second motif which seems to run through the insights of the saints refers to their remarkable ability to have done with the virtues of a dying society or a disintegrating culture, long before it becomes apparent to the world that its way is marked with the sign of death. They move out of the old while it still has glitter and glamour and they set their lives in a new context from which the new age, not yet born, takes sustenance and prepare for its time of birth. One can see this quite plainly in the early centuries of our era. While the collaspse of Greece and Rome were still far off, the saints withdrew, established little communities with new attitudes, new values, new ways of looking at life, new ways of relating to one another, new standards for measuring man, new dimensions for experience, new designs for society, new visions of history, new patterns of beauty and truth. Centuries later, it was these insights of the saints which informed the new culture and fashioned a new civilization when the old could no longer sustain the agony and imagination of man. Later, when the breakup of the medieval world occurred, there had already appeared men whose perspicacity and insight had already presaged both a new man and a new society.

Today I believe we stand in a similar situation. The virtues which developed the human consciousness in its individualistic phase and at the same time established the benefits of an industrialized society have now reached a point where they no longer contribute to the satisfaction of the individual in his search for fulfillment or to the stability of society. Extreme individualism and the technological culture are at odds. Virtues that produced the best things of our time cannot sustain them. The sense of life's meaning, its coherence and structural security, has been lost and the frenzied acceleration of the aggressive or materialistically productive virtues only exacerbates the crisis. And while it sounds strange, and a bit perverse or silly to say, I suspect it will not be the engineers or the economists who will lead us out of the chromeplated, over-stocked wilderness in which we are wandering, but the saints.

The third motif which can be found quite generally in the insights of the saints is their victory over time. Now in one sense this might be taken for an escape, as sometimes it is. But I am not speaking here of turning from the world into some kind of stratospheric utopia where the pseudo soul basks forever in a euphonic Nirvana. I am referring to something much more intrinsically imbedded in the very structure of our common life, but in no sense dominated by the harassment of time. In many ways this is a remarkable achievement. It accounts for, or at least describes, the rare ability of the saints to be content, without being complacent, and to be profoundly joyous without being deliberately optimistic. There is a great difference in these things. For instance, to be content implies an active will, a dynamic condition, whereas complacency is passive, a decidedly tired condition. Similarly, joy among the saints is utterly different from the wilful, deliberately coerced optimism so characteristic of those who imitate the saints' inner hilarity without sharing it.

Anyone observing our epoch sees immediately its anguish in respect to time. We are driven pellmell; we rush headlong from one thing to another; we have no time, though supposedly we have more leisure than any other people on earth; we are tortured and harassed by time, measuring it meticulously, using it feverishly. Yet the more fatigued and exhausted we become, the faster we travel, and the more compulsive our actions. We simply cannot stop, although action finally becomes a kind of galvanic activity with no other aim in view than to appear busy. Significantly, the Greek word to hurry means to coerce oneself. This coercion is the opposite of reconciliation with the world, which God made and with time with which he made it. The man who thinks himself saved, and is still under the domination of this frenzy of time's demonic pressure, does not know what salvation means. To find a place in the movement of time, to make one's peace with it, to travel its pace and to share its seemingly slow purposes, is indeed to be saved. But I must confess that I have found few ministers indeed who had conserved such an affirmative and peaceful relationship to time that they could have been said to have achieved the rarest of all virtues—true and lively contentment. Most of us have been cursed with the awful itch of time, the nervous twitch that comes from trying to be in two places at the same time, and the altogether not-there look of the man who is so constantly in flight from one swinging trapeze to another that he has lost the ability to stand in one place on the earth and collect himself.

Even as the saints choose between a lively contentment with the passing event and a rat race trying to keep up with things, so they know how to choose between joy and a brazen optimism. The reason is not hard to find. If a man joins himself to God's creation, pays humble attention to events as they occur, no matter how commonplace they are, he will soon be rooted in the deep soil where there are "rivers of water," and his leaf shall not wither, and whatsoever he doeth shall prosper. His cup will run over, and he will praise the Lord with a loud voice. Joy simply is the outcome of having roots in the right place; it's a fruit that cannot be produced without depth of soil. Our present mode of trying to live on the surface of things, of covering as much ground as possible, of getting through as many experiences as possible without stopping long enough to find out where we are or what it all means, is the very way to produce a joyless world, where our only consolation is a forced optimism. At least it covers our empty hearts and joyless days. We make believe we are enjoying life, when the truth is we wonder how long we can stand it.

Now the joy of the saint, which rises from deep roots in the living substance of the world, is a special mark of the ministry. Again I must say I do not mean the kind of Rotarian cheerfulness which can be cranked up for the occasion, or the sick evangelical smile which is supposed to win souls and hypnotize congregations. The joy of which I have been speaking as one of the insights of the saints is the power of a man to "celebrate" the breakthroughs which happen in our mortal journey, and to do it with such accuracy and imagination that men and women will know that God is a living God, actively at work in their affairs.

The word "celebration" is an old one in religious history, and the fact that we Protestants have allowed it to fall from our fingers ought not to blind us to the reality which it describes. Wherever there is real joy, not its facile substitutes, wherever an event rises in the soul of man and unfolds its meaning, discloses its mystery and might, wherever the routine breaks open and light breaks through, where anything is fulfilled in man's understanding or in his deeds, then joy abounds and the time for celebration has arrived. This is the moment of epiphany and the sanctuary is where it should be celebrated with song and praise. One of the reasons the services of the church so often are boring and deadly dull is that nothing is celebrated, or that what is being celebrated really does not touch the souls of men to a lively joy. God's world is not so poor, the circumstances of life are not so dull or shallow that worship need ever be conducted without good cause for celebration. As Gerard Manley Hopkins described it in his sonnet:

> The world is charged with the grandeur of God.
> It will flame out, like shining from shook foil;
> It gathers to a greatness, like the ooze of oil
> Crushed . . . .
> Nature is never spent;
> There lives the dearest freshness deep down things . . . .

The minister is one forever on the lookout for revelation, keen to discern the little epiphanies of God amid the commonplace events of ordinary men, tiptoe to see the glory which shines now and then in the soul of a nobody. When he sees it, then he should know how to celebrate it in prayer and praise, choosing just the right words, the right images, so that men's faith stands confirmed and their joy is made perfect. ℞

Harold Cooke Phillips

Harold Cooke Phillips was pastor emeritus of the First Baptist Church of Cleveland, Ohio, when he gave the 1964 Mullins Lectures. He holds the distinction of being the only person to present the Mullins Lectures twice: the first time was in 1953. Dr. Phillips was a popular preacher and lecturer. He presented the 1946-1947 Lyman Beecher Lectures on Preaching at Yale, later published as *Bearing Witness to the Truth*. Dr. Phillips' Mullins Lectures were prepared for oral delivery, and are presented here—with oral qualities intact—just as they were delivered.

The Eternal Word

This is my second try at the Mullins Lectures. The committee must have felt that, like Jonah, I needed a second chance. "And the word of the Lord came to Jonah the second time . . ." (Jonah 3:1). So like this prophet, but I trust with a less reluctant spirit, I return to this modern Nineveh, this "great city wherein are more than 120,000 persons that cannot discern between their right hand and their left hand and also much cattle" (in the slaughter house if not in the field). (Jonah 4:11).

Now let me tell you what I shall be trying to do. I shall not attempt to discuss preaching in any abstract or theoretical fashion. There are ever so many books that do that far more competently than I could. Rather I would like to share with you certain insights of the gospel which have gripped me and to suggest some principles or emphases that have guided me in my ministry. This surely sounds audacious, as though I were suggesting that my approach should be yours, as though I were setting up myself as a sort of model for you to copy! Needless to say, that is not my intention, unless you accept a certain definition of the word "model." It is said a woman once told her husband that he was a model husband. Quite flattered, he consulted a dictionary to see just how good he was. There he read: "Model: a small imitation of the real thing."

We begin today by thinking of "The Eternal Word." By this we mean "The Changeless Word in a Changing World." It is trite to say that we live in a world of rapid and seemingly ceaseless change. Indeed, there is a saying in the Navy, "If it works it's no good."

Our mechanical changes symbolize, if indeed they may not have helped to produce, the deeper changes in our ways of thinking and living. At any rate, questions our fathers thought had been answered for good and all are now on the witness stand undergoing the most critical cross examination. To problems under which our fathers had written Q-E-D our age affixes a question mark. What Walter Lippmann once called "the acids of modernity" have been at work. To be sure, if we take the long view, we shall see that there is nothing new about change as such. It is said that when Adam and Eve were driven out of the Garden, as they passed through the gate Eve said to Adam, "We are in an age of transition." Well, we have been "transitioning" ever since.

Into this world of flux and fluidity Christianity projects the idea of the Changeless, the Eternal. As the Psalmist wrote, "They shall perish, but thou shalt endure. Yea all of them shall wax old like a garment. As a vesture shalt thou change them and they shall be changed. But Thou art the same, and thy years shall know no end." God is from everlasting to everlasting, the Rock of Ages, his steadfast love and goodness enduring forever.

The apostles apply the same quality to the Christian faith. It is a faith "once for all delivered to the saints." It is an anchor that holds against the swirling seas. The unknown author of the Epistle to the Hebrews takes a further step, and a bold one, when he sees the changeless character of God and of our faith incarnate in one of whom he writes, "Jesus Christ the same yesterday and today and forever" (Hebrews 13:8). So we sing

Change and decay in all around I see;
O thou who changest not, abide with me.

These are comforting words for the believer, but confusing words to those who do not share the faith. They ask: "Why should religion be the only value that escapes the depression or inflation that has touched everything else? Why should it remain high and dry in some sort of Noah's Ark, when all else has been caught in the flood?" And if we insist that it has, are we not in danger of relegating our religion to an outmoded and irrelevant past? Might it not become a sort of dried up river bed from which the fast moving stream of life has been diverted? This is a question which as preachers we must face: how to preach the Eternal Word in an ever changing age. We shall face it from two sides, so to speak. First we shall discuss the fact of the changeless and then the nature of the changeless. First, then, the fact of the changeless.

This fact of the changeless Christ is, as I see it, supported by three considerations. The first is that Jesus still remains for us, as he was for the apostles, the center of our faith. Though we accept this in theory, we often deny it in practice. We act as though our faith were centered in a book, or a creed, or a church, or an ecclesiastical form. But we are wrong. The ultimate in our faith, as for the apostles, is not a book, however irreplaceable, nor a creed, however true, nor a church, however indispensable, nor an ecclesiastical form, however biblical, but a life, a person.

This is why those New Testament scholars who question the historic reality of Jesus and are telling us that we can know little or nothing about him are making the most crucial attack that could possibly be made on Christianity. For in truth if we can know nothing about the Jesus of history we can know nothing about genuine Christianity.

It is one thing to say that the portraits of Jesus given in the gospels represent the faith of the early Church concerning him. But it is quite another thing to say that these portraits are lacking in any objective historic reality, that they were created by the Church for utilitarian reasons to meet certain needs, or to withstand certain pressures consequent in the Church's contacts with its pagan environment. If that were true, then our gospels would not be motivated by truth but by propaganda, which as we know is a perversion of the truth. It is heartening to know there are several equally able and competent New Testament scholars who do not share this view—may their tribe increase!

At the center of our faith is a life—a person. And while it is true that from our relatively fragmentary records we do not know all we would like to know about him, we know the most important thing to be known about him or anybody: we know the kind of person he was, the spirit that motivated him, the hopes that inspired him, the goals for which he strove, the faith in which he lived and died.

But the fact of the changeless Christ, the Eternal Word, is seen in another way, namely, that his right to the spiritual leadership of mankind has remained unsurpassed through the centuries. The one unique value possessed by Christianity, but lacking in the other religions of the world, is Jesus Christ. Now to say this is surely not to say that Buddha, Confucius, Mohammed, and all the other religious seers were not the media of God's revelation, but it is to say that in Christ we have the fullest revelation of the Eternal; in the others rays of light from the sun. In him "the dawn from on high hath visited us."

For myself I cannot believe that this claim we Christians make for the unchanged spiritual preeminence of Christ is an indication of spiritual pride, or the result of our sentimental attachment to his person, or an example of wishful thinking. I believe this is so simply because it is so. We believe that Christ is the light of the world in a sense unmatched by any other spiritual seer. Were this not so, the whole purpose of Christian missions would be thrown off balance. Its nerve would be cut.

It would be impossible within the limits of this period to try to substantiate this claim. But I believe the path to its vindication would lie not so much in what Jesus said as in who he was. If "never man spake like this man," it was because never man lived like this man. "In him was life, and the life was the light of men." The authority of his words rests back on the authenticity of his life, and this because it was the life of God lived out in human flesh. As someone has put it, "Jesus had all of God in him that it was possible for a human being to have." "The Father that dwelleth in me . . ." was the phrase he used. That explains his unchanged spiritual preeminence among the sons of men.

There is, however, a third reason for our faith in the Eternal Word. It follows from our faith in the incarnation. The purpose of the incarnation was the redemption of man: "God was in Christ reconciling the world unto himself." But the world is not yet reconciled. Does God then change his purpose because man remains self-willed? Does he cease to be gracious because man will not cease to be rebellious? Surely that is not the nature of him whose love passes our knowledge. The changeless purpose of God in Christ is morally necessary to meet the changeless spiritual needs of man. Why should we doubt the possibility of enduring goodness when we do not doubt the actuality of enduring evil? Why should we doubt the unchanging nature of God's redemptive work in Christ when the evil in man remains the same yesterday and today and forever? "Where sin abounds there did grace much more abound."

It is a striking, but not always recognized fact, how little the changes of which we are so enamored have affected the deep and decisive areas of our life; no more than are the secret depths of the ocean affected by the surf and suds of the shore. Let me use a simple illustration. Suppose that George Washington should revisit the White House. How nonplussed he would be! If you told him he was wanted on the phone, he would give you a blank stare. If you asked him if he would like to try out the new helicopter, so constantly used by his successors, he would not know what you were talking about. If you told him that by pressing a button he could hear someone talking in London or that by pressing another he could actually see people at work or at play in Europe, he would probably conclude that this practical, hard headed country of his was now a veritable fairyland. Any little six year old boy in things "out there" could make the father of his country look like a numbskull.

But now suppose he had arrived during those fateful days that witnessed the tragic assassination of our wise and courageous President. He could have shared most fully our grief. Or if you should discuss with him one of the issues involved in integration versus segregation, isolation or international cooperation, he would "get you." If you talked with him about honor, integrity, self-discipline or moral values he would understand and might give you some pointers. Washington the city has changed; Washington the man . . .?

How much of our modern sophistication comes from our inability or unwillingness to distinguish between the variables and the constants in human nature—the changes "out there" and the unchanged realities within us. This is why we are prone to identify scientific progress with progress. But the only progress for man comes from changes within. The fact that we fly while our fathers lumbered along in a stage coach is not of itself progress, until one knows where we are going and why. The fact that we talk via radio or TV to millions while our fathers talked to hundreds is not progress; that depends on what we say. Too often these wonderful techniques are used to give nonsense a wider hearing. The fact that we have replaced David's slingshot with an atomic bomb is not progress, unless it be progress towards total destruction. As Helmut Thielicke writes: "What a strange, enigmatic breed we are! Presently we shall be flying in space, but at the same time we are threatening to blow up the base of this voyage into space, namely our own planet. We conquer space and time with our machines, but these machines appear to be conquering us. We change the face of the earth, but in our own faces are the same old runes of guilt, suffering, and death. Despite everything we have created, we are still the same as the men of old" (*How the World Began*, p. 4).

As a matter of fact, in the deep decisive areas of life modern man is about as modern as Adam and Eve. It is our failure to see this that explains the supercilious attitude of some moderns. A professor addressing the American Anthropological Association said not long ago: "A cultural system that launches satellites can dispense with God entirely." What an astounding statement! We would say that such a system needs God more than ever since it gives man more terrifying techniques for expressing his self-will. As Walter Lippmann has truly said, "The unregenerate man can only muddle into muddle." It is because of the unchanged nature of the evil in man that both faith and fact make us reach for God's unchanged redemptive grace in Jesus Christ, the same yesterday and today and forever.

So much for the fact of the changeless. We come now to the second part of our theme: the nature of the changeless. And here there is a difference of opinion. I thoroughly dislike and distrust labels. I seldom use them. I do not think God reads our labels but our life. Yet for clarity's sake let me say that our concept of the nature of the changeless is, broadly speaking, the issue that separates liberals and conservatives, modernists and fundamentalists, so called. It is the issue between the letter and the spirit.

It seems to me that the changeless may be regarded in two ways: there is a static changelessness and a dynamic changelessness. The Sphinx or the pyramids are examples of static changelessness. Despite the erosion of the wind and weather of the centuries, they remain essentially the same. A tree, on the contrary, symbolizes dynamic changelessness. The tree changes its appearance, its color, in response to the changing seasons. Yet it remains basically the same tree: its roots drawing sustenance from the soil, its leaves responding to the chemistry of the sunlight through thousands of years.

Take another example. Two plus two make four. They always have. They always will. That is static changelessness. A mother's love for her child might be an example of dynamic changelessness. The genuine love of a mother for her child never changes, yet what changed ways she has of expressing that love as the child passes from babyhood to maturity. When the child reaches man's estate she prays for him. But whether as a little child she teaches him to pray, or as an adult prays for him, she is expressing in changed ways her changeless love.

Now the difference between static and dynamic changelessness, between the Sphinx and a tree, a mathematical formula and a mother's love, is life. Static changelessness applies to dead things, dynamic changelessness to living things.

If this distinction is a valid one, then the question is in which category would we put our Lord. Does he belong to the static realm of death or to the dynamic spirit of life? Is he a kind of hitching post, erected somewhere in the Galilee of Bible times to which we are tethered, or is he a living guide leading us through untrodden ways? To ask the question is to answer it. Yet it is so basic a question that it might be well to validate our claim to the dynamic nature of our Lord's changelessness by reference to his own life and teaching.

There can be no doubt that the true nature of the changeless was the main bone of contention between the Master and his religious contemporaries. To his religious contemporaries religion was a sort of mummy embalmed in changeless death, in laws, many of which, at best, had become irrelevant, and at worst a burden grievous to be born. He would have none of it.

He told two parables, twin parables which made clear the difference between his new teaching and their static ideas. "No one sews a piece of unshrunked cloth on an old garment; if he does the patch tears away from it, the new from the old, and a worse tear is made. And no one puts new wine into old wine skins; if he does the wine will burst the skins and the wine is lost and so are the skins; but new wine is for fresh wine skins" (Matthew 9:16, RSV).

Further evidence may be seen in the fact that he left us not static laws for our guidance but dynamic principles. "Ye have heard that it hath been said by men of old time, but I say unto you." And what he said was not a law but a principle which could be interpreted and applied to meet the changing needs of man. "The law was given by Moses, but grace and truth came by Jesus Christ." "Grace and truth" are no two plus two concepts. They suggest realities that are fixed and yet flexible. There is a difference between the changelessness of law and the changelessness of love.

Again, it is not without significance that when the Master was asked a question he seldom, if ever, gave a direct answer, Often he answered a question by asking another. Did he want his questioners to think for themselves, guided by the spirit of truth, to ask and seek and knock? Nor can we forget his words, "I have yet many things to say unto you, but you cannot hear them now. However, when the spirit of truth is come, he will guide you into all truth and he will show you things to come" (John 16: 12-13).

Now if words mean anything it would seem that the Master did not regard truth as merely a frozen stream but as a flowing river. The river changes its depth, its speed, sometimes its direction as it moves across the land, but despite these changes it remains the same river. The water of life is not frozen or stagnant. Jesus' immutability does not mean immobility.

"I am the Way." The Way suggests movement. God is not dead. Not only has he spoken; he speaks. Every man has to decide whether faith for him is letter or spirit, static or dynamic. I wholeheartedly agree with the late Dr. Clarence Knapp of the First Baptist Church of Pittsburgh, whose recent and untimely death is a great loss to the Christian cause, when he said: "It is the static mind, the implacable spirit, which finds the new scene discouraging and frightening. It is the static mind and institution which will find themselves left behind as the main stream of the world's life moves on, left behind in the ineffectual eddies and pockets of life" (*The Announcer*, January, 1963).

It is well to remember that the Master did not say "copy me" but "follow me." "He goeth before thee." We speak of going back to Christ. But if we really go back we move forward. Christ is not back. As George Matheson wrote, "Thou art abreast of all the centuries. I have never come up to thee, modern as I am."

You want an illustration of all we have been saying? Very well, take one from the book of the prophet Zechariah. Jerusalem had been destroyed and was to be rebuilt. The prophet writes: "I lifted up mine eyes and looked, and behold a man with a measuring line in his hand. Then said I, 'Whither goest thou?' and he said, 'To measure Jerusalem, to see what is the breadth thereof and the length thereof' . . . Run, speak to this young man saying 'Jerusalem shall be inhabited as towns without walls' . . . For I, saith the Lord, will be unto her a wall of fire round about and will be the glory in the midst of her" (Zechariah 2: 1-5). Ah! the harm that has been done to the cause of truth by eager young men with their measuring rods intent on making demands of a new day conform to the measurement of the past.

This is true in history. It was measuring rods that were responsible for the unspeakable tragedy of World War II. It was because some eager young men and stubborn old men took their measuring rods, walked about the ruins of the world, intent on building the new Jerusalem, the new world, on the same old isolationish dimensions that had marked the one destroyed. If ever God spoke to man to move into the ampler areas of international cooperation and fellowship, it was in 1918 as humanity faced a ruined world. But we would not move. And so we died in the hideous catastrophe of World War II. Our measuring rods were too small for us.

Religiously might we be doing the same thing, making the same mistake? Are our measuring rods holding up the progress of God's kingdom? Are we acting as though the creeds were changeless, or our particular denominational organization or ecclesiastical practice changeless? Was Reinhold Niebuhr right when he accused the Protestant Church of triviality? He defines triviality as "disproportionate concern with the minutiae of religious observation, ecclesiastical organization, and sectarian tradition at a time when the whole generation is passing through a world revolution."

"In God we live and move . . ." and, as George Buttrick has said, "if we do not move we do not live; we die." Is there any evidence that God wants his Church to move in a new direction today? Let me mention one. For myself I cannot doubt that the ecumenical movement is one evidence of the leadership of the Holy Spirit. We love to sing, "Like a mighty army moves the Church of God." It does nothing of the sort. It moves like a bunch of isolated squads each carrying on guerrilla warfare against a common foe, which is too big for any denomination. The world is too strong for a divided Church!

I believe God wants this situation changed not only because it is wasteful and inefficient, not only because our preoccupation with our denominational machinery diverts our attention from the weightier matters. He wants it changed because it is sinful. It corrupts our witness. It is a denial of our gospel which says "Ye are all one in Christ Jesus." This oneness in Christ, this unity, does not mean uniformity. The late Harry Elmer Barnes used to taunt us with what he called "the Jesus stereotype," as though Christians came off the end of an assembly line all stamped with the same pattern. He never got that idea from the New Testament! The day should now be passed when any church, any denomination, should think it is a facsimile of the New Testament church. There is great variety in the New Testament. Its pattern is unity in diversity.

Has not the time come when we should not think of our denominations as though they were absolutes, but see them as means to an end, that end being the coming of the Kingdom. "Seek ye first the Kingdom of God. Then our chief concern will not be to be known as Baptists or Methodists and so on but to be known as Christian. "Ye are all one in Christ Jesus."

This will mean that we will not feel duty bound to put a Baptist Church or a Presbyterian Church and so on in every community that does not have one, when perchance that community already has more Protestant churches than it can support.

What, do you suppose, keeps us from the larger loyalty of putting first the Kingdom of God? Denominational loyalty or pride or maybe arrogance? These no doubt are contributing factors. But I believe there is something else. There is a genuine fear that if we as Baptists associate in inter-denominational enterprises we may lose our distinctive witness. But is not such a fear a sad reflection upon the validity and vitality of the truth we hold? Truth, as John Milton said, does not have to fear open encounter. Truth does not have to be coddled or hidden behind iron curtains, political or religious. Politically there were those who espoused our national isolation. They kept us out of the League of Nations, with disastrous consequences for ourselves and the world, and even now they would take us out of the United Nations. Religious isolation in the modern world is just as incongruous and ultimately self-defeating as political isolation would be. It is difficult to doubt that Christ wants unity among his followers. Did he not pray that men may all be one that the world might believe? A divided Church cannot speak with authority to a divided world. "Physician heal thyself."

This, then, is the Eternal Word. It is at once our theme and our authority. We preach the truth as it is in Jesus. This is not a static but a dynamic truth. It combines uniquely permanence and relevance, changelessness and change, anchors that hold and sails spread to catch the winds of God. We follow one who is called the Pioneer of Faith. Some of the paths he blazed in his day we have yet not had the courage to explore.

If the Church is true to her Lord she will never be left in the eddies, the pockets of life. She will be in the main stream of the world's life. He is the water of life, and life is not static; it moves. So must we. He goeth before you into the modern Galilee with its problems and perils. He is before us. Would that we had the wisdom, the vision, the courage to follow the leadership of his spirit! ᛒ

The Relevant Word

Perhaps a good example of the Eternal Word, of which we spoke this morning, as it combines changelessness and change may be seen in its continuing relevance. Judged by outward appearance, how completely different is the modern world from that in which the Master lived and taught. How radically changed! And yet, as I shall endeavor to show, his message is just as applicable, as relevant to our world, as it was to his.

There are of course those who do not think we should use the word "relevant" with the gospel. They do not like its connotations. I shall not argue the point except to say I do not agree, which, of course, is not argument! If one prefers another word which means the same thing, let him use it. But an irrelevant gospel could not be the gospel of Jesus the Eternal Word.

It could not be because this gospel came to us in a life. "The Word was made flesh." Moreover, the avowed purpose of his life was to impart life. "I am come that they might have life and that they might have it more abundantly" (John 10:10). When the emissaries of the imprisoned John the Baptist came seeking his Messianic credentials, Jesus' answer was not argument but evidence taken from life: "Go tell John the things which you do hear and see, the blind receive their sight, the lame walk, the lepers are cleansed, the deaf hear, the dead are raised up, the poor have the gospel preached to them" (Matthew 11:4-5). Something is happening to life.

If further evidence of the effect of the gospel on the life of the age were needed, it could be found in the crucifixion. If anyone questions the use of the word "relevance" with the gospel, it seems to me he should remember the cross. As the late and beloved Hal Luccock has written, "Jesus was not crucified for saying 'Consider the lilies of the field how they grow,' but 'consider the thieves in the temple how they steal'." It is evident that he aroused the bitter hostility and determined opposition of the social, economic, political and religious powers of his age. An irrelevant gospel would never have done that. And he predicted that his followers would be brought before governors and kings for his sake (Matthew 10:18), as they were and have been. But only a word that touched life deeply and widely could have evoked such relentless opposition. The cross, then, is a symbol of the involvement of our faith in all that most deeply affects life. Sir George McLeod of Iona puts it vividly: "I simply argue that the cross be raised again at the center of the market place, as well as on the steeple of the church. I am recovering the claim that Jesus was not crucified in a cathedral between two candles, but on a cross between two thieves; on the town's garbage heap, at the crossroads so cosmopolitan that they had to write his title in Hebrew and in Latin and in Greek, at the kind of place where cynics talk smut and thieves curse and soldiers gamble . . . That is where he died and that is what he died about" (*Only One Way Left,* p. 38).

A man might say, "I do not believe the gospel. It is wishful thinking. It is an escape from reality, but whatever it be it is not true." A man might say that. Or one might say, "I believe the gospel, but I do not like it. It's not for me. It demands a discipline which I am unwilling or unable to give. It sets the immediate against the ultimate. It asks me to see time in the context of eternity. But my motto is one world at a time." A man might say that. But I do not believe that anyone who understands the gospel could ever think it is irrelevant.

Now today I should like to mention three of the familiar but basic claims of the gospel which will show its enduring relevance to life. If we think of our troubled world as a turbulent river rushing along, these three facets of our faith are like precipitous rocks, if you please, rising out of and reaching up above the troubled waters. The waters cannot cover them, nor can they wash them away, nor can they be diverted from them. Indeed, they are the points about which the waters swirl and are most agitated!

Mark you, I am not saying that every man will make up his mind about these matters, for every man will not and does not. Some will say that they do not know enough to consider them abstractly. Others might say it's not their line. They have no interest in such matters. But those who say that do not escape their impact. For though not everybody may make up his mind about them, so deeply are they interwoven in the fabric of life that no man can avoid making up his life about them. And it is not the things we abstractly make up our minds about, but those we concretely make up our minds about, that are decisive.

I said that these facets of our faith were like rock projections, but that is not a happy simile. For rocks suggest static changelessness.

These concepts are dynamic. We have and can and do re-think them; we can reinterpret them to meet the ever changing conditions of life. Guided by the Spirit, we may, as our Lord said, be led into a fuller and clearer knowledge of the truth. But they remain as changeless verities.

One is the gospel's view of God. I maintain that God is inescapable. The question is not whether one believes in a God, but rather the kind of God in whom or what one believes. If not the God of the gospel, then assuredly some other.

When Paul took the gospel to Rome, he did not go to a godless city. One of the best preserved relics of antiquity is the Parthenon in Rome, erected to the gods, to Jupiter and Juno, Neptune, Minerva, Apollo, Diana, and the rest. There were no atheists in Rome. It has been said that there are no atheists in foxholes. Truth to tell there are no atheists anywhere. Oh, to be sure, there are many theoretical atheists, but there are no practical atheists, and unfortunately, God is not a theory.

When a man says, "I do not believe in God," what he means, though he never says so, is "I do not believe in the God you believe in." But believe in some sort of God he surely does. For who or what, after all, is God? God is man's reaction to the sum total of reality. God is what one thinks gives meaning to life, and so is that about which a man organizes his life. Was not Martin Luther right when he said, "Whatever, then, thy heart clings to or relies upon, that, I say, is properly thy God." Every man's heart belongs to something, relies on something, and that for him gives meaning to life. Our pantheism is no relic. It is open for business.What are some of our modern gods? Race, nationality, money, success, power, popularity, social status, the American standard of living, and others. We say that these are our gods because they control our conduct. In these we think we find reality, the meaning of life.

The Communists are said to be atheists. How one wishes that they really were! They are fanatical believers in a god made in their own distorted image of reality. Their ideology has become their idol. Indeed, Paul writes of those "whose god is their belly," those who live as though the meaning of life were found in the undisciplined indulgence of the senses. And if one should say, "But my heart turns to nothing"; life is "sound and fury, signifying nothing," then "no god" becomes his god. He organizes his life around that. He lives as though the meaning of life were found in its meaninglessness. God is not a theory.

Actually the real trouble with our world is not atheism but polytheism. It is not that we do not believe in a God; we believe in too many of them. Life is like a wheel. It has many spokes. But a wheel has a hub, something that holds all the spokes together and keeps life from fragmentation. Ploytheism ignores the hub. It picks up individual spokes and tries to make absolutes from these. This is why our world is threatened with disaster. Our gods have failed us. They are just not big enough to encompass reality. They are projections of our ego. As John Calvin once wrote, in words more true today than ever, "An immense crowd of Gods has issued from the minds of men," but all such are "only dreams and phantoms of their own brains" (Baillie, *The Sense of the Presence of God,* p. 176).

Ah, the relevance of the gospel! As relevant today as when Paul wrote to a world bogged down in the sinking sands of polytheism and said, "For though there be so-called gods in heaven or on earth, as indeed there are many 'gods' and many 'lords' yet for us there is one God, the Father, from whom are all things and for whom we exist" (1 Corinthians 8: 5-6). "For this reason I bow my knees unto the Father, from whom every family in heaven and on earth is named . . ." (Ephesians 3:14). "One God who has made of one blood all the nations of men to dwell on the face of the earth" (Acts 17: 26).

What a magnificent concept! But more than a concept. In Jesus this concept became alive—was "made flesh." He came to teach that the human race was a family under the universal fatherhood of God. If one could only say, "Accept this concept of God or you will have no God." But there is no such thing as "no god." Whenever the true God is dethroned, some lesser deity is enthroned. Who was it who said, "Destroy a man's faith in God, and he will worship humanity. Destroy his faith in humanity, and he will worship science. Destroy his faith in science and he will worship himself. Destroy his faith in himself, and he will worship Samuel Butler"? Or, I might add, a less worthy object!

We turn now to a second truth of the gospel as illustrative of its permanent relevance to life, namely, the gospel's view of man. If it is impossible for any of us to avoid making up his mind about God, it is equally impossible to do so about man. Long ago the Psalmist asked, "What is man?" Well, what is man? Is he a freak of nature, a cosmic accident, or might he be a child of God? Is the deepest truth about man biological, psychological, sociological, or might it be theological, man made in the image of God?

The answer to the question "What is man?" varies. There are those who seem optimistic about man and his future. They see him as a creature who, despite his setbacks, is destined to win out. To others man is a colossal accident, a misfit in a universe quite ignorant of and so indifferent to him, his needs, hopes, values. Upon him and all his race rests the shadow of doom "pitiless and dark."

Now the gospel shares neither of these views. Its view is neither shallow optimism nor cynical pessimism. Its view is realism. It gives us the only realistic diagnosis of the human situation.

That there is something basically and tragically wrong with us is too obvious to be argued. The first step in curing an ailment is a correct diagnosis. It's just no use to give a man a couple of aspirin tablets if what he needs is surgery. The gospel says the real trouble with us is that we are sinners. This does not mean that there is nothing good in us. It means that there is a Judas in the heart of each of us, some deep seated evil which constantly perverts our good intentions, our high resolves, betrays the truth, and makes us sell our birthright for a mess of pottage. I do not see how anyone who knows himself or understands what is happening to our world could possibly doubt the truth of that diagnosis.

Something happened this past summer when I was in Jamaica which made me think, wonder. A man had lost a leg. After about two years he found it was necessary to have the other one amputated. He went to his doctor. The doctor said, "I must speak frankly. If I amputate this other leg you will die. If I do not amputate it you will die." He chose to have it removed. A week later he died.

I say that made me wonder. Is that the condition we confront with reference to our chronic disease, "the body of this death"? "You are damned if you do and damned if you don't." Are we hopeless? Is there no cure for the body of this death?

The gospel says, "Yes, there is. But the first step on the road to a cure is the frank recognition of the fact that you cannot cure yourself. Your salvation from the sin which so easily besets you lies not in what you do but in your acceptance through faith of what God in Christ has done for you." In a word, the gospel says to modern man, "You are not self-sufficient."

And that's the pill we find it hard to swallow. That's the rub. To tell modern man, who has mastered nature and is now bent on mastering space, who puts satellites and men in orbit, that he is not self-sufficient; well, it's hard for him to accept that. While we have the right to be justly proud of our scientific exploits, please do not be misled by them. For the real problem of man will not be solved by his mastery of space but by his mastery of himself. As we have said, the real problem of man does not lie in space, not on the moon, not even on the earth. It lies deep within man himself, in what the Apostle calls "the mystery of iniquity." Man cannot cure this disease by himself because the very self he would use as the means of his redemption is the self that needs to be redeemed.

Of course there are those who seem sincerely to believe that there is nothing deeply wrong with man which a little education will not put right. All glory to education! We cannot have too much of the right sort. But those who place their faith in secular education *per se* face the rather disturbing fact that our major problems and perils today come not from the ignorant but from the educated. Man constantly uses the very knowledge which is supposed to save him to carry out his devilish designs. The education that saves us is not just that of the mind, but of the heart, the conscience, the will, the total self. And this is done as the self submits to and receives the power, the grace, the forgiveness, the love of the Eternal as mediated through Christ our Lord.

The gospel's view of man is therefore realism. It sees man as he is, a sinner, but it never loses sight of what man by the grace of God may become. It looks beyond actualities to possibilities. Its view of man is therefore one of enduring hope. "Thou art Simon. Thou shalt be Peter." It sees man in the light of the God-man, the incarnation. As Barth puts it, "Every man on earth must be regarded from the point of view of this particular man" (*Against the Stream*, p. 186). In his light we might say with Peter, "Depart from me, for I am a sinful man, O Lord." Yet the very quality that repels us draws us. For the image of God in us, though defaced, is never quite effaced.

In his book, *Dear Mr. Brown*, Harry Emerson Fosdick tells of a young officer who during the First World War came to him with a problem. Said the young man, "At home I had never visited a brothel, but here in France with my fellow officers I have gone twice to look on. The first time I hated it; the second time I tolerated it; and I know that were I to go again I would participate in it, and so, before I went, I thought I would have a talk with you" (pp. 14-15).

Ah, what is man? Who said, "There is no peace in the worst part of me because there is goodness in the best part of me"? And is this goodness the chance product of a merely physical cosmos, an accident, or might it be a revelation of God? Every man who lives will by his life answer that question. And whether he admits it or is even aware of it, he will confront the relevant Word of God. Barth is right: "Every man on earth must be regarded from the point of view of this particular man."

Consider, now, a third facet of the gospel's relevance. Suppose you were standing atop a high building looking down on a moving mass hurrying about. You would know that each individual was going somewhere, activated by some purpose good, bad, or indifferent. But what about the total mass? Has mankind any collective destiny? Where is history going?

There are those who say that it is going nowhere. History moves in a circle. It has no goal. It is the result of purely fortuitous accidental forces, going it blind! Man walks a treadmill. He is not going anywhere. The human adventure is ultimately "a tale told by an idiot." "Sound and fury signifying nothing."

The gospel sees this differently. It says history has a goal. The whole creation may groan and travail in pain, as the Apostle says, but the pain has a purpose: "the revealing of the sons of God" (Romans 8: 19-22). Man is not a wanderer but a pilgrim. The human adventure is not like flotsam and jetsam on the restless ocean, but a ship. It has a course, a harbor, and a pilot!

What is the goal of history? Every Sunday we voice it when we pray, "Thy Kingdom come." Whatever be our interpretation of that phrase, whether completely eschatological or totally ethical, or a modification of both, it means the rule of God, the ultimate sovereignty of God, the reign of righteousness, truth and love in the hearts of men. It is therefore a frontierless, universal Kingdom. This is history's goal.

It seems a fantastic illusion. As one contemplates our modern world with its iron curtains, its warring ideologies, its vicious propaganda of hate and lies and cruelty, its reliance on weapons of incredible destructiveness, its "balance of terror," the Kingdom our Lord preached, lived, and for which he died must seem not the inspired vision of a seer but the ravings of a deluded visionary. But is it really?

Let me share an experience I had some time ago. I was in Rome. I could not help thinking of the Rome Paul viewed—the kingdom of Caesar. How magnificent it must have seemed, how powerful and how permanent—the Eternal City! I went out to the Coliseum with my camera. Paul did not have one. I though of the time when the elite and the populace filled those now dilapidated and deserted seats to be entertained as helpless, defenseless Christians were devoured by wild beasts. Such was "the kingdom of Caesar."

But now rising there amid the ruins someone had placed a huge cross. This symbolized another kingdom—the Kingdom of God. I recalled the words of the familiar hymn:

> In the cross of Christ I glory,
> Towering o'er the wrecks of time.

I recalled the words: "Spires outlast spears. Altars are more lasting than armaments. To the man who thinks, life is comedy; to the man who feels, life is tragedy; but to the man who believes, life is victory" (*Notable Sermons—American Pulpit*, p. 193). That cross said something which history has repeated with monotonous regularity, namely, that kingdoms founded on force, motivated by fear, dominated by the lust of power are not the goal of history. They do not symbolize ultimate reality, hence they do not and cannot endure. In our lifetime have we not seen many of them fall? Our modern world is unstable, precarious, its future uncertain precisely because it is patterned too largely after the kingdom of Caesar.

But the Kingdom symbolized not by the sword of Caesar but the cross of Christ, that we believe is here to stay because it represents Reality. It speaks not of the sovereignty of man, which is an illusion, but of the sovereignty of God. It bespeaks the hope that the end of history is not catastrophe but consummation.

Has it occurred to you that, while theologically the Master's vision of the human race as a family remains an unrealized dream, scientifically it has become a reality? The barriers once erected by space or distance have crumbled. Our technological achievements have "broken down the middle wall of partition between us." What happens in the remotest region of the world or in the tiniest of nations (Cyprus with its half million people) concerns the world as truly as the fate of one member of a household affects the family. Don't ask for whom the bell tolls; it tolls for thee.

But while science has given us proximity, it cannot create community. Proximity without community spells peril! As the world shrinks physically man must mature spiritually, grow in understanding, brotherhood, good will, and grace if we are to live together. Unless we learn to live together it seems probable that we may not live at all. No wonder the late Arthur Compton, Nobel prize winner in physics, could say, "Science has given us a world in which Christianity is a necessity."

For what is the alternative? Let Charles A. Ellwood, the noted sociologist, answer: "We must have a Christian world, or we shall have social chaos" (Harry Emerson Fosdick, *Dear Mr. Brown*, p. 102). These words were written before the invention of the atomic bomb. Today he would not say "social chaos" but "social suicide."

Do you see now why we speak of the gospel as "the relevant Word"? These three aspects of the gospel which we have all too inadequately mentioned, the reality of God, the nature of man, and the destiny of history, cannot be evaded any more than we can evade life. The turbulent waters of our age have not washed them away. It has not flooded them out of sight. It cannot be diverted from them. As a matter of fact, they are the inevitable points around which the waters rage in ceaseless agitation.

But now we face a sad and really distressing fact. We quoted the noted physicist as saying that in the kind of world science has given us Christianity is a necessity. But the sad truth is that the world has no such idea. The world does not take the Church, the bearer of the Word, seriously. It thinks that Christianity in general and the Church in particular are all right for those who like that sort of thing. The Church provides a solace for the pious, or a garb of respectability, an innocuous decoration like parsley sprigs on a dish. The minister is invited to business luncheons to give the invocation and pronounce the benediction. But the main course? Indeed, the world seems to think, as do some ministers, that when our Lord said he was to be the light of the world he meant a tail light!

Why is this? Are we to lay all the blame on the world for its indifference to the Church, or perhaps to blame ourselves also? I say this in no censorious spirit. I am just as involved in the relative ineffectiveness of the Church as anyone. But the truth is that "the light shineth in the darkness, but the darkness comprehended it not" (John 1:5).

There is no ready or simple answer to this ancient problem. But I wonder: is part of our ineffectiveness due to the fact that we have been more concerned about the lamp than the light? So involved in keeping the institution running that we have lost the vision of what it is running for. Does the earthen vessel seem more important than the treasure?

Or can it be that, all unwittingly, we have become so much like the world, prating its prejudices, comforming to its standards, as to become an echo of the world's voice rather than the voice of God to the world? Or can it be that we are so involved in tithing ecclesiastical mint, anise and cummin as to forget the weightier matters?

There is another possible reason, and this may be the main one. There are two statements in John's gospel, one in the first chapter, the other in the eighth, which we have not kept in balance. One text refers to the Master as "the true light that lighteth every man coming into the world"—the personal emphasis. In the other text the Christ of the fourth gospel says, "I am the light of the world"—the social emphasis. Can it be that, by and large, in our preaching we have overstressed the personal emphasis to the neglect of the social? The Master's life encompassed both foci—neither one escaped him. He said to the demoniac, "Go home to thy friends and tell them ..." He also said, "Go ye into all the world." He said to Simon Peter, "Simon, I have prayed for thee." He also prayed, "Thy Kingdom come." He wept at the grave of his friend Lazarus. He also wept over a city that knew not the things that belonged to its peace. One half of the gospel is not the gospel of Jesus Christ.

Have we allowed the relevance of the Word to the individual, "the true light that lighteth every man," completely to divert our attention from the relevance of the light that illumines the world? Is our emphasis too exclusively personal? No! Christianity can never be too personal. But I tell you what it can be. It can be too private. And when the gospel becomes a private matter, then it does not matter! Unless the gospel begins with the individual it does not begin. But if it ends with him, it ends.

Let me illustrate. Sir George McLeod was once scheduled to address a public meeting in Durban, South Africa. Just before the meeting a man came to him and said, "I hope you are going to give them the gospel red hot." Dr. McLeod explained that he was going to speak about the social implications of the gospel in Durban. "Social implications?" said the man. "What is wanted is the gospel red hot." Not dismayed, Dr. McLeod continued, "Then what are you gospellers doing about the ten thousand Africans and Indians who have not a decent shelter in Durban this cold night?" "Them?" said the man. "I wish the whole damned lot were sunk in the harbor." An extreme case? One hopes so! But it illustrates what happens to the relevant gospel when it begins and ends with the individual, when the personal gospel degenerates into a private gospel.

I know, all too well do I know, how one's involvement in the affairs of the local church, our immediate tasks, tends to obscure our ultimate purpose. We must pray and so work that our mundane tasks will not rob us of the vision without which as ministers our lives are lost in shallows and in miseries. In preaching we must not forget the world that God so loved. The true light that lighteth every man shines with only half its radiance unless we remember that it is also the light of the world. The preacher is not the chaplain of a private club. The problems of the world must be in our minds, its needs on our hearts. If not, our God is too small. The "hot gospel" which ignores our involvement in the total life of man is not hot, not even warm; it is frozen stiff! ꙮ

The Word of God

Whenever one hears or uses the phrase "The Word of God" he instinctively recalls that learned and creative thinker, Karl Barth—"the most famous Protestant theologian of the twentieth century." I am not a student of Dr. Barth, though I gratefully acknowledge the salutary influence he has had, and continues to have on our theological thinking. I believe the late Archbishop of Canterbury, William Temple, speaks for many of us and writes truly when he says, "The error of the Barthian school of theology—for that it contains error when judged by the canons of either natural reason or Christian revelation I cannot doubt—is, like every other heresy, an exaggeration of truth. To deny that revelation can, and in the long run must, on pain of becoming manifest as superstition, vindicate its claim by satisfying reason and conscience, is fanatical" (*Nature, Man and God*, p. 396).

It has often happened that some thinkers have had to go too far, in order to get the rest of us to go far enough. I have no doubt that this is true of this remarkable man.

The phrase, "the Word of God," is the ever recurring theme of the Bible. It has a history into which we cannot now go. "It covers the whole gamut of the divine activity in creating, sustaining and redeeming the creaturely order. Thus the Word is the characteristic mode of creation and revelation" (Rust, *Salvation History*, p. 25ff.). We are concerned now with its New Testament expression. Here the Word is not a word given to the prophet, but a life. Here the Word becomes flesh. Here "the Word of God is not given to Jesus as something distinct from him. It is Jesus himself" (p. 26). We shall think of the Word of God as Christ embodies it. How shall we as preachers describe this Word?

This question is important because it is, broadly speaking, one's relationship to this phrase, one's acceptance or rejection of its implications that determines whether he is a Christian man or just a religious person. There is a difference. A Christian is a religious man, but a religious man is not necessarily a Christian. "Man is incurably religious." Truth to tell every man, is in some sense religious. When you say a man is religious you say so much that you say nothing. Such men as Hitler, Stalin, and their modern counterparts were all religious, fanatically so. A religious man may be a tyrant, a secularist, or a saint. The act that makes a religious man a Christian is found in his relationship to "The Word of God."

We are to speak tomorrow evening of "Communicating the Word of God." But before we communicate anything, we should know what it is we seek to communicate. What then is the Word of God? Someone has said "God may have other words for other worlds, but for this world, the word of God is Christ." And that is true. "In the beginning was the Word . . . And the Word was made flesh and dwelt among us . . . full of grace and truth" (John 1:14). But let us see if we can be more specific.

I propose to mention three words, which as I see them give specific meaning to the Word. As I see them, there are no doubt other descriptive words that could be used.

The first is the Word given. This claim runs through the New Testament. "God so loved the world that he gave . . ." (John 3:16). "The gift of God is eternal life through Jesus Christ" (Romans 6:23). "For by grace have you been saved through faith, and that not of yourself: it is the gift of God" (Ephesians 2:8). Paul is very explicit on this point. He tells us that the word he preached was not after man nor did he receive it from man, but that it came by the revelation of Christ. He insists on the word revelation. "It pleased God . . . to reveal his son in me . . ." (Galatians 1:15-16). "How that by revelation he made known unto me the mystery . . . Which in other ages was not made known unto the sons of men, as it is now revealed unto his holy apostles and prophets by the spirit" (Ephesians 3: 3-5).

Now what was the crux, the heart of this revelation? What did Christ the Word reveal? It was, I believe, the nature of God. Christ the Word was given to reveal the nature of God. This brings up the touchy question of the relationship between discovery and revelation, between man's attempt to know God and God's will to make himself known, between man's search for God and God's quest for man. Job asks,"Canst thou by searching find out God, canst thou find out the Almighty unto perfection? Is it high as heaven what canst man do? Deeper than hell, what canst thou know? The measure thereof is longer than the earth and broader than the sea" (Job 11: 7-9).

This is true. But it surely does not mean that man had discovered nothing valid nor valuable about the nature of God prior to his revelation in Christ. Who would dare to say that Amos, or Isaiah, or

Hosea, or Jeremiah and other seers or prophets have not illumined for us the nature of the Eternal? The author of the Epistle to the Hebrews assures us on that point. The question then is "What did Jesus the given Word, reveal about God which the prophets had not discovered?"

The Jewish scholar Montefiore says that everything Jesus said about God can be found somewhere in the sayings of the Rabbis, everything except one thing. Nowhere in Judaism is God described as one who aggressively seeks the lost. He writes, "The Rabbis welcomed the sinner in his repentance, but to seek out the sinner, and instead of avoiding the bad companion to choose him as your friend in order to work his moral redemption, this was, I fancy, something new in the religious history of Israel" (Moses Haim, *The Religious Teaching of Jesus*, p. 57).

It is not possible to pursue this further except to say that while this distinguished scholar is no doubt technically right, he is as I think, wholly wrong if he limits our Lord's originality to this one specific fact. For the uniqueness of God's revelation in Christ is not to be found simply in what he said about God, but in what he himself revealed through his life—the whole concept of *agape*, self-giving love he incarnated. Moreover, originality does not consist simply in saying what is new or different, what nobody else has ever said. It consists also in illuminating, re-interpreting, criticizing, evaluating what has been said. And that is what our Lord did with his religious tradition.

While therefore we do not belittle the importance of man's effort to discover God, we say the Word is "given because in Christ his teaching, his life, God has revealed what man could not discover." Man's effort to discover is met by God's purpose to reveal. "The Given Word."

The fact that the Word is given illumines a great Christian truth, namely that the initiative is always with God. As Augustine said, he is "beforehand" with our souls. "We love him because he first loved us." We find him, because he first seeks us. "God was in Christ reconciling the world unto himself." The initiative is with him.

This should keep us humble. "For we preach not ourselves but Christ Jesus the Lord and ourselves your servants for Jesus' sake."

Now let us mention a second mark of the Word of God. I confess I had difficulty in finding a word that would express what I feel—the word I finally hit upon is "definitive." It makes a tremendous claim—but no other word seems adequate.

The dictionary defines definitive as "decisive, unconditional, final." By it I mean that the Word of God is the Word without which no other words ultimately make sense! Now as I have said, this is a tremendous claim. Many people, most people, do not believe it at all. And many of us who profess to believe it, give it only lip service. The question then arises, "Is it true?" What right have we to make so sweeping a claim? I propose to mention, very briefly, three reasons.

For one thing we say God's Word is definitive because it is addressed to man, who is the definitive force in the world. That is why God addresses him—he is the key. In the book of Genesis the definitive nature of man is made clear. There we read, "And God blessed them and God said unto them, be fruitful and multiply and replenish the earth and subdue it and have dominion over the fish of the sea and the fowl of the air and everything living that moveth upon the earth" (Genesis 1:28). By the same token in our attempt to conquer space we are but carrying out the Eternal's intent—to "subdue" and "have dominion." We sometimes say with the poet, "Where every prospect pleases and only man is vile." But it is man, be he vile or virtuous, that is the definitive factor on this planet. The kind of world we have is determined by the kind of people we are.

The history of the world, in its final analysis, is nothing more or less than the history of man; what he thinks, what he does, what he dreams and plans, how he behaves. At the heart of history stands man, this seemingly puny, transient, yet powerful definitive being. The Word of God is definitive because it is addressed to man who is the definitive being.

But let us mention the second reason. We said that the kind of world we have is determined by the kind of people we are. But what determines that? What determines whether we convert the Father's house into a den of theives or make the wilderness and solitary places grow and blossom? "Out of the same mouth proceed blessings and cursings." But what determines whether we bless or curse, whether we rob, plunder, kill, destroy the earth, or use our amazing capacities constructively, to uplift and bless humanity?

The answer lies in our character, and character is a spiritual phenomenon. In short, the definitive fact about man, this definitive being, is the degree of his moral and spiritual maturity. The master once said to his disciples who would call down fire from heaven to destroy a Samaritan village, "Ye know not what manner of spirit ye are of" (Luke 9:55). Spirit, that is the key to man's destiny. When you know the spirit of a man, you know the man, so the spirit of an age determines its character.

One always hesitates to speak of the spiritual as distinguished from the material. For it would be so wrong to think that there is some sort of iron curtain between them; or to imagine that they are like oil and water that do not mix, when actually there is the free interplay between them. Body and Soul are all of a piece.

This is why it is hard to understand why so many people think of the spiritual realm as the realm of fantasy, illusion, as though the spiritual were unimportant, unreal. When it is actually an inescapable reality. It is definitive.

Take democracy. A political phenomenon of course. Yet is there any doubt that the success of democracy depends on character, on our moral and spiritual maturity? We speak of education for democracy, but is there any doubt that educated crooks, clever, self-seeking politicians are our most subtle danger? The success of democracy depends ultimately not on our political know-how, but on our character. A spiritual reality.

Take the United Nations. A noble experiement. The fulfillment of the poet's dream of "The Parliament of man the federation of the world." Will it work, will it endure? The answer lies in the spiritual realm. Whether the nations possess enough moral and spiritual maturity, to put the welfare of mankind above selfishness and pride and lust.

The atom—surely there is nothing spiritual about that! The theoretical physicist in his laboratory splits the atom—this is purely a scientific matter. How one wishes it were! It has actually posed the profoundest spiritual problem man has ever faced. It has given modern meaning to the words of the ancient writer, "I call heaven and earth to record this day against you that I have set before you life and death, blessing and cursing, therefore choose life that thou and thy seed may live" (Deut. 30:19). And what pray tell will determine our choice? Our degree of spiritual maturity. I would venture that there is no problem that involves mankind, be it economic, political, social, international, that ultimately does not lead to his spiritual condition.

However we look at it, our world is nothing more than the soul of man in projection.

If then we say that the Word of God is the definitive Word, we make that claim, not only because it is addressed to man, the definitive being, but also because it speaks specifically to the definite aspect of his being—his character, his moral and spiritual nature. This determines the kind of people we are and so the kind of world we inhabit.

But there is a third reason, and this is really the heart of the matter. The Word of God is the definitive Word, not only because it is addressed to man, but because it came in a man.

Is it enough to say that the future of man on this earth depends on his growth in spiritual maturity? How does he know whether he is growing or not? Has he any way of measuring this? Is each man to be his judge in such matters? This brings us to the mystery of the incarnation. For if we believe that Christ is God's Word made flesh, then Christ must be the definitive man among the sons of men, and Christlikeness becomes the definitive mark of man. And so the definitive Word becomes the redemptive Word.

Man is a measurer. He constantly uses standards of measurements from an ordinary yardstick to some highly complicated scientific apparatus. But is there any standard against which he can measure himself? The Greeks said "Man is the measure of all things." But by whom or what is he the measurer, measured?

Sometimes we are prone to measure ourselves by things. We say a man is worth so many dollars and so on—obviously this is an inadequate standard. We cannot measure life by things. A man cannot measure himself by that which is below him!

Most of us are prone to measure ourselves by that which is on our level. Paul speaks of those who measure themselves by themselves (2 Cor. 10:12). But this Narcissus-like performance is a highly ambiguous one. For the self is not one but many. Moreover the end result of this is self-centeredness and pride which are self-destructive.

Paul also speaks of those who compare themselves among themselves (2 Cor. 10:12). You measure yourself by others. Millions have fallen into this fallacy of "keeping up with the Joneses!" This is really the worse kind of slavery. And we are prone to adopt it not only in inconsequential matters, we actually let society set our standards for us. We find that if everybody is doing it, then it must be the thing to do. But unfortunately this, all too often, turns out to be a case of the blind leading the blind. I once heard a minister say, "Sixty-thousand people can be wrong." So indeed they can! As a matter of fact, I think that in matters of deepest moment, majorities are always wrong!

If we really believe in the incarnation, we cannot be content to measure outselves by what is below us, nor horizontally by what is on our level. We measure ourselves by that which transcends us—by Christ, the God-man—the definitive Word of God. This is the testimony of those who strive for spiritual maturity. As Barth says, "Every man on earth must be regarded from the point of view of this particular man."

> O Lord and Master of us all,
> What 'ere her name or sign,
> We own thy sway, we hear thy call,
> We test our lives, by Thine.

It is for these three reasons that we dare make the claim that the Word of God is the definitive Word.

There is a third mark. The Word is given. It is definitive. But the Word of God is also a living Word. Paul speaks of "living epistles." A dead Word could not produce "living epistles." Hence the living Word is the redemptive Word. He distinguishes between the "living Word" and the "written word." He says "You are a letter that has come from Christ. . . . A letter written not with ink but with the spirit of the living God, written not on stone tablets, but on the pages of the human heart" (2 Corinthians 3: 1-3, English Bible). If words mean what they say, then it is obvious that the Apostle identifies the living Word with Christ, not with a book.

The Book is invaluable. We love it. We should be lost without it. It is irreplaceable. It is indeed a lamp to our feet, a light to our path (Psalms 119: 105). But since there is so much bibliolatry about, I must, even though "bringing coals to Newcastle" press the distinction, between the "living Word" and the "written word." The "living Word" whatever else it be, must be the word of truth. "I am . . . the truth." By this test not every word in the Bible is the Word of God.

The distinction we are making was made by Martin Luther. He said, in substance, that the Bible is not the Word of God, but contains the Word of God. Were you to have asked him, "How then does one distinguish between the Word of God in the Bible and the word of man?" He would have said "Test it by the spirit of Christ. Whatever in the Bible is not in harmony with the spirit of Christ is not the Word of God." He said that the Bible is the crib in which Christ is lain. He carried this test to unwarranted extremes. He called the Epistle of James the "Epistle of straw," because it does not contain the name of Christ. But since the living Word is the word of truth, his test is still valid.

Emil Brunner makes one same distinction. He writes: "For real faith in the Bible, such as we find in the Reformers, the Bible is like a certain area of ground, in which you can find gold, now go and find it. But orthodoxy declares 'All the ground is gold. Gold and ground are identical, you need not search . . . .' Into what diastrous difficulties it led one believer, soon became evident" (*The Word and The World*, pp. 94-95).

The Bible itself makes the distinction we are discussing. In the book of Deuteronomy, the eighteenth chapter and the twenty-first verse, the writer hears God say: "And if thou say in thine heart, 'How may we know the word which the Lord hath not spoken?' When a prophet speaks in the name of the Lord, if the word does not come to pass, or come true, this is the word which the Lord hath not spoken, but the prophet has spoken it presumptuously." Here again, if words mean anything the writer clearly distinguishes between the Word of God, the Word of Truth, and the word of man which he terms "presumptuous"—or more kindly we might say, "mistaken" or ill-formed."

If further evidence were needed our Lord himself could give it. He did not treat his Bible, the Old Testament, as though every word in it was, in very truth, the Word of God. Matthew reports him as endorsing the law in its entirety, every jot and tittle of it (Matthew 5:18-19). Yet in actual fact did he not disregard many of the ceremonial laws of the Bible, at the cost of bitter and determined opposition? Could not his words to the Pharisees be applied here also? "Every plant which my heavenly Father has not planted will be rooted up" (Matthew 15:13). The evidence, as it seems to me is irrefutable. The Bible, *in toto*, is not the Word of God, but contains the Word of God.

During my undergraduate days at Denison University, our lovely Garden of Eden, the Denison campus, was invaded by a serpent—an atheist. He brought with him to our campus any number of pamphlets which he freely distributed to the students. The pamphlets sought to blacken the character of God. He had gone to the Old Testament and picked out all the unsavory incidents he could find: unmoral, immoral, submoral, trickery, treachery, deceit, adultery, incest, murder—they are all there! "Your God" he said, "condoned, allowed all this—this is the God you believe in."

I was going to preach that week end, so I took his pamphlet with me thinking to read it on the train. I began to do so but soon stopped. I feared that if I finished it, it would finish me, and I would not be able to preach!

Now I could read that without, as we say, "batting an eye." For I know that every word in the Bible is not the Word of God. This does not make the Bible less of a book, less an authoritative or trustworthy guide. Frankly, it has made it more so for me. It is no less a Divine book, because it is so human, so genuine, so honest a portrait of human life. When Cromwell sat for a portrait he said to the artist, "Paint me just as I am, warts and all." That is the picture the Bible portrays, not make believe, touched up, faked, but a genuine, true, valid picture of man in his dealings with God, and God's dealings with him.

The Apostle Peter writes, "Holy men of God spoke as they were moved by the Holy Ghost" (2 Peter 1:21). Quite true! But though "holy" they were still men; men of their age, conditioned by its culture, sharing in its life, exposed to its errors. The Holy Ghost did not put them in a vacuum, nor did the Holy Ghost treat them as a ventriloquist does his puppets, by making them no more than echos of his voice, helpless objects of his manipulative skill.

The fact is that God did not reveal his truth to man all of a sudden, as light comes into a dark room when one turns a switch. His truth came rather like the breaking of the dawn. At first but dimly seen on the distant horizon but growing brighter and brighter into the perfect day. God could communicate his truth to men only *through* men, as they were prepared to receive it.

The same principle helps us in dealing with the outmoded scientific ideas of the Bible. It is well to remember that Moses was not a physicist nor Joshua an astronomer. If one should think that in rejecting the cosmology of the Bible one has to throw out the baby with the bath, let him read Helmut Thielicke's book *How the World Began.* A book which shows how the first chapters of the Bible can be dealt with "through more fruitful categories than those of demythologizing or a flattened out literalism."

This committed and skillful preacher draws the water of life, the living water, from the dried up and abandoned wells of our fathers' scientific immaturity. He finds living bread in the scientific chaff which the winds have driven away. How truly did Paul write, "For the Word of God is not bound . . ." (1 Timothy 2:9). It is no more bound to the outmoded scientific ideas of the Bible than was it to the imprisoned Paul. As Charles Hodge, distinguished theologian of his time put it, "Their inspiration no more made them astronomers than it made them agriculturalists" (*Protestant Thought and Natural Science*, p. 235). As one of the Fathers puts it, "The Bible tells us how to go to heaven not how the heavens go."

Take the book of Jonah as further illustration of the truth. For how many is that epoch-making little book little more than a glorified fish story! As far as the living Word is concerned it makes no difference whether Jonah swallowed the whale or the whale swallowed Jonah. After all the author got Jonah in the sea, and he had to get him to shore. The whale provided the most convenient if not the most comfortable means of transportation. But the living Word in that little book shrinks the whale to the size of a minnow! It would be wise to heed the word of one of the Fathers who said, "Press not the breasts of holy writ too hard, lest they yield blood rather than milk."

Now if what we have said is true, then it seems to me that as preachers, we are not being true to ourselves, our people, or to God if we do not little by little try to lead our people out of the obscurantism of bibliolatry into the light of truth. It is our duty to help them distinguish between the living Word, the Word of God, and the mistaken "presumptuous" word of man. We must help them see the difference between the gold and the ground, the building and the scaffolding, the picture and the frame, the treasure and the earthen vessel. If we refuse this task, then in the words of the Apostle, we are "handling the Word of God deceitfully" (2 Corinthians 4:2).

Such then is "The Word of God" as a preacher sees it—given, definitive, living.

But how can we communicate it? That is the question we shall try to answer tomorrow evening. ℞

Communicating the Word of God

We spoke at our last session on "The Word of God." We described it as being "given," "definitive," "living." However we describe it, it is the preacher's theme and authority. "How shall they hear without a preacher?" (Romans 10:4). The preacher is the bridge, the connecting link, between the Word and the people. He communicates the word, through his words. Today we make some suggestions aimed at helping us in this task.

There is, of course, a technical side to preaching, a "know-how." We sometimes say of a man that "he knows how to preach." Sermons often fall short, not because the preacher has nothing to say, but because he does not know how effectively to say it. This knowing how is so important that we have professors of homiletics to instruct us in the art of sermon preparation.

Into this aspect of the matter we shall not now go, except to say that some sermons are like swamps—they ooze out all over the place. Others are like rivers—the difference between a swamp and a river is that the river has banks. These give direction and movement. Some sermons are like the world before the Eternal intervened—they are without form and void and darkness is upon the face of the congregation!

Let us be thankful then for our teachers in homiletics, but remember that communicating the Word of God involves more than the mastery of techniques. This is why our teachers in homiletics are concerned not only about how we preach, but what we preach—the content of our sermons. It is, broadly speaking, this matter we shall now discuss.

I suggest that we take the Master as our guide, for indeed we could have no better guide. How did he communicate the Word of God? To discover his method let us limit our thought to three incidents in the Gospels. Our approach then will be selective, not exhaustive. Our theme will be bounded, limited, to three specific individuals with whom the Master spoke. But these individuals represent or symbolize three types of people whom we try to reach.

The three individuals I have chosen are the woman of Samaria, Nicodemus, and Peter. All familiar ones. You will recall that they were all different. The woman's problem was moral, Nicodemus' problem was intellectual. We are not told if Peter had a problem. Since he was a working man, a fisherman, and at work, maybe he was preoccupied. However, Jesus, who knew what was in man, called him, and he came.

Since these people were all different, the Master used, as we shall see, a different approach to each one. His approach to the woman would have been lost on Nicodemus. His command to Peter would have been ill-advised if addressed to the woman. Effectively to communicate the Word of God, we must be concerned not simply with our subject but with our object. In fishing for men we must use not only a net but sometimes bait. All fish do not take the same bait!

I am reminded of a story that Dr. Albert Schweitzer tells in his autobiography. He says that the preacher whose church he and Mrs. Schweitzer attended in Africa, never preached a sermon without mentioning the evils of alcohol. Surely a timely theme, but not for every Sunday. One Sunday morning the preacher announced that the next Sunday he would preach on the creation of the world. Mrs. Schweitzer whispered to her husband, "Well at least we shall be spared the evils of alcohol." To which the doctor replied, "I am not so sure, you do not know the versatility of the homiletic mind." Next Sunday came—the preacher, in his sermon, mentioned the six days of creation and the creative activity of the Almighty on each of the days; then he paused and asked, "Does the Bible tell us he created alcohol?" And he was off on his well-worn theme!

It has been said that every preacher has only one sermon, one major emphasis, which he preaches in a hundred different ways. This may in a sense be true. We might say that Harry Emerson Fosdick's emphasis was to make religion intellectually respectable; to show that you could be a Christian and yet be an intelligent, educated man. Billy Graham's emphasis is the power of God to redeem the individual from sin. Reinhold Niebuhr has punctured our illusions. He has broken the bubble of our self-righteousness. He has made the old word, "There is none that doeth good, no not one" relevant. But it is one thing to say that every preacher, generally speaking, makes his own approach, or emphasis, and quite another to say that he monotonously harps on one string. These three incidents we are considering will show that our Lord never did that.

Now to be more specific. Take his approach to the woman of Samaria. She symbolizes those whom we immediately recognize as sinners. She was a bad character, a harlot. How did he communicate the Word to her? He did so by putting his finger on her moral pulse.

See how he did this. The conversation, as you will recall, was pitched on an elevated plane. It was profoundly theological. It began with a discussion of living water, inner spiritual resources. It proceeded to a discussion of worship. Should one worship in Mount Gerazim or Jerusalem? A question which involved a statement of the nature of God as Spirit. And it ended with reference to his messiahship.

The striking fact, however, is that right in the midst of this weighty theological discussion Jesus interrupted her by saying, "Go call thy husband and come hither." The woman must have thought, "Why bring that up?" She had no husband or more accurately, five husbands. It must have seemed to her a shocking thing to bring her down to earth, when her mind was occupied with such elevated thoughts.

Listen to the words of the Gospel. "Sir, give me this water that I thirst not, neither come hither to draw. Jesus said unto her, 'Go call thy husband. . . . .' ." As much as to say, "all our discussion of the living water, or the meaning of worship, or the nature of God, or the promised messiah, avails nothing if not related to, brought in contact with, the moral realities of your life."

It would seem from the record, that the turning point of this story was reached when the Master touched this moral nerve: "Go call your husband."

In speaking of the moral nerve we are not of course thinking just of sex but of all unethical practices which are basically immoral—of the dishonesty of Zacchaeus, the greed of the rich fool, the cruelty of the wicked husbandman, the selfishness of Dives, the indifference of the Priest and the Levite. In short, all we mean by the ethical teaching of Jesus.

There are some theologians who do not think very highly of morality. They speak of it as though it were an illegitimate offspring of nature, rather than the mark of God on the soul. They inveigh, and rightly so, against moralistic preaching—moralistic preaching is bad preaching and one hopes he has not done much of it. But we must distinguish between moralistic preaching, and preaching that comes to grips with the moral and ethical issues of our time. As the late Dr. John Baillie has written: "There is a difference between moral religion which is the best religion, and moralistic religion which is a delusion" (*Interpretation of Religion*, p. 309). One can be moral without being Christian, but he cannot be Christian without being moral. We must not allow the inadequacies of moralistic preaching to commit us to the no less inadequate practice of theological preaching, unrelated to, uniformed by the moral realities of our age. The mouthing of pious-sounding words, time-worn cliches, will not do. Theological preaching invovles more than the meticulous use of theological language.

We bewail, and rightly so, the spiritual illiteracy of our people. We could bewail just as much their moral illiteracy. Will the theological God be real to one who has not encountered the moral God? I wonder. Will the incarnation of God in Christ be apprehended by one who has never heard God in the still small voice? Will the mystery of the Cross reach one who does not see the meaning of the Ten Commandments? "If I have told you earthly things and ye believe not, how shall you believe if I tell you heavenly things?" (John 3:12).

They tell of a priest who once asked a gypsy if she knew the Ten Commandments. She replied, "Father it's this way. I was going to learn them, but I heard they were going to abolish them." It seems that for many they have been abolished! Is it not a disturbing fact that this age which has witnessed a resurgence of religious interest, as seen in increased church attendance, church building, and church budgets, this same age also witnesses to an alarming and widespread deterioration of our moral life in high places and low?

There is, of course, no simple explanation of this. Many factors may be involved. But one cannot help but wonder whether the church in general and us preachers in particular may not be partly responsible. The trouble is not that we preach theology. That is our Gospel. It is that our theology has not been sufficiently informed by, related to, and involved in the great moral issues of our age.

Theology may soar aloft like an airplane into the blue yonder, but remember that the plane takes off from the earth, and against the wind. Remember too that it stays aloft and is guided in its flight by its contact with earth. Neither a theology that is otherworldly, nor a morality that is earthbound is adequate. How wise was the Master! He sought to communicate the Word of God to this woman by relating her theological concern to the moral realities of her life. "Go call your husband."

Preach theology, but unless our theology be pious cliches time-worn, without relevance, vitality, conviction, power, it must be related to, involved in, the great moral issues of our age.

Consider now how he sought to communicate the Word to Nicodemus. He was as we have stated a different person, and Jesus used a different method. The woman was a bad character. Nicodemus was a good man. Her problem was moral. His was intellectual. Unlike some intellectuals, he was not sophisticated, clever, or cynical. He was a sincere seeker after truth, troubled with honest doubts. "How can these things be? How can a man be born when he is old?" How did the Master deal with this honest doubter?

He was patient and sympathetic. He did not say, "Nicodemus, I said you must be born again and that's that. You may take it or leave it." On the contrary he tried to make the new birth understandable, intelligible. See how he did this? He likened the mystery of the new birth to that of the wind, unpredictable, mysterious, cleansing, freshening, and it is gone! Again, he reminded Nicodemus of the adumbrations of the new birth in his own tradition. Did not God say through Ezekiel, "A new heart will I give you . . . and I will take away the stony heart. . . and I will put my spirit within you"? (Ezekiel 36:25-29). Did not the Psalmist pray "Create within me a clean heart O God, and renew a right spirit within me"? (Psalms 51:10). "Nicodemus, art thou Master of Israel and knowest not these things?" (John 3:10). And further he brought in the testimony of experience. As though he said to him, Nicodemus, the new birth is no fantasy, no illusion. Its truth is verified by human experience. "We speak what we do know and testify what we have heard and seen" (John 3:11).

Thus did the Master try to explain, to make understandable the truth of his claim. It is as though he were saying, "Nicodemus, I do not want you to believe this just because I say so, not even because the Bible says so. I want you to believe it because it is so, because it is true."

This raises the question, "What are we doing for, saying to, the Nicodemus of our age, the honest questioner? Have we quite forgotten him? When we prepare our sermons we think of the woman of Samaria, the bad immoral people who need to be made good. But have we no word for the morally good people, perplexed with honest doubts? If some Nicodemus attended our church some Sunday morning would he leave it feeling, "This is not for me. It is for bad people who need to be cleaned up. It is for those who are in the fold.

306 / Preaching with Purpose and Power

But not for me." Have we a message for those whose problem is not that of goodness versus badness, but of truth versus falsehood? When we prepare our sermons do we ever say to ourselves, "I am saying this because I believe it is true. Now how can I help others to see the truth of it? How can I make the Gospel intelligible?"

It would, of course, be presumptuous to suppose that we can always help the honest doubter. The late F. W. Norwood of the City Temple in London, said at the end of his fruitful ministry, "I have spent all my life explaining things." Doubtless, some of his explanations did not explain. It has been said that God is never found at the end of an argument. "I thank thee Father that thou hast hidden these things from the wise and prudent, and revealed them to the simple-minded" (Luke 10:21). Moreover, we must remember that often the Spirit of God reaches Nicodemus when our words do not.

Having said this let us say further that even though we may not always be able to help him, we should try not to hinder him. Some things we do may be a hindrance to Nicodemus.

In what I say from now on, many of you, perhaps most of you, but I hope not all of you, will disagree. Though I speak as a Baptist, I am not presuming to speak for all Baptists. The man who can speak for all Baptists is not yet born and his parents are dead!

Are we doing anything that may hinder Nicodemus, make him turn away from the church?

For one thing our use of traditional phrases often lack reality. This is a hindrance to the honest questioner. Take the words "lost" and "saved." These are surely valid concepts, but do we not often use them too loosely, as though we were speaking of black and white?

I once heard a minister say in a sermon that if one stood at a certain corner for twenty-four hours, two hundred thousand lost souls would pass by. I could not help wondering where he got his statistics!

We are wont to think that lost people are always bad people. Our Lord did not think so. He told three stories to explain the word lost— The Lost Sheep, The Lost Coin, The Lost Son. But only the son was willfully bad. The lost sheep was not bad. He was not vicious. He would not have attacked you like a tiger. He was just thoughtless, just wandered away. The lost coin was not bad. It was not counterfeit. It was a good coin in the wrong place. There was a gap between its potential and actual value. But its material value was still there. I think we hinder Nicodemus, drive him away if we tell him he is lost as was the prodigal when he is not. Have we any word for those who are not morally bad, and yet, like the coin or the sheep, might be lost?

And so with being saved. This is a timelessly valid truth, but do we not often make it too mechanical, perfunctory? Is salvation a static fact, or a dynamic process? Was Luther right when he said, "A man never is a Christian, he is always becoming one"? But you will remind me that the scriptures say, "Believe on the Lord Jesus Christ and thou shalt be saved" (Acts 16:30). But too often such professed belief is verbal, not vital. I must remind you the scriptures also say, "the devils also believe and tremble" (James 2:19). Some of these very people who profess to believe and have joined the church are staunch segregationists; they deny by their life what they profess with their lips. Are they saved?

And not only matters of race. How many of us who profess to believe and belong to the church lack compassion, understanding love. We are smug, proud, self-righteous. Are we saved? ". . . Now if any man have not the spirit of Christ, he is none of his" (Romans 8:9). "Why call ye me Lord Lord and do not the things which I say?" (Luke 6:46). "By their fruits ye shall know them" (Matthew 7:20). "Not every one that saith unto me 'Lord Lord' shall enter into the kingdom of heaven, but he that doeth the will of my Father who is in heaven" (Matthew 7:21).

Again, I think the modern Nicodemus is hindered by our neglect of the teaching function of the church. He wants more information, more light, and he is not getting it. ". . . He opened his mouth and taught them" (Matthew 5:2).

The teaching function is being neglected, as it seems to me, because of our limited idea of evangelism. In a sense every sermon should be evangelistic. But should not evangelism mean more than we popularly conceive it to be? Does it not mean more than coming forward and deciding for Christ? When Apollos, a Jew of Alexandria, came to Ephesus, we are told that Aquila and Priscilla met him and "expounded unto him the way of God more perfectly" (Acts 18:26). Was that not a part of evangelism? Is not the minister who gives some thought and time to making those who are nominally Christian more Christlike doing the work of an evangelist? Our concept of evangelism is almost exclusively quantitative—how many. The kind I am speaking of is qualitative—what sort. We need both. But the second is too largely neglected. "These ought ye to have done and not to leave the other undone" (Matthew 23:23).

Can we afford to neglect it? Is the future of Christianity determined by the size of the dough or the quality of the leaven? Have we got into a sort of rut in our preaching of evangelism? I am reminded of a man who bought a cello. In learning to play it he almost drove his wife to distraction. He held down one string and moved his bow back and forth on it, thus sounding only one note. His wife went to a concert given by a professional cellist. When she returned she told her husband he was not going at this the right way. The professional cellist used all the strings and moved his fingers up and down. To which her husband replied, "Oh, he is looking for the note. I have found it!" But the most melodious note, if played continuously, becomes monotonous and therefore ineffective.

But this harping on one string to the neglect of the teaching function of the church is not the only hindrance to Nicodemus. It has another result that may be just as bad, if not worse. It means that those who are members of the church do not grow in grace and in the knowledge and love of God. "The hungry sheep look up and are not fed." The Apostle speaks of "the unsearchable riches of Christ." But these are often unexplored. And because the other strings of the Gospel are not sounded, the average church member may develop a smug, self-righteous spirit. He may mistake the one note for the full orchestration. To change the figure he may feel he has reached the end of the line, when actually he has only started the journey. By all means be evangelistic, but enlarge the idea to include Nicodemus.

Do not forget Nicodemus. For when we do, we forget more than Nicodemus. We forget the spiritual growth and development of our people. We forget ourselves—our own spiritual growth.

Consider now the third individual—Peter. And now I am going to get into more hot water—hotter water! The woman's problem was moral. Nicodemus's problem was intellectual. If Peter had some specific problem, we are not told what it was. Perhaps as I have suggested, it was preoccupation. He was a working man and was at work, in the act of casting his net into the sea when he was called. He was a man of action. Was that why the Master asked him to do something? He assured him he would still be a fisherman, only he would catch men, not fish. Be that as it may.

Now what is the important lesson for us in the call of Peter? Is it not this: that we should remember that in communicating the Word of God, the heart of the Gospel is loyalty, commitment to a person? All Jesus said to Peter was "Follow me." And to follow Jesus does not mean to walk behind him. It means to share his purpose, his faith, his spirit. He presented Peter with no creedal or ecclesiastical test. It was not until near the end of his ministry that, at Caesarea Philippi, he said to Peter, "Whom say ye that I am?" And Peter replied, "Thou art the Christ, the Son of the living God" (Matthew 16:15-16). But had he put that question to Peter when he called him by the lake, he would not have been able to answer it.

Is it not significant, too, that in the post-resurrection story Jesus seems to emphasize that the heart of the Gospel is attachment to a person? He asks Peter three times, "Lovest thou me?" "Lovest thou me?" "Follow me." That is the supreme test of a Christian. It would appear that Jesus who "knew what was in man" saw the possibilities in this fisherman. He wanted him, his life, and so he asked, "Are you willing to follow me?" "Do you love me?" That was all. But that was enough.

Is there anything we may learn from this in communicating the Word of God. I can only tell you what it suggests to me. It suggests that all Protestant denominations, our own included, often put the emphasis in the wrong place. We have tests which we deem more important than one's loyalty to Christ. Let me now speak of our denomination which I know best.

When I had the privilege of teaching homiletics here two years ago, one of the truly able students in my class preached from a text in Ephesians (4:5). "One Lord, one faith, one baptism." In the course of his sermon he said, "We Baptists have turned that around to read, One Baptism, one faith, one Lord. But this inversion is a perversion." I believe that Tom Hearn was right. It is a perversion of the Gospel to put so much emphasis on the form of baptism that in the minds of many it obscures the more important demands of the Gospel.

Lest you should misunderstand me, let me say that on no less an authority than Karl Barth, I believe immersion is the scriptural form of baptism. I believe further that if rightly understood and taught it can have deep theological meaning, signifying, as it does, the burial and resurrection of our Lord. Moreover, I believe that if performed with dignity and reverence it can be a beautiful and meaningful experience for all. If done badly, it can be positively awful! I would say further that one who, understanding its significance, refuses it, misses something important in his spiritual life.

But having said all this, there are three things I will not do. I will not make a fetish of it. There are some Baptists, south and north, who seem to feel that if one has been immersed, he is bound for the kingdom of heaven and nothing can stop him. I rather believe the old country preacher may have been right when he said, "Some of you are going to hell dripping wet!"

Nor will I make it the test of one's obedience, love, or loyalty to Christ. "If any man have not the spirit of Christ, he is none of his" (Romans 8:9). And being immersed, unfortunately, is no assurance of the possession of that spirit. It follows from this that I could not make baptism an obstacle to Christian fellowship.

I would not make it a bar to fellowship within the local church. Many a Peter, whose life the church needs, is kept out because he does not see the significance of this act. The late Dr. Cornelius Wolfkin used to say: "The baptistry should be at the altar, not at the door." "Come in, Peter. We need you. You do not see the significance of this act now any more than could you have made your confession when I called you by the lake. But if you are willing to follow me, come in. Baptism, Peter, is not an initiation. It stands on a higher level. It is a privilege. The church, Peter, is not a museum for exhibiting saints. It is a school for sinners. If you love me and are willing to confess me and follow, me come in." "But Master you commanded that I should be baptized." "Yes I did, Peter. But there are other commands I deem more important. I said, 'Love your enemies. Do good to them that hate you and pray for them that despitefully use you (Matthew 5:44). I said, Forgive 'unto seventy times seven' (Matthew 18:22). I said some disturbing things about selfishness, about neighborliness, about brotherhood, about the greatest being the servant. Peter, if you love me, will you follow me? Then come in. I need you."

If you have read Karl Barth's little book, *The Teaching of the Church Regarding Baptism,* you will know what great importance he attaches to it. Yet in this very book he writes:

> The power of Jesus Christ, which is the only power in baptism, is not dependent upon the carrying out of baptism. Baptism has the necessity of a command, which cannot fail

to be heard . . . . It has not the necessity of an indispensable medium. The free word and work of Christ can make use of other means. That the church is commanded to use this means, cannot signify that Jesus Christ himself is limited to it" (p. 23).

In the Cleveland church that I served we had open membership. Every year we took in some on confession of faith in Christ without baptism. I cannot feel we did wrong. If Peter loves the Lord and is willing to confess and follow him, it seems wrong to keep him out. Open membership is an old story to many British Baptists. It is practiced in many American Baptist churches, of which the Riverside Church in New York City is perhaps the most notable example. It is not that the churches that practice it minimize the significance of baptism, but rather that they do not give it a place of primary importance. Nor did Paul. "One Lord, one faith, one baptism" (Ephesians 4:5). If the Master could say that the sabbath was made for man, not man for the sabbath, would he not say the same of baptism? Life comes first. "Is not the life more than meat...?" (Matthew 6:25).

But we make this symbol also a bar to fellowship between the churches and denominations. And that is worse. Why? Is there a valid reason why our denomination should not be associated with the World Council? Something happened when the body of our martyred president lay in state which impressed me. I noticed that as the mourners passed by his casket, they used different ways of expressing their grief. Some walked by and gave a passing glance at his casket. Some stopped and bowed. Some stopped and saluted. Some made the sign of the Cross. Some wept. The announcer made a striking comment. He said, "They are all saying it a different way, but they are all saying the same thing." Suppose someone in that procession had said, "I won't walk in fellowship with you unless you all salute. That is the only way to say it." Would we not think him a queer fellow?

Yet is that not comparable to what we do when we refuse, as a denomination, to have full fellowship with other denominations? Are we not putting more importance in the way we say it, than what is being said? "One Baptism, one faith, one Lord"—It is a perversion. "Ye are all one in Christ Jesus" (Galatians 3:28). To deny that is sinful.

I just cannot escape the feeling that this great denomination of ours, south and north, living in this day of upheaval, this perilous, "this grand and awful time," should have a more vital image, should stand for something more significant, more revolutionary, than our observance of an outward form.

I have said enough; maybe you will be thinking that I have said too much. It is said that a minister once used the word "procrastination" in a sermon. One of his parishioners asked him what the word meant. He replied, "That is one of the fundamental Baptist principles." Well I have used another principle tonight. Freedom of conscience, freedom to say what the Spirit moves you to say, praying meanwhile that it is not an evil spirit!

The Apostle admonishes us to speak the truth in love. Have I spoken the truth? All I would say is that I have spoken what seems to me to be the truth. And one hopes that he has spoken in love.

The key to the communication of the Word of God is the communicator—the preacher. That is another matter into which we cannot now go. Except to say, let us pray God that we shall always bring to this task of preaching the best of our mind and heart. That we will not give to the task of preparation the leftovers of our time, or leave the ministry of the Word to serve tables. Remember, our sermon is our life in projection. Our best, God knows, is none too good. Let me close with a short poem.

Years ago Edward Shillito, an Englishman, wrote the column for *The Christian Century* signed Simeon Stylites. He was followed by the late and beloved Hal Luccock of Yale who meant so much to me and made the column often the finest then in *The Christian Century*.

Dr. Shillito had a little poem in his column once which he called, "Saturday Prayer for a Preacher." Let me close with this.

> If through my perjured lips Thy voice can speak,
> If through a sinner Thou canst save from sin,
> Go forth my Saviour, through my words to seek
> And bring Thy lost ones in.

> I offer Thee my hands with recent scars
> Raw with the scars, deep cut by gyves of sin,
> Ply them in prisoned souls to break the bars
> And by me, Lord, pass in.

"O God to us may Grace be given
To follow in their train."

Index of Names